RUSSIA'S IRON AGE

STALIN ADDRESSING OFFICERS AND MEN OF THE RUSSIAN FLEET

RUSSIA'S IRON AGE

By

WILLIAM HENRY CHAMBERLIN

Author of "Soviet Russia"

With Illustrations

BOSTON
LITTLE, BROWN, AND COMPANY
1934

THE ATLANTIC MONTHLY PRESS BOOKS
ARE PUBLISHED BY
LITTLE, BROWN, AND COMPANY
IN ASSOCIATION WITH
THE ATLANTIC MONTHLY COMPANY

TO SONYA

Wife, comrade, and co-worker during many Russian years

INTRODUCTION

The Soviet Union during the last five years has undergone more fundamental and sweeping changes, in daily life, in psychology, in economic and social organization, than some countries which have experienced externally more spectacular revolutions. The decisions of the Soviet leaders to drive forward the industrialization of the country at a feverish pace, to take away from the peasants the individual method of farming the land, to banish the last remains of private ownership and initiative from the economic life of the country, to institute a gigantic all-embracing system of centralized state economic planning, affected very much more than the economic life of the country. They modified a thousand aspects of the country's life, from the character of its contemporary literature to the methods of recruiting labor.

All these changes were brought about with such uncompromising and ruthless disregard of the human cost involved that the period which witnessed them may fairly be called Russia's Iron Age. Such features of Soviet life as the erection of a far-flung network of new factories and electric power plants, the widespread employment of forced labor, the compulsory regimenting of the peasants in collective farms, the great famine of 1932–1933, did not exist at the time when my *Soviet Russia* was originally written in 1929, and they tend to make many parts of this work of purely historical value at the present time. Even the revised edition of *Soviet Russia* could not fully convey an impression of the sweeping transformation of many phases of Russian life.

So my main reason for publishing a new book on contemporary Russia is the distinctive and important character of the developments which have taken place there during the last few years. The preparation of the present book has also been facilitated by the fact that I am on the eve of leaving Moscow for another field of journalistic activity.

It has become almost a commonplace to say that the elements of stress and strain in Soviet life during recent years have been so great as to suggest a state of war. And censorship is an inevitable handicap of the war-time correspondent. More than once during recent years I have had occasion to feel that it was impossible to convey to my readers an absolutely uninhibited, full, and rounded description of the dramatic and sometimes tragic events which I was witnessing. The present book is designed, in some measure, to remedy this deficiency, to give a complete account of the Iron Age from its beginning to the present time.

I have a deep-rooted antipathy to the "Me and Russia" type of book, and I think nothing is more pathetic or more futile than a systematic effort, whether conscious or unconscious, to describe Soviet developments in the tone either of an indictment or of an apology. At the same time I have naturally been strongly moved by many of the experiences of the country in which I have lived for more than a decade, and by reproducing some excerpts from a personal diary I have given my readers some idea of my own reactions to various aspects of the Soviet régime.

I should like to express gratitude to the editors of the *Christian Science Monitor*, the newspaper which I have represented in the Soviet Union since 1922, for permission to incorporate in the book some passages which have appeared in the form of correspondence in the *Monitor*.

WILLIAM HENRY CHAMBERLIN

Moscow, *March* 1934

CONTENTS

ILLUSTRATIONS

RUSSIA'S IRON AGE

I

THE IRON AGE

THE last few years in Russia have been an Iron Age, both in a literal and in a figurative sense. The drive for the industrialization of the country has been to a large extent a drive for more iron and more steel. And the methods by which this industrialization and its twin process, the forcible collectivization of peasant agriculture, have been carried out have been iron in their ruthless crushing of resistance. Soviet planned economy is very much more than an effort to plot the graph of national industrial and agricultural output. As it went into effect it brought about on a more and more sweeping scale a destruction of old landmarks and the erection of new ones, a substitution of new habits for old ones, an annihilation or, to use the familiar Soviet word, a "liquidation" of individuals and of whole classes which could not be fitted into the framework of the new régime.

The whole quality of Soviet life has been transformed since 1929, which Stalin himself characterized as "the year of great change." It has become at once more dynamic and more pitiless. Instead of the relatively easy-going atmosphere which prevailed during the years from 1921 until 1928, when the country was gradually drifting toward a higher standard of living without undertaking any very ambitious projects of new construction, one has always, since then, been conscious of an atmosphere of struggle, stress, and strain.

The frequent use of war metaphors in Soviet descriptions of the five-year-plan period has been fully justified by the realities of the situation. Under the conditions which developed between 1929 and 1934, every new big factory or electrical power plant was a fortress to be stormed in the face of such obstacles as the poor technical training of many of the workers and engineers, the irregular and insufficient supply of food and raw materials. In the agricultural field the use of military terms was still more appropriate; the annual process of extracting grain and other foodstuffs from the reluctant peasants assumed more and more the character of a ruthless requisitioning foray; and it was only in 1933, after the end of a great catastrophe in the shape of a major famine during the winter of 1932–1933 and the spring of 1933, that some easing of the situation was felt.

The Iron Age has laid its transforming hand equally on inanimate things and on human beings. It has blown up the solid, golden-domed Cathedral of the Redeemer in Moscow and has given in its place a project for the largest public building in the world, to be called the Palace of Soviets. It has torn down scores of the pretty little churches which formerly lent a picturesque touch to the winding side streets of Moscow and has set up all over the country the monuments of the new materialistic faith: blast furnaces and turbines and tractor stations.

It has not spared such traditional things as the days of the week and the names of historic places. As a result of the introduction of a six-day week (the main object of which was to get rid of Sunday as the regular day of rest) the average Soviet citizen no longer reckons in individual days, but only in dates. As if to mark the final and definite breach with the past, there has been an orgy of renaming towns. St. Petersburg, after being first rechristened Petrograd, is now, of course, Leningrad. Nizhni Novgorod, the old Volga town which was once the scene of a huge annual fair that attracted merchants from many Eastern countries, is now Gorky, in honor of the unofficial Soviet writer-laureate. Stalin is commemorated in Stalinsk (formerly Kuznetzk), one of the new Siberian steel and mining towns, in Stalinabad (formerly Dushambe), in far-off Central Asia, in Stalingrad (formerly Tsaritsin), on the lower Volga, a town where he organized the defense during the civil war, and in Stalinogorsk (formerly Bobriki), southeast of Moscow, where a new chemical plant has been constructed. One of his chief lieutenants, Ordzhonikidze, has given his name to the town of Vladikavkaz, the former Tsarist military stronghold in the unruly Caucasus, and Zinoviev recanted his heresies fast enough to permit his native Ukrainian town, Elizavetgrad, to retain its new name of Zinovievsk.

The Soviet plunge into planned economy has affected very vitally the everyday lives of the hundred and sixty million inhabitants of the Soviet Union. It has created new towns, built up around industrial plants, on what were formerly open stretches of Ukrainian or Siberian steppe. It has depopulated formerly flourishing Cossack villages, where the people refused to bow their necks to the yoke of collectivization, and scattered their wretched inhabitants among the timber and construction camps of North Russia and Siberia. It has taken distinguished professors and scientists and broken them on the wheel of its sinister sabotage trials. It has taken youths from the deserts of Central Asia and the mountains of the Caucasus, won them away from Mohammed and the Koran to Marx and Lenin, and trained them to be engineers and scientists. It has broken the heart and the spirit of many a peasant who could not conceive of life without his individual piece of land. It has given to the youth of the country, including the peasant youth, a considerable range of opportunity, a chance to become aviators, writers, factory and farm directors.

In short, the Soviet Union under Stalin has lived through an era not dissimilar in spirit to that which Russia experienced in the time of Peter the Great. The stage is much larger; the setting is different; but many essential features are very much the same. Modernizing changes which in other countries or under a different form of government would probably have come about gradually, without tearing up the lives of so many people by the roots, have been driven through with varying degrees of success by the will of an absolutist ruler, so sure of the rightness of his policy that he took little account of the immense amount of suffering which its execution caused.

Russia has always been a country of contrasts. Within its vast area one could always find the hottest summers and the coldest winters, the most highly developed Europeanized intellectuals and the most primitive Asiatics, large up-to-date industrial and agricultural enterprises and methods of farming which have changed little since the Middle Ages.

If the Revolution has tended to eliminate or to reduce some of these pre-war contrasts (the masses are certainly more literate to-day, while the new educated class is just as definitely inferior, on the whole, to the former Russian intelligentsia in breadth and depth of culture), it has created new ones, especially during the tense and stormy years of the Iron Age. A mere list of some of the outstanding

Soyuzphoto

A GIANT TURBINE IN THE NEW CHEMICAL PLANT AT STALINOGORSK
(FORMERLY BOBRIKI)

events and characteristics of that period will convey some idea of its contradictions, of the very varied appeal which it makes to the consciousness of the foreign spectator.

The building of a large number of industrial plants of all kinds, especially of steel, chemical, machine-building, and electrical power works. A clear failure of railroad transportation to keep pace with the programme of industrial construction, and a persistence of the abnormally low standard of quality which has always been a characteristic of Soviet production. The abolition of industrial unemployment and the general introduction of the seven-hour working day, with a six-hour day for underground and harmful occupations. A decline in the material standard of living of the workers and employees to a point where many of them are on or below the living standards of British or American unemployed. The pouring of an increasing stream of tractors, harvesting combines, and threshing machines into the Soviet fields. Simultaneously with this a breakdown of food production, mainly attributable to the policy of forced collectivization and to the way in which it was carried out, that brought the towns to a narrow subsistence minimum and the villages over a very wide area of Southern and Southeastern Russia to stark starvation. The introduction generally of compulsory elementary education and the expansion of higher and middle education, along with the institution of a number of trade and professional courses. A persecution of the old technical intelligentsia which from 1929 until 1931 assumed incredible proportions, leading to the arrest and banishment of thousands and to the shooting of hundreds of people on charges of sabotage and espionage, often supported by the flimsiest of evidence, or

by no published evidence at all.   The provision of preferential reception in summer rest homes and of reserved seats
at the opera for those members of the working class who
rank as *udarniki*, or model workers.   The widespread condemnation to forced labor, often under very hard and in-
human conditions, of persons unfortunate enough to fall
into the expansive and elastic category of "class enemies."
The non-application of the death penalty for ordinary crime
and the attempt to reclaim ordinary criminals and delinquent
waifs, in many cases by humane treatment and educational
methods.   The passing and frequent application of a law,
quite unthinkable in any Western country, which prescribes
the death penalty for any theft of state property.

One could go on multiplying apparently contradictory
facts of this kind indefinitely.   And all of them, the worst
along with the best, have a common psychological origin: the
fanatical conviction of the Soviet leaders that their system
and their policies will ultimately create a terrestrial paradise
in the shape of "a classless socialist society" — a conviction
which is quite unshaken by the fact that the inauguration
of this paradise has required the shooting of thousands, the
deportation and starvation of millions, who stubbornly failed
to recognize its prospective benefits.

The present masters of the Soviet Union, the leaders of
the Communist Party, smashing opposition to their will with
all the ruthlessness of the most absolute Tsar, are driving
toward the goal of building up a kind of human society
which will differ very substantially from anything that has
hitherto been known.   They are laying the axe at the root
of some very old and deep-rooted human impulses: the
will to believe in something outside of and beyond the present
material world, the peasant's instinct for personal ownership

of the land which he tills, the old-fashioned home and family life.

In the place of these old impulses they are striving to create new habits, new morality, new types of human beings. They are endeavoring to make group loyalties — to the Communist Party, to the Union of Communist Youth, to the Soviet state, to the much vaguer "working class of the world" — take precedence over personal loyalties to family and friends. While the motive of personal gain is by no means overlooked, indeed is heavily emphasized at the present stage of development, there is an effort, backed by an unrivaled governmental propaganda machine, to dramatize labor achievement, to give to the director or the outstanding workers of a successful factory or institution, along with the higher salaries or wages which they can have under the Soviet system, a liberal measure of public and social applause as a substitute for the physical ownership of factory, shop, or land, which of course is rigidly forbidden.

The drama of Russia's Iron Age, broad in scope, fascinating in novelty, passionate in faith, terrible in some of its tragedies, has been played on a gigantic stage. Sheer bulk would make the Soviet Union impressive. Covering an area of 21,200,000 square kilometres, almost one sixth of the surface of the globe, it is the largest continuous land mass under single sovereignty, being more than equal in size to the United States and China rolled into one. In area the Union of Soviet Socialist Republics is exceeded only by the far-flung British Empire.

In considering the Soviet Union one must think in terms not of an ordinary country, but of a continent. Indeed the European part of the country is larger than any other

European power; the Asiatic part larger than any single state in Asia. From Russia's western frontier to the Pacific is a distance of over five thousand miles; from the ice-free port of Murmansk, north of the Arctic Circle, to the mountain ranges and high plateaus of the Pamir, in Central Asia, is a journey of almost three thousand miles.

One can find within the Soviet Union all the climatic differences that exist all over Europe. There is less physical contrast between Sweden and Italy than there is between the endless forests and frozen tundras, or marshlands, of the Russian North and the hot deserts of Turkestan, where irrigation makes possible extensive cotton plantations and oases bloom with rich fruit.

In population the Soviet Union, with a little over 160,000,000 inhabitants,[1] is exceeded only by India and China. In natural resources it is comparable with the United States and with the British Empire, regarded as a unit. China is another huge land mass, but lacks effective control of many of the regions which are still formally included within its geographical frontiers, and is apparently much poorer than the Soviet Union in such vital sources of mineral wealth as coal, iron, and oil.

Stretched out over such large parts both of Europe and of Asia, Russia has always had a foot in each continent without belonging definitely to either. Its cultural forms and aspirations have been European. Its governmental methods and its low living standards have suggested Asia. This

---

[1] Some Soviet estimates put the present-day population as high as 168,-000,000. I think such estimates overlook such factors as the increased death rate and the lowered birth rate, which have inevitably accompanied the hardships of recent years, and still more the tremendous famine mortality in Southern and Southeastern Russia during the first half of 1933. Officially, to be sure, the famine did not occur.

dualism has not been removed; in some respects it has been intensified by the changes which the Revolution brought about. As a result of the World War and the civil war the more Westernized portions of the former Tsarist Empire, Poland, Finland, and the Baltic Provinces, split off and set up independent national states. The Soviet centre of population and industrial gravity is very definitely being pushed toward the East, toward Asia, partly by strategic considerations, partly because the main sources of undeveloped mineral wealth now lie in the Urals and east of them. It is in the Ural territory and in Western Siberia that the Soviet Government is placing the main foundation stones of its edifice of industrialization.

Whether one is walking through the streets of Moscow or attending a Soviet Congress or sitting in a station waiting room, one can scarcely fail to be impressed by the essentially Eurasian character of the Soviet Union. For along with the tall, large-boned Russians one sees a great variety of faces and figures that belong to the East: slant-eyed Tartars from the Volga and the Crimea, yellow-skinned Mongols from Eastern Siberia, tall, rangy, olive-skinned mountaineers from the Caucasus. Old racial and religious inhibitions are breaking down among the younger generation which has grown up since the Revolution, with the result that racial intermarriage is becoming more common and the considerable strain of Eastern blood which could always be found among the Russians is increasing.

One should not be so carried away by the vastness of the Soviet Union as to lose sight of some of the serious natural disadvantages which have always retarded its development and held down its standard of living. A considerable part of its area, especially the frozen stretches of Northern Russia and Siberia, and large arid and desert tracts in Central Asia, will never, in all probability, support a considerable population. The Soviet Union is landlocked, with a scanty ice-free seacoast and inadequate harbor facilities. The value of its huge Siberian rivers is substantially reduced because they flow into the Arctic Ocean. Its great central plain is singularly poor in rock, which helps to explain the immemorial and atrocious condition of most of the country's roads.

Russian industrial development is seriously handicapped by the vast distances which not infrequently separate plants from their sources of raw material. Such machine-building centres as Leningrad, such textile towns as Ivanovo-Voznesensk and Vladimir, are located thousands of miles away from the main sources of cotton and iron and are dependent upon long hauls over a chronically overburdened and defective transportation system. There is no convincing evidence that Russia possesses exceptionally large reserves of gold, copper, and other nonferrous metals. As against the fertility of the famous "black earth" belt which runs through parts of Central Russia, Ukraina, and the North Caucasus, one must set the shortness of the Russian agricultural year, the habitual extremes of heat and cold, the liability of some regions which are extremely fertile in good years to severe drought.

Yet, when one has made full allowance for these negative physical factors of the Soviet Union, one cannot escape the conclusion that a country with its vast size and population, with its proved and potential extensive resources in coal and iron, oil and timber, platinum and manganese, with its varied agricultural possibilities, is capable of very significant development, especially in its Asiatic regions, where much

Soyuzphoto

Soyuzphoto

TYPES OF RUSSIAN DELEGATES AT THE PARTY CONGRESS

known mineral wealth is awaiting efficient exploitation and new discoveries are not unlikely.

Under any kind of strong government, under any social and economic system that did not amount to mere chaos, Russia would be a power to be reckoned with in world politics and economics. And just for this reason the new social and economic order acquires both greater chances of survival and greater historical significance than a socialist revolution might have in a country which was more dependent on the outside world.

The Soviet Union is by no means self-sufficient as yet; paradoxical as it may sound, its economic dependence on foreign countries is at least temporarily increased by its strenuous efforts to cast off this dependence. For the aspiration of the Soviet Union, in its Iron Age, is to manufacture its own tractors and agricultural machines, its own automobiles and blast furnaces; and the process of equipping the plants which will carry out these manufacturing processes calls for increased purchases abroad of machines and equipment which cannot yet be produced inside the country.

But, given the docility of the Soviet population and its capacity to exist on an abnormally low standard of living, the Soviet Union has fair prospects of becoming ultimately more self-sufficient than most countries, especially if it finally overcomes its agrarian crisis. If a socialist order can be built up in any country, Russia would seem to be the logical place in which to try out the experiment. The United States has perhaps equal or greater prospects of self-sufficiency and, of course, an infinitely more efficient and developed technique of industrial production. But the likelihood of a socialist revolution on the Russian model in the United States is so remote, timorous critics of the

New Deal notwithstanding, as to be practically nonexistent.

The Soviet Union is now setting about a task that bears considerable resemblance to that which the United States undertook at the end of the Civil War: the tapping and opening up of new land and undeveloped natural resources. Russia's East corresponds in some measures to America's West in the seventies and eighties of the last century.

Yet the differences between Soviet and American lines of development are certainly more striking and significant than are the physical points of resemblance between the two countries. America's appeal was to the initiative, the freedom, the hard work and good luck of the individual. The typical American pioneer was the farmer, attracted by the offer of a homestead for the taking; the hunter and trapper, exploring and opening up the mountain fastnesses; the gold prospector, willing to risk certain hardship for a possible fortune.

Very different is the eastward push of the Soviet Union. America was built up by individuals; Russia is being built up by the state. Only a few of the present-day Soviet pioneers are going entirely of their own volition, or in search of personal fortune. The young engineer who goes to work in Kuznetzk or in Magnitogorsk or in some other hard and bleak post is fulfilling a semi-contractual obligation which he owes to the state organization which helped to support him during the period of his education. Should he leave his work he would be held up to scorn as a "deserter from the labor front," and might be excluded from his trade-union and blacklisted if he sought further employment.

A good deal of the common labor that goes into the construction of the new plants in Siberia and the Urals is the forced labor of "kulaks" (formerly well-to-do peasants) and other "class enemies," who have been driven from their homes and forcibly enrolled in construction gangs. Another element in the labor force of the factories, railroads, and timber camps consists of peasants who come not as individuals seeking employment, but as contracted laborers sent by their collective farm in agreement with the management of the enterprise. No individual fortunes in the Soviet Union can be made through gold "strikes" or through discoveries of other precious metals; everything goes into the pockets of the omnipotent state.

The Soviet peasant who migrates to Siberia to-day does not travel on his own account and at his own risk in a covered wagon with his family and belongings, planning to settle wherever land and living conditions seem most favorable. He is in the vast majority of cases a member of a group, destined for membership in a collective farm, which, in the eastern marches of Siberia, in proximity to the unsettled Manchurian frontier, may very well recruit its strength from ex-soldiers and be prepared to fulfill a rôle quite similar to that of the military colonies which Russia's mediæval Tsars established along the Oka River to beat back the raids of marauding Tartars.

In short the two countries, the United States in the nineteenth century and the Soviet Union in the twentieth century, which were faced with the problem of settling new land and opening up natural resources on a Continental scale, chose diametrically opposed methods of development. America employed the maximum of individualism, the Soviet Union the maximum of state control and planning. Another decade or two of Russian pioneering should furnish material for interesting comparisons and contrasts.

And this is only one of many aspects of Russia's Iron

Age which should make the country absorbingly interesting outside its own frontiers. For reasons which will become clear in the course of the book I do not personally share the idea that the Soviet Union constitutes either a great challenge or a great menace to Western countries.

But now, as in more than one era of its past history, Russia is an amazingly fascinating spectacle to the imaginative observer. On this vast Eurasian plain, behind a smoke screen of favorable and unfavorable propaganda which becomes thicker as events themselves become more tense and ruthless, one of the major dramas of history is being played out. One can see in it elements of world significance: the working out of a fanatical theory which brings about vast changes in life and thought and at the same time dooms millions of its opponents to destruction. One can also see in it typically Russian traits, notably the resurrection, under new forms and behind the masks of new phrases, of such typical old-fashioned Russian conceptions as the absolute right of the state to use individuals and destroy them, as it likes, for the achievement of its ends.

More than at any time in its history the Soviet Union to-day fairly bristles with questions. What is the result when a state takes over every branch of production and distribution and endeavors to plan everything in the country's future development, from the amount of coal to be mined to the number of moving-picture performances to be given? How far can a new dogma, armed with unlimited resources both for repression and for propaganda, change human nature in general and Russian nature in particular? What happens when a huge modern steel plant is erected in the heart of a territory that was formerly grazing ground for Asiatic nomads? What of the growing elimination of all religious belief, especially in the younger generation? Are people happier when the state plays such an enormous rôle in their lives, undertaking to find work for everyone, directly or indirectly prescribing what they may eat and wear, whether they may travel, what books and newspapers they may or may not read? Or would the average human being prefer the lottery of private capitalism, with its glittering prizes and its blanks lumped together, with its greater individual opportunities and uncertainties, with its greater freedom from external restraint?

These questions are not static; they are being worked out with the passing of time. And the answers to many of them depend on individual training, temperament, and background. But there they are, raising their heads and pressing for reply at every turn of Soviet life.

I have lived in the Soviet Union during one of its most dynamic periods, during the first years of its Iron Age, when a single year sometimes seemed to crowd in as many events as a decade of life in other countries. I have seen some of the greatest triumphs of the Iron Age in terms of steel and concrete and witnessed some of its greatest tragedies in terms of human beings. For, whatever may be the case in a possibly milder future, the first outlines of Russia's new system of planned economy have been written on the living bodies of the present generation as sharply as if with a sword. To describe what changes the Iron Age has wrought in the Soviet Union and in the lives of the peoples who inhabit it is the purpose of the forthcoming chapters.

II

COMMUNISM: THE FAITH WITHOUT GOD

PRESENT-DAY Russia can never be understood psychologically, except on the premise that its rulers are dominated by an intense, burning faith in the rightness of their ultimate goal which gives them a feeling of entire self-righteousness in applying any means, however ruthless, that may seem necessary in order to reach this goal. Indeed it is just in Russia, which rejects and condemns all the familiar forms of religion, that one finds one of the strongest organized faiths in the world. For Russian Communism, as it has developed during the sixteen years which have passed since the Revolution, displays in striking degree all the psychological traits, if not of a new religion, — and both Communists and members of religious organizations would be inclined to protest against this definition, — at any rate, of a new crusading faith.

Communism has its body of doctrine in the works of Marx, Engels, and Lenin; its creed and catechism in the *politgramota*, or course of instruction in Communist political and economic ideas, which is drilled into every school child; its ecumenical councils to determine matters of faith and discipline in the Congresses of the Communist Party. Its insistence on the complete subordination of the individual to the requirements of the cause, its absolute intolerance of heresy and dissent, its conviction of a world Messianic mission — all these traits of fanatical believers in new dogmas are conspicuously characteristic of the Russian Communists.

Some years ago I was talking with an enthusiastic young woman Communist who was a member of the factory committee at a large electrical-equipment plant in Kharkov, the capital of Ukraina. A copy of Karl Marx's *Capital* lay on the table. Pointing with reverence to the volume, my companion said: "Whenever we encounter any difficulty in the management of the factory we look into that book and find the solution." A skeptic might cherish justifiable doubts as to the efficiency of Marx's classical work as a panacea for leaky boilers and broken-down turbines, and an older and more sophisticated Communist would probably not have endowed it with such magical powers. But the young woman's remark was typical of the attitude of unquestioning faith which has been instilled into a considerable part of the Soviet younger generation.

Mysticism among Communists is a term of abuse. Yet it is ironically curious to see certain mystical tendencies of older religions reproducing themselves in the new faith of Communism. Pilgrimages to shrines and tombs of saints are rare in Russia to-day, although sometimes one may see an old peasant woman walking through a monastery which is now used as an antireligious museum, obviously regarding its ikons and other religious ornaments — which have been preserved for historical or artistic considerations — as objects of worship. But in these times there is a daily stream of pilgrims to the granite mausoleum in the Red Square, where the embalmed body of the founder of the Communist faith, Vladimir Ilyitch Lenin, lies in state.

The ikon corner, with its gilt portraits of saints and

Biblical scenes, is going out of fashion in Russian homes, although it has by no means altogether disappeared. In its place is the new shrine, the Lenin corner, where portraits of scenes in the life of the Bolshevik leader, from the time when he was a small boy to the last scene in the mausoleum, are hung up, along with copies of his writings and texts from his works. So far as external appearance is concerned, the enormous parades that take place in Moscow on the two main revolutionary holidays, May 1 and November 7, might be old processions of the Cross, on an enlarged scale. Instead of ikons and religious banners one sees portraits of revolutionary leaders amid the mass of red streamers, each one proclaiming the achievements of some factory or institution or some Soviet slogan.

Most religions have cherished the conviction of a world mission; and Russian Communism is no exception to this rule. The Communist leaders have always regarded their revolution as at once a prelude and a stimulus to similar upheavals in other countries. Failure of insurgent movements in other countries to proceed along Communist lines and absorption in problems of internal reconstruction seem to have appreciably diminished the belief of the Soviet leaders in the imminence of revolutions on the Russian model; but belief in the world significance of the Russian Revolution remains an article of faith to which at least lip service must be paid, and a missionary organization in the shape of the Communist International exists to spread the gospel of Marx and Lenin in infidel countries.

What is the substance of this new faith, which commands the allegiance of the articulate part of Russia's hundred and sixty million inhabitants? It originated in the economic and social theories of Karl Marx, who himself gave a revolutionary interpretation to the dialectic method of the German philosopher Hegel.   The latter envisaged human history as a process of perpetual change and struggle, in which synthesis proceeds from the clash of thesis and antithesis and historical values are relative, what is progressive in one age becoming reactionary in another.

Applying this method to an analysis of economic and social relations, Marx arrived at the conclusion that the bourgeoisie, the owners of private capital, who had been a progressive, even a revolutionary class during the last stages of the feudal system, had now, in the era of capitalist industrial production, become a reactionary force, which must be swept away by the new class that had been called into existence by the emergence of the capitalist form of production.   This class consisted of the wage-workers, or proletarians, who, in the words of the Communist Manifesto, promulgated by Marx and his collaborator, Friedrich Engels, in 1848, had "nothing to lose but their chains."

Marx saw the main root of economic evil in the "surplus value" which, in his opinion, the employing or capitalist class extracted from the labor of their employees.   This surplus value, in Marx's opinion, could not be consumed and therefore tended to pile up unproductively, until the situation was relieved by a periodic crisis of slack production and unemployment.   He believed that the private profit system carried within itself the seeds of its own destruction by leading to these inevitable devastating crises and by bringing more and more wealth into the hands of fewer and fewer people.

He advocated the violent overthrow of the existing order by the proletariat and the substitution of a new society, dominated at first by the industrial working class, in which private ownership of the means of production would be forbidden. Ultimately this new society would become classless, and would be guided by the principle: "From each according to his abilities; to each according to his needs."

The majority of the organized Socialists all over the world in pre-war days regarded themselves as disciples of Marx. But the revolutionary cutting edge of his doctrine tended to become blunted in countries where the industrial workers felt that, after all, they had something to lose besides their chains, and where the middle class and the peasantry (the significance of which in a modern developed industrial state Marx seriously underestimated) revealed a tendency to turn to Fascism when a crisis seemed to become unmanageable.

At first sight Russia, with its small industrial working class and its relatively backward pre-war industry, might have seemed stony soil for Marx's ideas. But there were compensating factors of which Marx's greatest disciple, Vladimir Ilyitch Lenin, leader of the Russian Revolution and founder of the Soviet state, took full advantage. The Russian middle class was small in numbers and politically ill-organized. And great masses of the peasantry, the largest element in the Russian population, were too poor to have acquired in full measure the instinct for private property which places definite bounds to the political radicalism of the peasant or farmer in other countries.

Lenin was a theorist as well as a practical leader. While he was a thoroughgoing Marxist in his economic outlook, he imparted a definite and distinctive quality to Russian Communism, as distinguished from pre-war and still more from post-war socialism, by his elaborations of Marx's teaching and by his emphasis on just those more militant aspects of the writings of Marx and Engels which West

European socialists were inclined to minimize and gloss over.

Lenin's theory that capitalism developed at an unequal pace in various countries led him to the conclusion that a working-class revolution could be carried out successfully in one country, that the world capitalist system could be broken at its weakest link.   Marx and Engels had proceeded on the assumption that socialist revolutions would occur more or less simultaneously in the more developed countries.

Lenin also put forward the conception that capitalism had entered on its final stage of competitive imperialist systems, which would lead to international wars, out of which, in turn, would proceed revolutions. When the World War broke out Lenin had nothing but scorn for pacifism; his slogan was: "Turn the imperialistic war into civil war."

Other ideas which were very much in the foreground of Lenin's teaching were that there could be no gradual peaceful transition from capitalism to socialism, that the old state machine must be smashed and a new one, manned largely by workers, must be built up. Lenin's conception of the function of the state has exerted a basic influence on Soviet development. To him any state is an agency for the suppression of one class by another. In a phrase which is typically Russian in its sweeping extremism Lenin summed up the question as follows: "While there is a state there is no freedom. When there is freedom there will be no state."

The Soviet state, therefore, according to Lenin, must be an agency for the suppression of the dethroned capitalist class. The seizure of political power by the working class could not, in his opinion, lead to the immediate establishment of a classless socialist society. During an intervening

period of unspecified length a system which he described as
the dictatorship of the proletariat must prevail. During
this period all the means of production — factories, mines,
transportation, banking, and such — would be socialized.
The state would ruthlessly suppress any attempt on the
part of the former propertied classes to resist the social
changes or to regain their lost power.

Finally, on some millennial day, classes themselves will
disappear, and the need for the state as an engine of repression will also vanish. Then and only then fullest
liberty will prevail. Lenin is no dreamer of Utopias. One
will look in vain through the dozens of volumes of his
collected works for any detailed picture of what human
society will be under socialism. Fanatically convinced of
the correctness of Marxism as a law of human progress,
willing to give his own life and to take unnumbered lives of
other people in order to establish a political and economic
order based on Marxian principles, Lenin seems to have
felt that it would be futile to peer too deeply into the
future, to trace the outlines of the human society which would
emerge after the fierce period of class struggle was over.
Plato and Thomas More have no successor in the Bolshevik
leader, who permits himself only such dry and fleeting
glances toward his ultimate goal as one sees in the following
sentences: —

The expropriation of the capitalists will inevitably yield a tremendous development of the productive forces of human society.
But how soon this development will go farther, how soon it will
reach the point where there is no more division of labor, where the
contrast between mental and physical labor is destroyed, where
labor is transformed into "the first necessity of life," this we
do not and cannot know.

Stalin, although he is to-day the supreme recognized interpreter of Marx, Engels, and Lenin in the Soviet Union, has added little to the doctrinal basis of the Communist faith. His idea that socialism may be successfully built up in a single country may be regarded as an adjustment to existing facts; it was politically far more expedient to describe the system which is growing up in Russia as socialism than to make the realization of socialism dependent upon the coming of a more and more uncertain international revolution.

Like more than one religious system in the past, Communism may be and often is extremely ruthless simply because ruthlessness is so logical — if one grants all the premises of the new faith. If "capitalism" is synonymous with exploitation and war, why not starve or deport to unpleasant places those peasants who are so blind and stubborn as to cling to private "capitalist" methods of farming? If the outside world is continually and surreptitiously plotting for the overthrow of the Soviet state, what is more reasonable than to give the Gay-Pay-Oo full power to deal summarily with spies and *saboteurs*? If a few innocent people suffer in the process, this is a mere incident, mildly regrettable, perhaps, in a vast process of historical reconstruction. By a very similar line of reasoning, mediæval saints and scholars defended, if defense were regarded as necessary, the contemporary practice of "liquidating" heretics. What was a little transitory pain, inflicted upon the heretics, in comparison with the eternal torments which might overtake masses of people if they were seduced from the true faith by the insidious heretical teaching? The problem of whether a rational and humane social order can some day, as if by magic, develop out of a régime of terrorism and espionage seems to cause the average Communist as little concern as the mediæval inquisitor felt when he handed over a new batch of heretics to the secular arm to be burned for the greater glory of the Christian Church.

The Communist faith has its organized body of believers: the All-Union Communist Party. Early in 1934 the Party, which had just passed through a rigorous *chistka*, or purge, numbered in its ranks 1,872,488 members and 935,298 candidates, or applicants for membership on probation. A third rank has recently been introduced, that of "sympathizer." Individuals who do not qualify for the preliminary test as a candidate, but who are unobjectionable, are given the rating of sympathizers.

Foreign visitors to Russia are sometimes surprised at the fact that an organization of less than 3,000,000 members and candidates can exercise absolute power in a country of 160,000,000 inhabitants. Part of the explanation, of course, lies in the fact that the Soviet régime spares no resource of propaganda or of terrorism in maintaining itself in power. Moreover, the organized Communist strength is not adequately measured by the figures of Party membership. There are about 4,500,000 Young Communists, youths between the ages of fourteen and twenty-three, to say nothing of almost 6,000,000 Young Pioneers, children still younger.

It is significant that requirements for admission to Communist organizations become stricter according to the age of the applicant. Any child can put on the red scarf that is the distinguishing mark of the Young Pioneers. Any working-class boy or girl, barring some objection on the ground of delinquent moral conduct or imperfect grasp of Communist ideas, can join the Union of Communist Youth;

and admission into this organization is only a little more sparingly granted to Red Army soldiers, peasants in collective farms, and children of employees. Only youths who are branded with the stigma of "bourgeois" parentage find it difficult to be accepted as Young Communists; and even they may gain admission if they solemnly renounce and break off relations with their unworthy parents and throw themselves actively into the work which is expected of every Young Communist.

The Communist Party, on the other hand, is deliberately held down in numbers through a policy of severe entrance requirements, rigid discipline, leading to fairly frequent expulsions of members and occasional wholesale purgings, when Party members whose conduct is found unbecoming a Communist are dropped from the ranks or reduced to the rating of "candidates" or "sympathizers." The Party passed through a general purging in 1933, and incomplete preliminary figures show that the percentage of expulsion was 17, while an additional 6.3 per cent of the Party members were demoted in status.

Public confession, a practice of more than one religious sect, is a conspicuous feature of a Party purging. The sessions of the examining commissions, consisting of Party comrades of unimpeachable orthodoxy and long standing, are open to anyone, and are apt to be crowded. Every member of the local Communist Party branch is called on to give an account of his life and work; and any spectator, whether Party or non-Party, who has anything to say against him or on his behalf is also given the floor. The result is that one often gets interesting first-hand pictures of human conduct and of the ethical standards which are prescribed for Communists in the course of the purgings.

Here, for instance, is a worker in a rubber factory named Firsov, up for examination. At first his record seems quite exemplary. He attends his Party meetings regularly and has been rewarded as an *udarnik*, or shock-brigade worker. But then, in the course of the discussion, in which his fellow workers participate, it turns out that after he had returned from Siberia, where he had been sent by the Party to help organize collective farms, he had criticized the Party policies in private conversation, expressing the heretical ideas that too much grain was being taken from the peasants, that the speed of industrialization was too great, and that there was no real war danger. For prudential reasons he had not expressed these ideas at Party meetings; but the damaging facts came out at the purging, and he was sentenced to expulsion.

Karpov, summoned before the purging commission in one of the numerous factories which are named after Stalin, is found guilty on another count. He had a good character as a skilled worker. But he had married the daughter of a man of the pariah disfranchised classes (former aristocrats, merchants, traders, landowners, priests, and so on), and he helped his wife's brother and father to find work, concealing their class origin. This is regarded as "deception of the Party" and Karpov is cast out.

The first duty of the Communist is absolute, unquestioning obedience to the orders which he receives from his Party superiors. After this, in the list of Communist virtues, would follow, in roughly approximate order: favorable influence on his fellow workers, efficiency at the task to which he has been assigned, a grasp of at least the simpler fundamental doctrines of Marx and Lenin.

Tennyson's well-worn line, "Theirs not to reason why,"

has become an increasingly appropriate slogan for Russian Communists. Party discipline has always been strict and Party leaders like to quote with considerable unction Lenin's phrase that "the Party is not a debating society." During the Iron Age, when the hardships and difficulties of the country considerably increased, the disciplinary régime became more and more severe. Not only the professing of heretical views, but *primirenchestvo*, or an attitude of toleration for people who hold such views, is regarded as cause for exclusion from the Party, which often involves the loss of the public post which the excluded person has been holding.

That criticism does occasionally crop up is evident from some cases which find their way into the Soviet press. So one Demenkov, secretary of the Party Regional Committee in Chukhloma, a small town near Ivanovo-Voznesensk, protested in letters to the Party newspaper, *Pravda*, and to the provincial Party Committee against the proposed pace of collectivization in Chukhloma, declaring that it could not be realized without extreme pressure on the peasants and a repetition of the excesses which had occurred in a preceding winter. In one of his letters Demenkov let slip the phrase: "We are so used to circulars and stamps that we fear our own thoughts."

This freethinker from Chukhloma was quickly disposed of; he was removed from his post and excluded from the Party, and the chronicler of his fate, a certain E. Shestakova, drew the following moral from it: —

The Ivanovo-Voznesensk organization must learn the political lessons of the Chukholma affair and increase its Bolshevik vigilance and ideological intolerance for the struggle with opportunism and tolerance of opportunism.

A Communist worker in the Leningrad factory *Dvigatel* named Grushetsky committed an even more heinous offense, according to *Pravda*, which quoted him as saying that "the Party invented sabotage and the people who were shot allegedly for creating hunger were innocent victims." Needless to say, Grushetsky quickly vanished from the ranks of the Party, and with him went the president of his factory committee and another sympathizer among the workers.

A discussion which was initiated at one time among the local Party branches of one of the Moscow wards elicited the following unorthodox comments on the part of various Party members — comments which were cited for the purpose of indignant refutation and which, in all probability, did not make for the political advancement of the persons who uttered them: —

We have no meat because we began to liquidate the kulak before we created a base for meat supply. . . . The material position of the workers is deteriorating. . . . Our pace of development was excessive and the liquidation of the kulaks was untimely. . . . You can talk only about the favorable side of things; if you talk about difficulties you become a Right deviationist and are out of harmony with the decisions of the Party. . . . To talk about difficulties in the Party is forbidden.

Such subdued mutterings, however, are quickly suppressed, and the well-oiled Party machine rolls on. The voices of criticism which were formerly heard at Party Congresses, but which became fainter and fainter as Stalin tightened his grip on the mechanism of power, have now been silenced entirely. At the last Party Congress, which was held in January and February, 1934, the chorus of approval from the delegates was so loud that Stalin and Kaganovitch, who delivered two of the main reports, decided not to make the formerly customary secondary speeches, devoted to answering points which had been raised in debate. Not for nothing was the Congress preceded by a rigorous purging, which expelled or demoted about a fifth of the Party members.

Expulsion from the Party, it should be noted, is a much more serious penalty than it would be in a country where a man who had fallen out with his political organization could simply retire to private life. In Russia there is very little "private life" to which a Soviet citizen could retire, because, whether he be factory director or engineer, skilled workman or clerk, scientist or professor, he is in the employ of the all-embracing state. Moreover, many of the higher executive and administrative posts may only, in practice, be occupied by Communists. Expulsion from the Party is, therefore, a severe blow to a man's career, to his prospects of advancement in life.

Highly placed Communists who deviate from what is generally known as the "Party line" — that is, the programme and policies dictated by Stalin — can only regain admittance to the Party, if their offense has been so serious as to entail expulsion, by consenting to go through a form of public recantation. The last Party Congress witnessed the declarations of a number of repentant sinners, some of whom, Zinoviev, Kamenev, and Preobrazhensky, had incurred the penalty of expulsion, while others, including Rykov, Bukharin, and Tomsky, had merely been removed from former high posts. Incidentally, one of the most amusing historical analogies I have encountered in Russia is the amazing similarity between the formula of recantation which Galileo adopted when he was faced by the Inquisition and the similar formula with which Zinoviev begged for re-admission to the Party. Galileo promised to become an informer in the future; Zinoviev expressed abject regret that he had not been an informer and denounced his acquaintance, Sten, to the Central Committee of the Party in the past. Galileo said four centuries ago: —

I abjure, curse and detest the said errors and heresies . . . and if I shall know any heretic or anyone suspected of heresy, I will denounce him to this Holy Office or to the Inquisition of the place in which I may be.

Zinoviev said in 1933: —

My sin before the Party is very great. I, who could learn directly from Lenin, and after this from Stalin, went off the road and placed myself in the position of an apostate. If I had been in quite healthy, direct, simple relationship with the Central Committee, I should have been obliged to inform it on the very day when Sten showed me the counter-revolutionary programme and platform.

Class is as much of a fetish in contemporary Russia as race is in contemporary Germany. While the ultimate aim of Communism is to abolish classes, its immediate policy is to make the most careful and jealous inquiry into the class origin of every applicant for work, of every Red Army recruit, and, of course, of every applicant for admission to the Party. Under the new Party constitution applicants are divided into four categories, as follows: —

1. Industrial workers with a labor record of at least five years.
2. Industrial workers with a labor record of less than five years, agricultural laborers, Red Army soldiers, if their parents are workers or collective farm peasants.

3. Collective farmers, members of handicraft coöperatives, and teachers in elementary schools.

4. All other employees, including professional men, intellectual workers, office employees, and so forth.

Conditions of admission, as regards the number of required recommendations from Party members and length of probation, are easiest for persons in the first category and become progressively harder up to the fourth. Special restrictions, which could only be surmounted with the greatest difficulty and in infrequent cases, are imposed on the admission to the Party of persons who have ever belonged to any other political organization.

It would be a naïve mistake to imagine that each individual Communist enjoys an equal share of the absolute power which the Party, as an organization, wields. The tendency of recent years has been at once to strengthen the dictatorship of the Party in the country and the dictatorship of the Party leaders over the rank and file. The Party Congresses, which are formally elected by the membership (under careful guidance from above), are held with increasing infrequency and possess no real power of initiative.

More authority is vested in the Central Committee of the Party, which is reëlected by each Congress, the list of candidates being prepared by the Party leaders. It now consists of seventy-one members and sixty-eight candidates. Together with another large body, the Commission of Party Control, it meets in plenary session several times in the course of a year; and these gatherings pass resolutions on the most important current problems. While the Central Committee, which includes most of the outstanding Party and Soviet functionaries, has primarily executive functions, it is the business of the Commission of Party Control to investigate and check up on the fulfillment of Party decisions, and also, with the aid of local commissions, to look out for Party discipline and morale and to expel unworthy and heretical members.

Above the Central Committee in actual power, although nominally elected by it, is the Political Bureau, a group of ten men which really directs the powerful and complicated machine of power which has been built up in Russia. Its members are Stalin, Kaganovitch, who is Stalin's chief lieutenant, Premier Molotov, President Kalinin, War Commissar Voroshilov, Commissar for Heavy Industry Ordzhonikidze, Commissar for Transport Andreev, Kirov, Kossior, and Kuibishev.

A decision of the Political Bureau, which meets much more frequently than the Central Committee, is the last word, whether it be a question of selling the Chinese Eastern Railroad, starting a big new copper plant, initiating a new policy in the country districts, intensifying or slackening Communist propaganda in this or that foreign country. Stalin, of course, dominates the deliberations of the Political Bureau; indeed one might depict the Soviet régime as a pyramid, with the Political Bureau representing the top and Stalin standing on the very apex.

The objectives of the Communist Party leadership are to keep the Party membership relatively small, while at the same time securing for the office holders, who constitute an important element in the Party membership, a basis of rank-and-file support by creating fairly large Party branches in industrial establishments and in Red Army units, and somewhat easing the admission requirements for peasants who belong to collective farms. The Party control of the Soviet executive machinery has naturally become firmer than ever during the recent years of stress and strain. The independence of local Soviets, especially in the country districts, has been substantially curbed; and wide, somewhat indeterminate powers have been vested in the so-called political departments, which have been set up all over the countryside under the direction of men who are appointed directly by the central Party authorities. When the president of a local Soviet or of a collective farm fails to carry out the policy of the central government, he is not infrequently deposed by summary order, and his successor may be appointed without the rather empty formality of consulting the peasant "electors."

As a new faith, Communism has naturally created its own very distinctive standards of morality. What may seem quite right and normal in a "capitalist" society is often grossly wrong, according to Communist ethical standards, and *vice versa*. Failure to understand this point leads to much misunderstanding of Soviet psychology.

A British traveling companion recently asked me what had become of the substantial citizens of pre-war Russia, the men who owned factories, banks, mines. I replied that it had gone very hard with them, that some had been shot during the civil war or later, on sabotage and treason charges, that many had fled abroad, and that those who could still be found in Russia were mostly living in obscure poverty, fearful, most of all, lest attention be called to their pre-war position. My companion shook his head sadly. "What a pity," he said. "I am sure these men were mostly very good citizens."

From his standpoint they doubtless were. From the point of view of a Young Communist who has been brought up on heavy doses of class hate they were little better than fiends in human form, whose "liquidation" had been one of the most meritorious achievements of the Revolution.

Communist morality is intensely pragmatic and utterly contemptuous of absolute standards. Whatever is beneficial for the advancement of Communism at any given time is good. Whatever retards it is bad. This attitude is particularly noticeable in the matter of truth telling. If an amiable falsehood serves the purpose of soothing a foreign visitor or fooling the more gullible part of the Soviet population better than an unpleasant truth, the telling of the falsehood becomes not only unobjectionable, but a positive matter of Communist moral duty. The pragmatism embodied in Benjamin Franklin's thesis that honesty is the best policy has somehow never taken deep root in the Soviet Union.

The Communist attitude toward personal morality is also strictly utilitarian. Loose living and excessive drinking may be considered cause for the expulsion of a Party member; but the expulsion would be motivated by some such practical reason as "discrediting the Party in the eyes of the masses." The idea that an action or a line of conduct may be right or wrong in itself is quite foreign to the Communist, in so far as he is indoctrinated with the philosophy of a Party. The sole standard is the advancement of the Communist cause. This is why the same local Communist official, with an equally good conscience (assuming that his human feelings have been completely obliterated by his schooling in Party dogma), can push forward a baby-saving campaign, in the form of the opening of new nurseries and kindergartens, and a baby-killing campaign, in the form of driving kulak families from their homes and deporting them to places

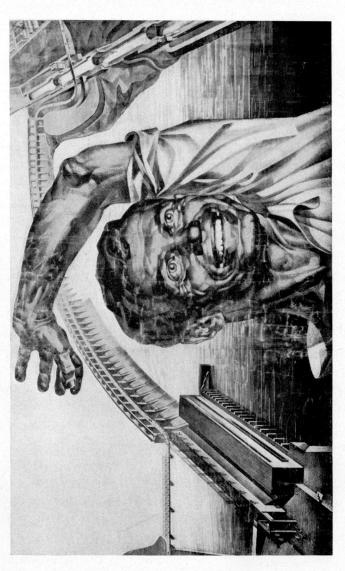

A Soviet Poster Celebrating the Completion of the Dnieper Dam

where work is hard, food is scarce, and mortality rates are high.

Despite, or perhaps because of, the missionary efforts of the Communist International, Communism shows little sign of becoming a world faith.   In Russia, on the other hand, it is firmly based on a double foundation of intensive propaganda and extreme repression.   It has already performed many historical functions.   It has swept away many archaic remnants and cobwebs of superstition.   It has given Russia a powerful, if often clumsy and misdirected, shove toward industrialization.   To the masses of the country, along with many hardships and deprivations, it has given new opportunities for education and advancement.

The world has witnessed many outbursts of disciplined fanatical fervor before the advent of Russian Communism. One can trace plausible psychological parallels between the Party which was founded by Lenin and the early Mohammedans, the English Puritans, the Order of Jesuits.   The general experience of such outbursts is that, while they often achieve remarkable results and appreciably mould the course of contemporary development, they cannot, in the very nature of things, be permanent.   Sooner or later the first fervor of fanatical idealism cools down; and the further fate of the doctrine depends on the solidity of the organization which it has called into being, on the smooth working of the new routine of life which it has introduced.

There seems no reason to believe that Communism, the materialistic faith of the twentieth century, will prove an exception in this respect, or that it will succeed in instilling into the whole membership of the Communist Party, much less into the whole Soviet population, that mood of complete personal abnegation and self-devotion which one finds now and then in the veteran "underground" revolutionary of pre-war days or in the more ardent of the younger Communists. It is significant of the more prosaic trend of the present time that the "Party maximum," the arrangement under which Party members were limited to a fixed maximum salary, so that a high government official often received less than a non-Party engineer or expert, has now been abolished and replaced by a tax which amounts to 3 per cent on all Communist incomes in excess of five hundred rubles a month. (One quite despairs of rendering the value of the Soviet ruble accurately in terms of foreign currency, if only because there are many kinds of rubles, which vary greatly in purchasing power. The average wage of an industrial worker is about a hundred and twenty-five rubles a month.) Indeed so great is the emphasis at the present time on the need for efficiency that the Communist is regarded as serving his Party best if he qualifies for a high wage as a skilled factory worker or for a substantial salary as a capable administrator.

What distinguishes Communism from the fanatical, authoritarian religions with which it has so many points in common is, of course, its rigid, dogmatic, and uncompromising exclusion of any element in life lying outside the confines of the present material world. This, over a long period of time, may prove to be its fatal weakness. One, perhaps two generations may find sufficient food for imagination and enthusiasm in the idea that they are building up socialism, remaking their country and the world.

But ultimately it seems improbable that any amount of steeping in Communist propaganda can banish from Russian minds the questioning aroused by the problem of death in the individual life, by the prospect of the death, at long

last, of the planet on which we live.   Is it possible to find
the answer to such questionings by the most diligent search
in the pages of Marx's *Capital?*   Or will the tendency to
seek desperately for some non-materialistic interpretation of
life assert itself, despite the most watchful efforts of Soviet
orthodox propaganda and censorship?   This may in the end
prove one of the most fundamental problems which history
will present to the Soviet Faith without God.

III

THE DRIVE FOR INDUSTRIALIZATION

THE history of old Russia is the history of defeats due to backwardness. She was beaten by the Mongol khans. She was beaten by the Turkish beys. She was beaten by the Swedish feudal lords. She was beaten by the Polish-Lithuanian gentry. She was beaten by the Anglo-French capitalists. She was beaten by the Japanese barons. All beat her for her backwardness, for military backwardness, for cultural backwardness, for governmental backwardness, for industrial backwardness, for agricultural backwardness. She was beaten because to beat her was profitable and could be done with impunity. . . . That is why we must no longer be backward.

This is how Stalin, in a speech which he delivered early in 1931, summed up the categorical imperative behind the fierce drive for industrialization at any cost of material deprivation and individual suffering which has been the main dominating fact of Soviet policy during the last few years. And in the winter of 1932–1933, when people were already beginning to die of hunger in Ukraina and the North Caucasus, typhus, the familiar dreaded epidemic disease which often accompanies hunger, raised its head even in Moscow. The terrific strain of that time was reflected in laws prescribing the death penalty for theft of state property and dismissal with loss of food card for one day's unauthorized absence from work. Yet Stalin cherished no doubt that what had been achieved was worth the cost. In summing up the results of the five-year plan he laid stress on the new industries which had not existed or had existed on a very small scale before the inauguration of the plan and which were already beginning to function — tractor, machine-building, chemical, automobile, aviation.

Russia's drive for industrialization has been accompanied by the adoption of a system of intensive planning of the national economic and social development. The first Soviet five-year plan came to an end on December 31, 1932, after being shortened in practice to a four-and-a-quarter-years plan. Although the second plan is supposed to run from 1933 until 1937, its details were only published in definite form early in 1934.

Viewed in retrospect, the inauguration of the five-year plan may be considered one of the three most important dates in post-revolutionary Russian history, the other two being the Bolshevik Revolution on November 7, 1917, and the adoption of Lenin's New Economic Policy in March 1921. What was most important was not the five-year period, but the practice of governmental planning, which brought with it, by a kind of inevitable logic, the wiping out of private trade and of private farming, neither of which could be fitted into the framework of a rigorously planned economy.

An outstanding feature of the five-year plan was a rapid forcing up of the figures of industrial production at an annual rate of increase. The output of coal was to grow from 35,400,000 tons in 1927–1928 to 75,000,000 tons in the last year of the plan; the output of pig iron from 3,300,000 tons to 10,000,000 tons; the output of steel from 3,900,000 tons to 10,000,000 tons; the production of oil from 11,600,000 tons to 22,000,000 tons. An even greater increase was projected for agricultural machinery. All in all, industrial output was supposed to increase by more than two and a half times before the end of the plan; and sweeping increases were proposed for the industries which produce goods for immediate consumption, such as textiles, as well as for the so-called "heavy" industries — iron, steel, coal, metallurgy, machine-building.

The State Planning Commission, or Gosplan, which framed this vast blueprint of national development, left no detail unmentioned. The standard of living was to rise; every industrial worker at the end of the plan was to receive 70.5 per cent higher real wages; everyone in the cities was to be eating 27.7 per cent more meat, 72 per cent more eggs, and 55.6 per cent more dairy products by the time the plan was completed, while the corresponding figures for the peasants were 16.7 per cent, 45. 2 per cent, and 24.7 per cent.[1]

In agriculture the plan called for a substantial increase in the country's supply of live stock and in the production of grain, cotton, sugar beets, and other crops, with a growth of the acreage yield. There was also to be a beginning, although only a beginning, of the process of transforming the small peasant holders into members of collective farms, where land, machinery, and working cattle would be socialized.

The results of the plan were extremely varied, ranging from striking achievement in some fields of industrial production and new building to dismal and unmistakable

[1] All these figures are taken from the useful summary of the aims of the first five-year plan, published in *Pyatiletni Plan Narodno Khozaestvennovo Stroitelststva SSSR* ("The Five-Year Plan of National Economic Upbuilding of the Soviet Union"), 1929, by the State Planning Commission, pp. 127–163.

failure in the effort to raise the general standard of living. To some extent the student of Soviet economics during recent years has been left without a compass, because the stability of the ruble was one of the first casualties of the struggle for industrialization, with the result that all calculations in regard to wages, salaries, standard of living, and actual volume of production, when this is measured in terms of rubles, tend to become vague and approximate. Moreover, many of the better known and more experienced Russian statisticians (one may mention Groman, Kondratiev, and Kaffenhaus) have been arrested and removed from office on charges of sabotage; and an ominous slogan, "Statistics on the Class Front," has been proclaimed.

While the Soviet Government, if only for its own information, doubtless tries to obtain as accurate a picture of the real output in various branches of national economic life as may be possible, some of the methods used in computing agricultural statistics seem decidedly strange and unreliable,[2] and the suppression or the withholding over long periods of time of unfavorable statistics has become increasingly common. For several years, for instance, it was impossible to obtain official information about the size of the grain crop or the number of live stock; and the official summary of the fulfillment of the five-year plan which has been issued in English by the State Planning Commission leaves out any detailed figures about the textile and nonferrous metal industries, where production results fell especially far short of the plan, and is furthermore grossly misleading inasmuch as it assumes that the ruble of 1933 is equal in purchasing power to the ruble of 1928.

[2] In the following chapter I discuss in more detail the new Soviet method of compiling harvest statistics.

Stalin made the official claim that the five-year plan had been fulfilled by 93.7 per cent. In making this claim, however, he reckoned merely the volume of industrial production, which was far more favorable than the fulfillment of the plan as regards the food supply of the population. Even in this field, however, the actual results are somewhat obscured because just those industries where the most sweeping gains are claimed in many cases reckon their output not in more or less hard-and-fast tons, but in elastic rubles. This applies to general and agricultural machine building and to chemicals. More solid quantitative comparisons for several of the leading branches of industry work out as follows: —

	1927–1928 [3]	Estimated output for last year of the plan	Output in 1932
Coal	35,400,000 tons	75,000,000 tons	64,200,000 tons
Oil	11,600,000 tons	22,000,000 tons	21,400,000 tons
Pig iron	3,300,000 tons	10,000,000 tons	6,160,000 tons
Steel	3,900,000 tons	10,000,000 tons	5,890,000 tons
Copper	28,300 tons	84,700 tons	47,200 tons
Cotton thread	2,871,000,000 metres	4,700,000,000 metres	2,540,000,000 metres
Superphosphates	151,400 tons	3,400,000 tons	612,800 tons

It may be seen from this table that while, with the important exception of cotton thread (here are evident the effects of the stoppage of the former imports of American cotton before the Soviet Union was able to extend its own cotton plantations sufficiently to make up for the loss), substantial gains by comparison with 1927–1928 have been realized, these gains have in many cases, especially in the very vital iron and steel industry, fallen far short of the demands of the five-year plan.

[3] These figures are taken from the statistical tables at the end of the first volume of *The Five-Year Plan of National Economic Construction* (the official Soviet work on the first five-year plan) and from official Soviet reports on the output of industry in 1932.

A grave defect of the first plan, which is still keenly reflected in the difficulties of Soviet economic life, has been the failure of railroad transportation to keep pace with the vastly increased needs of industry. For three years, 1931, 1932, and 1933, the figure of freight-car loadings has remained practically stationary between 50,000 and 55,000 a day; and, while there has been a big increase in the amount of freight and the number of passengers carried since 1927–1928, the chronically overstrained condition of the transportation system is reflected in an abnormally large number of accidents, ranging from major wrecks, with scores of human victims, to minor breakdowns and delays. So, during six months of the year 1930, 14,046 railroad accidents occurred, as against 10,572 during the same period of time in 1928–1929.[4] There was no noticeable improvement during later years; and early in 1934 there were a number of very serious wrecks, followed by special demonstration trials and the infliction of death sentences and terms of imprisonment upon those employees who were found responsible for the accidents.

One prominent Communist after another has lost his administrative reputation by undertaking the thankless post of Commissar for Transport. In the summer of 1933 a realization of the fact that the amount of freight transported and the average daily runs of freight cars and locomotives, during the first six months of 1933, were all off by 5 or 10 per cent, in comparison with the same period of 1932, led the Communist Party Central Committee to take vigorous action.

A number of highly placed officials were dismissed; stringent orders for greater operating efficiency and discipline

[4] *Cf. Izvestia* for September 24, 1930.

were issued; political departments, recruited from staunch and reliable Communists and endowed with wide disciplinarian and executive powers, were established on the railroads. In a speech, the Commissar for Transport, Andreev, pointed out that new inventions and devices for the "rationalization" of railroad traffic had often led to unfavorable results, and even to the damaging of many locomotives and cars, either because they were intrinsically unsound or because they were inapplicable to Russian conditions. Moreover, so much attention was paid to new railroad construction that old lines were neglected, and the road beds in some sections fell into such disrepair that trains can no longer traverse them safely at high rates of speed.

Andreev also pointed out that the human element in the operation of the railroads had been overlooked. Thus, at a time when every available executive and engineer was needed on the lines, about two thirds of the higher railroad officials were employed in central offices where pay was higher and responsibility less arduous. Andreev also said some sharp words about Communists, appointed to high posts, who could not or did not learn the technical side of their work. Finally there was the familiar Russian complaint of "bureaucratism."

"How could it happen," asked the Commissar for Transport, "that the vast majority of the Communist managers on the railroads did not notice the enormous failings?" And he answered his own question: "People are literally drowned in the sea of red tape, bureaucratism, papers, figures, and orders, and have lost all sensitiveness to defects."

So transportation, which was not pushed forward at the same pace with industry during recent years, has become a sort of narrow bottle neck, which limits the progress of industry and agriculture and which might assume the proportions of a national disaster in the event of war.

With all the shortcomings that marked Russia's drive for industrialization (the continual failure of various branches of national economy to keep in step with each other, the frequent cases of inefficient management and poor coordination, and unsatisfactory quality of output), the progress which the country achieved in some fields may fairly be called remarkable. During the last five or six years production in many important branches of industry has been doubled or more than doubled; big new modernly equipped plants have sprung up, sometimes in the most remote and primitive parts of the country; the U.S.S.R. is beginning to make its own automobiles and trucks, its own tractors and harvesting combines.

I had an excellent opportunity to become acquainted on the spot with many of the achievements and failures, the problems and hardships, of the campaign for industrial upbuilding in the course of a trip which took me to the leading industrial centres of the Ural region. This rich industrial and mineral territory, where Europe imperceptibly merges into Asia, might well be called the heart of the Soviet five-year plan. The pace of new construction is faster there than anywhere else in the Soviet Union. Within the boundaries of the Ural region one can find, in various stages of construction and operation, Russia's largest steel plant, its largest chemical factory, its largest machine-building works, its largest copper smelter, and its largest heavy-tractor plant. These are all new enterprises, started since the inauguration of the five-year plan. Whole new cities, unmarked on the maps which were published a few years ago, have grown up around these industrial giants. The pre-war population of the Ural towns has in many cases increased from two to six times.

Although the Ural territory has most of the natural resources that are necessary to make it a self-contained economic unit, the Soviet economic planners, who are endeavoring to divide the country into specialized economic regions, link it up very closely with the adjacent regions of Western Siberia, Kazakstan, and parts of the Bashkir Republic and the middle·Volga region in the vast so-called Ural-Kuznetzk Combination.

Behind this sweeping programme of industrial development are considerable treasures of natural wealth. The Ural region is one of the world's main producers of platinum and asbestos; it is rich in iron and copper, in potash and phosphorus and precious stones. It has enormous forests. It is relatively poor in coal and there is an effort, which incidentally places an additional burden on the country's overburdened railroad system, to exchange the surplus iron ore of Magnitogorsk, site of the country's largest steel plant, for the coal of the Kuznetzk Basin in Central Siberia, some fourteen hundred miles away.

Strategic as well as economic considerations have marked out the Urals and Western Siberia as the main field of new Soviet industrial development. The chain of plants which stretches from Magnitogorsk in the south to Berezniki in the north lies from 1500 to 2000 miles away from the Soviet western frontier and still farther away from the eastern frontier. From the military standpoint, therefore, these new factories, each of which, incidentally, possesses definite potential war utility, are almost impregnable and are secure against hostile air raids.

The huge Magnitogorsk iron and steel plant, built up

since 1929 on a stretch of what was formerly bare steppe land, and already revealing the contours of one of the largest factories of its kind in the world, is at once the greatest, the most dramatic, and the most symbolic enterprise carried out under the five-year plan. It might well be regarded as the *pyatiletka* (five-year plan) incarnate: a strange combination of soaring ambition, driving energy, faltering and sometimes highly defective execution, large-scale building, hard and primitive living conditions, idealism, and ruthlessness.

Magnitogorsk at first conveys a confused series of impressions: heaps of bricks, timber, sand, earth, and other building material, thrown about in characteristically Russian disorderly fashion; long lines of low wooden barracks for the construction laborers; towering new industrial structures, with belching smokestacks.

The best way to bring some pattern of order into the chaos is to climb up the famous Magnet Mountain (so called because of the magnetic quality of its vast stores of ore) which gives the plant and the town their name, and take a panoramic view of the plants and houses which are sprawled out over an area of many square miles on the plain below, against the background of the low, but sharply etched main range of the Ural Mountains, which rises some forty miles to the west.   The town is a product of an ultramodern industrialization, yet curiously enough one's first impression is that of an Asiatic city.   At the time of my visit there was no semblance of paving, and the strong winds from the surrounding steppe lands raised thick clouds of penetrating dust, one of the surest signs of an Eastern town.

There are no mosques or minarets or churches or chapels or other religious edifices in this stronghold of Soviet metallurgy. (It was a Communist boast that this "socialist city" had started out without a single church and also without a single vodka shop. Later it was found necessary to compromise on the sale of vodka.) But the illusion of the Eastern city is preserved by the high industrial structures which overshadow the new town: the long outline of the coke plant; the serpentine intertwinings of the blast furnaces; most of all, perhaps, the high smokestacks of the steel-producing open-hearth furnaces.

When it is completed (Soviet industrial projects have a way of dragging on far beyond the time limits laid down in the original projects) Magnitogorsk will be equipped to produce annually 2,500,000 tons of steel and a somewhat larger quantity of pig iron. Mining operations in the neighboring mountain, which is estimated to contain at least 300,000,000 tons of ore, with an iron content of 65 per cent, will furnish 11,000 tons of ore a year, enough to feed the blast furnaces not only of Magnitogorsk, but of several other large plants.

Forty-two nationalities are represented among the builders of Magnitogorsk. This is just one of the complex elements involved in constructing a modern steel plant in the steppes of Asia. The representatives of varied nationalities range from the experienced American or German engineer, who gives his orders through an interpreter, to the illiterate or semiliterate Kirghiz or Bashkir, who finds it difficult to understand what his Russian foreman may be saying.

Magnitogorsk is located in a region where Russian settlers began to mingle with the nomadic peoples of Central Asia; and not a few of the barracks in which construction workers are housed are occupied by men with swarthy skins and Mongolian faces, who speak Russian brokenly, if at all. Most of the non-Russians are in the less skilled

Soyuzphoto

The Coke Furnaces at Magnitogorsk, Russia's Largest Steel Plant

branches of labor, although I met a Tartar named Galliulin, who, with the "brigade," as working gangs are called in Russia, had set up a world's record for the laying of concrete.

The human relations that grow up around the building of such a huge plant as Magnitogorsk are perhaps even more interesting than the inanimate objects toward which all this labor is being directed — blast furnaces, open-hearth furnaces, electrical power installations, coking ovens. About the time of my arrival the local Communist Party secretary, Karklin, declared in the course of a speech: —

Construction here has gone on and goes on under conditions of fiercest class struggle. The class enemy tries to delay the pact, to sabotage on different sections of building and operation.

"Sabotage of the class enemy" in Russia is all too easy and familiar an explanation for the results of bureaucracy, technical incompetence, and overambitious planning. At the same time there were individuals among the tens of thousands of laborers at Magnitogorsk who had suffered enough to make them desire to throw obstacles in the way of the construction task in which they were very unwilling participants.

Among the motley host of workers one could find two extremes. There was a considerable force of organized Young Communists, always ready to fling themselves into the breach if some part of the building were lagging, willing to work under the hardest material conditions without reckoning hours. They gave the management of the works a valuable reserve of disciplined enthusiasm.

At the other end of the scale were the unfortunate kulaks, or formerly well-to-do peasants, who, after being stripped of their possessions, were sent here, sometimes with their families, to work for the success of a system that is based on their ruin. My first encounter with forced labor in Magnitogorsk was on the littered ground of the coking plant, where forty or fifty boys, fourteen or fifteen years old, were digging and carrying sand. Their working day was limited to the four hours which Soviet law permits for adolescents, but they complained of having to walk four or five hours from the settlement where they lived to their place of work, of having no opportunity to go to school, of the irregularity with which bread rations were given out.

Later I met some of the fathers of these conscripted children, most of whom had been exiled from homes in the neighborhood of Kazan, outside the eating house where they were given one meal a day, in addition to the ration of two pounds of black bread. Their menu, on the day when I was there, consisted of a watery soup, with a few pieces of potato and cucumber floating about on the top, and *kasha*, or grits. They were working the ten-hour day which had been imposed on all the construction workers in order to rush through as much building as possible during the summer months. They spoke with some bitterness, not altogether repressed by the presence of a plant official, of the cruelty with which they had been driven from their homes, of the filthy and crowded condition of the barracks in which they were housed, of the lack of water with which to wash, and of the epidemics of typhus and typhoid fever which had carried off many of their children.

Employment of forced labor at practically no wages and at very minimum subsistence rations has been practised at almost all the large new Soviet factories. There was the same story at the Cheliabinsk tractor plant, at the Berezniki chemical works, at the Dnieprostroi hydroelectric power plant. Not only kulaks (of whom there were hundreds of thousands of families), but other persons who fell into the all-embracing maw of Soviet "class justice" could be found at this construction work. I talked with a peasant who had been packed off to hard labor because, in his own words, "I made too much noise at a meeting of the collective farm and said we were n't getting enough to eat," and to a worker who had been sentenced to imprisonment for breaking a machine. The canal which, along with a chain of lakes and rivers, links up the Baltic with the White Sea, and which was completed in the summer of 1933, was built entirely by the forced labor of criminal and political prisoners, under the supervision of the Gay-Pay-Oo. Forced labor has been a most important element in industrial expansion under the five-year plan. Its use adds one more note of vivid contrast — the effort to rear a modern industry, based on European and American models, on a foundation of Asiatic serfdom.

In the event of war, Magnitogorsk would obviously be a useful national asset. The experience of all the belligerent countries showed with what ease large steel plants may be utilized for the manufacture of shells and munitions. There is a similar military potentiality in the Cheliabinsk tractor works, designed for the manufacture of heavy ten-ton tractors, of the type required for hauling logs in forests and for use in especially tough soil. This plant on short notice could be set to making tanks.

In Sverdlovsk (formerly Ekaterinburg), the capital of the Ural territory and scene of the slaughter of the last Tsar and his family, a large, heavy machine-building plant has been opened. A Soviet engineer who showed me over the works remarked that it was closely based on the Krupp plant at Essen, and added significantly: "We can make everything that Krupp ever made, for war as well as for peace." Farther to the north, amid the tranquil forests along the Kama River, is a chemical factory at Berezniki, designed ultimately to produce half a million tons of chemical fertilizer a year. It turns out nitric acid, sulphuric acid, chlorine, ammonium sulphate, and ammonium nitrate. Regarding the last of these products, a foreign expert remarked: "It 's a mighty good fertilizer in time of peace — and a mighty good explosive in time of war."

Although the Ural region has relatively developed faster than any other part of the Soviet Union, the sweep of industrialization has caught up the entire country. A big new industrial territory is growing up around the huge Dnieprostroi hydroelectric power plant, far and away the largest installation of its kind in Europe, if not in the world. Dnieprostroi, which was formally opened in October 1932, is really a combination of three projects. First of all, a huge dam, 2500 feet long and 170 feet high, has been laid across the Dnieper River about 200 miles from its mouth and a few miles north of the town of Zaporozhe (the former Alexandrousk). Raising the level of the river by 120 feet, the dam makes the Dnieper navigable for a stretch of almost 1300 miles, by submerging the turbulent rapids which formerly blocked all shipping north of Zaporozhe and hundreds of years ago afforded a test of the skill and daring of the wild, independent Cossacks of the region, when they tried to shoot the rapids in canoes. Beside the dam, on the right bank of the river, is the hydroelectrical power station, with normal generating capacity of 756,000 horsepower and an ultimate generating capacity of 900,000 horsepower. The

station gave its first current in 1932, but is not yet functioning at anything like full capacity, partly because the group
of factories which are supposed to absorb the new power
lagged considerably behind the station in the process of construction. These factories include a steel mill, a coking
and chemical plant, an aluminum factory, and a ferro-alloys
works. When all these are finished the Soviet Union will
possess a new, powerful, industrial-military base, more exposed to attack from the west, to be sure, than the remote
chain of Ural plants.

A roll call of other remarkable five-year plan construction achievements would include tractor plants, each with a
capacity of 50,000 a year, in Stalingrad and Kharkov; an
automobile works at Gorky (the former Nizhni Novgorod),
modeled on Ford's Dearborn factory, but very much smaller
in capacity and thus far enormously inferior in smoothness
and efficiency of operation; a ball-bearing plant in Moscow; a steel mill at Stalinsk (formerly Kuznetzk), in Central Siberia; a large agricultural machinery works at Rostov-on-the-Don. These are only a few of the more important of many hundreds of new industrial and mining and
electric power enterprises, while old factories in a number of
instances have been completely reconstructed and enlarged.

Efficiency of operation and quality of output remain weak
spots in the Soviet drive for industrialization. The Commissar for Heavy Industry, Ordzhonikidze, paid a visit of
inspection to the big new steel works at Magnitogorsk and
Stalinsk in the summer of 1933 and published extremely
sharp criticisms of what he found in both places. Magnitogorsk had been projected as one of Russia's first "socialist
cities," free from all the ills to which "capitalist" cities are
supposed to fall heir. What the Commissar for Heavy

Industry discovered was that not one permanent house had been fully completed, that sewerage was conspicuous by its absence, that there were evidences of great neglect and dirt. The workers' barracks are dirty, the roofs leak in some cases, the dining rooms are filthy, and "there is also such a disgraceful thing as cheating the workers in weighing out their bread rations." All this bore out my own impression that Magnitogorsk combined two kinds of filth — the dust and utter lack of sanitation of an Asiatic city and the grime of a Western industrial town.

Ordzhonikidze had more harsh words about the functioning of the works. He commented on the large number of parts of the plant which had been started without being finished. These unfinished construction jobs, combined with lack of technical knowledge and skill among the workers and poor labor discipline, led to "frequent accidents which often threaten to inflict serious destructive effects upon individual machines and even upon the whole plant." Stalinsk was apparently little better. Here Ordzhonikidze spoke of the negligence evinced in not preparing the equipment for winter conditions, with the result that many machines became unusable for months as a result of freezing, and of the number of accidents, large and small, which had not been properly investigated, with a view to preventing their repetition.

An American engineer, who had fulfilled very responsible consultant functions at two of the largest and most important of the new Soviet plants, once burst out in the course of a private conversation: "I don't believe any honest foreign engineer could do anything but laugh at the idea of this country ever becoming really industrialized. Look at the crazy things I 've had to try to stop them from doing at Y," and he proceeded to outline a long list of technical slips and blunders. "You came to Y from X," I said; "how is the X factory getting on?" "Better than I expected," he replied. "They are getting out more production than I thought they could after the first months of operation, when some machine was breaking down almost every day, and the tubes of the boiler plant were always burning out." "Then maybe you are too pessimistic about Y," I suggested. "Of course," he replied, "once you have built a factory you can get some output from it, no matter how many mistakes you make. But you have to take some account of the cost. Why, a factory like X or Y in America, faced with hard competition, would be bankrupt in six months."

There are certainly very few Soviet factories which could hold their own in a technical competition if they were suddenly transplanted to America, England, or Germany. A new zinc plant at Ordzhonikidze, in the North Caucasus, four years after its construction began, is turning out five tons of zinc a day with a staff of 300 office workers and 1600 factory hands. A foreign visitor observed that a similar plant in St. Louis, after a similar period of construction, was producing fifty tons of zinc a day — with a force of sixteen office workers and 170 manual workers. This was undoubtedly an extreme case, with special circumstances. Russian labor productivity is unquestionably much lower than American, but not as low as these figures would suggest. But the illustration does show that a new plant in the Soviet Union requires far greater labor power to produce much smaller results than would be necessary in more technically advanced countries.

However, the element of cost and efficiency, which seems all-important to foreign engineers who have been trained in the school of merciless, high-speed competition, is not of such immediate importance in the Soviet Union as it would be in a country where the individualist system still prevailed in economic life. In the long run, to be sure, the Soviet leaders themselves are quite ready to recognize that the "capitalist powers" will beat them unless they develop a superior technique of production.

But when every industrial plant belongs, in the last analysis, to the huge state supertrust, mismanagement does not bring as a consequence a shutdown or a stoppage of production. When incompetent operation of a factory becomes too glaringly obvious, the Soviet authorities swoop down with Draconic penalties, not only dismissing the luckless director, but sometimes also putting him in prison. The factory then goes on as before under new direction. In the last analysis losses are borne by the national economy as a whole. The bill for the enormous new capital investment represented by the five-year plan is paid by the whole Russian people in the form of a distinctly lowered standard of living. To the rulers of the country the increase in its military capacity, the gradual freeing of it from dependence on foreign markets for such things as automobiles, tractors, agricultural and industrial machines, seem worth the price which has been exacted. If the masses of the people dissent from this view, they have extremely little opportunity of making their dissent effectively known.

Some foreign observers of the Soviet Union are inclined to criticize industrialization as an unnatural and uneconomic policy and to predict its failure on the ground that the Russians, by nature, are an incorrigibly untechnical people. I think these views are exaggerated. When nature provided Russia with extensive national resources it marked out the country for ultimate industrial development.

And it is a grave mistake to imagine that Russian industrialization dates from the inauguration of the five-year plan
or that the Communists deserve credit for modernizing an
utterly backward country. Pre-war Russia got a late start
in the industrial field, but the pace of its advance in periods
of world prosperity was very fast. The country's size, resources, and population made possible a scale of development,
in some respects, that would not have been practicable in
the smaller, more cramped and closely settled European
countries. Russia's rate of building railroads during the
nineties of the last century exceeded that of other European
countries at their most intensive periods of development.[5]
Russia's railroad mileage increased from 49,174 kilometres
in 1905 to 58,821 in 1913.[6] Between 1928 and 1932 the
increase was from 76,800 kilometres to 82,000 kilometres.[7]
The annual average during the Soviet period was somewhat
greater; but the pre-war building was more solid and left
fewer odd jobs to be cleaned up in later years. Russian
industrial production increased from 6,177,900,000 rubles
in 1912 to 7,357,800,000 rubles in 1913,[8] a rate of increase
of 19.1 per cent, which compares not unfavorably with that
of the last three years in the Soviet Union.[9] It must also
be borne in mind that pre-war Russian rubles were a con-

[5] *Cf.* Tugan-Baranovsky's classical economic history, *Russkaya Fabrika
v Proshlom i Nastoyashchem* ("The Russian Factory in Past and Present"),
p. 273.
[6] *Finansovo-Ekonomicheski Ezhegodnik* ("Financial-Economic Annual"), Petrograd, 1914, p. 515.
[7] *Cf.* Soviet magazine, *Bolshevik*, November 30, 1932, p. 43.
[8] *Dinamika Rossiskoi i Sovietskoi Promishlennosti* ("The Dynamics of
Russian and Soviet Industry"), Vol. I, Part III, pp. 13–177.
[9] The rates of growth of the large Soviet industries during 1931, 1932,
and 1933 have been officially stated, respectively, as 22.6 per cent, 11 per
cent, 9.1 per cent.

siderably more solid unit of reckoning than Soviet rubles of recent vintage.

So what seems open to criticism in the Bolshevik policy of industrialization is not the policy itself (which would have been inevitable under any ordered political and economic régime), but the overstrained pace and the unnecessary sacrifices which this caused. As for the supposedly unmechanical character of the Russian people, it should be borne in mind that peoples, like individuals, learn by doing. The low educational qualifications and the lack of technical experience of the typical new peasant recruit to industry [10] have undoubtedly contributed their share to the numerous worries of the Soviet industrial manager. But technical knowledge and aptitude cannot be considered matters of pure intuition; they may quite conceivably be created over a period of years.

The difficulties of achievement under the five-year plan were enhanced by the fact that the Soviet Union received no aid of any consequence in the form of investments of foreign capital. The sole form of help from abroad was in the form of so-called technical aid contracts, under which foreign firms and individual engineers and experts were engaged to draw up plans for new enterprises and to supervise, to some extent, the execution of these plans. American aid was employed, especially in the automobile, tractor, steel, and electrical industries; more German specialists were employed in the machine-building industries. This kind of coöperation began to fall off more and more, however, as the Soviet Government found itself increasingly short of foreign

[10] One of the funniest and also truest of Low's series of Russian cartoons shows a peasant girl fumbling around in a factory and bears the caption: "Peasant Recruit to Industry Tries to Milk a Steam Hammer."

currency. At the present time only a very small number of foreign specialists are still engaged on a *valuta* or foreign-currency basis. Work is available at salaries payable in Soviet rubles; but, as the ruble has no value whatever outside of Soviet territory, the foreigner who accepts a ruble contract is really agreeing simply to work for maintenance; and such an arrangement does not, of course, attract men of the highest qualification.

The year 1933 was a sort of bridge between the first and the second five-year plan. Many of the characteristic features of the first headlong drive for industrialization were discarded or modified, either because experience had shown their inadvisability or because changing economic conditions required new methods of approach.

The first five-year plan emphasized quantity output and new building on a grandiose scale; the second plan shifts the emphasis to quality of output, to the completion and efficient operation of the many unfinished giant enterprises of the first plan. While the original plan did include provisions for raising the living standard of the population, these were soon forgotten in the fierce struggle for the maximum amount of new building; and actually there was a severe deterioration of the standard of living as a result of agricultural shortages and the sacrifices which were imposed as the price of rapid industrialization. The second plan puts an improved standard of living very much in the foreground of its objectives, and calls for the development of the industries which minister to the direct needs of the consumer at a faster pace than that of the heavy industries.

The framers of the first plan suffered acutely from what is called in Russia "giant-mania" — that is, from the delusion that the bigger the factory or the farm the better it would be.

The second plan is based on a clear realization of the desirability of more decentralization. The first plan, especially up to 1931, appealed primarily to enthusiasm, to the desire of the workers to "build up socialism." While the propaganda appeal is by no means neglected now, the present tendency is to lay much more stress on such prosaic incentives as differential wage scales and piecework methods of payment. The first plan was based on an almost blind faith in the magical power of the machine. The second plan has a much clearer vision of the importance of the human being in industry.

The original five-year plan, and still more the upward revisions to which it was periodically subjected, grossly overestimated the country's capacity for increasing production. The second plan has been much more cautiously framed. It is significant that whereas the revised version of the first plan called for 17,000,000 tons of pig iron in 1932 (the actual output was 6,200,000), the second plan prescribes an output of only 16,000,000 tons in 1937. The preliminary estimates of the second plan, published in 1931, laid down fantastic figures — 62,000,000 tons of pig iron, 650,000,000 tons of coal, 125,000,000 or 150,000,000 tons of oil — for realization in 1937. In the final authorized version of the plan these figures have been sweepingly cut to 16,000,000 tons of pig iron, 152,500,000 tons of coal, and 46,800,000 tons of oil. Extravagant and futile planning has finally bred some measure of discretion.

The most noteworthy features of the second five-year plan, which will govern the country's development until 1937, are the increased attention to railroad transportation, the shift of emphasis from the heavy industries to those which produce consumers' goods, the eastward swing of the country's development, and the tendency to place newly projected factories near their sources of raw material. About 7500 miles of new railroad lines are to be built; the number of locomotives is to increase from 19,500 to 24,600 and the number of cars from 552,000 to 803,000, while many stretches of line are to be furnished with electrical power. With a view to making good the promises that real wages should be more than doubled during the second plan (real wages did not increase, but heavily declined during the period of the first plan, as a result of the shortage of foodstuffs and commodities), it is proposed to build 313 large factories of various kinds for the manufacture of consumers' goods (textile mills, shoe factories, glass works, and so on) and 350 food factories (such as canning and refrigerating plants, sugar mills, candy factories). These figures do not include small and middle-sized enterprises.

Many of the new textile plants are to be built in Central Asia, the country's main source of cotton; and this will have the incidental effect of bringing industrial habits to the primitive Uzbeks and Turcomans who live in that part of the world. The eastward trend of Soviet industry and population is emphasized by the fact that, according to the second plan, the eastern regions of the country (Siberia, the Ural territory, Kazakstan, and Central Asia), by 1937, are to produce a third of the country's pig iron, as against a fourth in 1932; about a fifth of the electrical energy, as against 6.5 per cent in 1932; a tenth of the output of machinery, as against a twentieth in 1932.

The heavy industries are not to be neglected during the second plan, although they will not be advanced so fanatically at the expense of the living standards of the population. Two new plants for the manufacture of three-ton trucks in Ufa and in Stalingrad are on the programme, along with a copper-smelting works on Lake Balkash, in Kazakstan. Perhaps the biggest new enterprise will be a huge hydro-electrical power works at Kamishin, on the lower Volga, which will make possible the irrigation of an extensive area on the left bank of the Volga which is suitable for wheat growing, but is subject to frequent drought. Two other hydroelectric plants will be constructed higher up on the Volga, in the vicinity of Jaroslavl and Gorky; and canals will link the upper reaches of the Volga with the Moscow River (thereby assuring Moscow's water supply) and the lower Volga with the Don. The first of these canals is already being built with the forced labor of "class enemies"; and one suspects that there will always be "class enemies" in Russia — so long as canals remain to be built.

Whether the second plan can fulfill its promise to give the population two and a half or three times as much food and manufactured goods as they received in 1932 (so great was the shortage and, in some regions, the actual hunger in that year that a doubling or trebling of food and manufac-tured goods would not imply a state of glowing prosperity) would seem to depend largely on whether the country's agricultural crisis has been definitely overcome. For the Soviet Union is primarily dependent on itself both for food and for most of the raw materials — cotton, wool, hides, which are necessary for the expansion of the consumers'-goods industries.

That the Soviet Union will still be far short of the realiza-tion of its cherished dream of "overtaking and outstripping America" in technical achievements after the end of the second plan is evident from the fact that the plan, even if it is fulfilled, will provide the country with 580,000 automobiles and trucks by 1937 — a little over 2 per cent of the American figure.

The five-year plan wrought vast changes in agriculture as well as in industry. And if in industry the unmistakable addition to the national stock of industrial equipment, the increased military capacity, the growing economic independence of the outside world, may seem to balance the great sacrifices which were imposed on the population, the picture in agriculture is much darker. The Russian peasants have experienced a protracted double tragedy, a tragedy compounded of the forcible uprooting of old habits and instincts and of increasing material deprivations, a tragedy which reached its climax in the terrible famine of 1932–1933, and which is only now beginning to yield to more hopeful prospects. But this is a subject for separate description.

IV

THE ORDEAL OF THE PEASANTRY

EVER since 1929, when the Soviet rulers declared what has
proved in practice a war of extermination against private
farming, the Russian peasants have lived through a tremendous ordeal, comparable in violent change and suffering only
with the crowded years of social upheaval, civil war, and
famine which marked the period from 1917 until 1921.
What has happened may be described as an agrarian revolution from the top, driven through against the passive opposition of the majority of the peasants whose lives it affected.

No one with first-hand knowledge of the Russian village
can well believe that the average peasant, left to his own
free will, would have given up his holding for membership
in one of the new *kolkhozi*, or collective farms. The best
evidence on this point is the fact that less than 2 per cent
of the peasant households entered collective farms during
the years of the New Economic Policy, between 1921 and
1929, when the choice between individual and collective
farming was genuinely free.

One cannot travel far in the Soviet countryside to-day
without seeing tangible signs of sweeping change. The
familiar strips of land which signalized individual holdings
have given way — especially in the broad steppes of the
south and southeast — to the wide compact fields of collective and state farms. The hum of the tractor is heard

more frequently; the threshing machine and the harvesting combine are more common sights.   There are other changes which make a less favorable impression: if there are more tractors on Soviet fields, there are far fewer horses and cows, pigs and sheep; and the harvesting combines which are supposed to symbolize the march of progress in agriculture sometimes find the going hard in the seas of weeds which are found on many state and collective farms.

In the human sphere the transformations that one would find on revisiting a country district in Ukraina or in the North Caucasus after an absence of several years are even more revolutionary.   In a very literal sense the last have become first and the first have become last.   The former *batrak*, or farm hand, who used to be at the bottom of the primitive village social hierarchy, may now be the manager of a collective farm, directing the work of hundreds of his fellow villagers.   There has been a considerable influx of urban Communists, most of them ex-workers, into the villages as directors of the state and collective farms and heads of the important political departments which were instituted early in 1933.

There has been a huge "liquidation" of the more well-to-do and incorrigibly individualistic peasants, loosely and conveniently dubbed "kulaks."   They have been packed in freight cars and shipped off in hundreds of thousands, if not in millions, for forced labor in timber camps, on canals, in new construction enterprises.   And during the winter of 1932 and the spring of 1933 stark famine stalked through great areas of Ukraina and the North Caucasus, the lower and middle Volga, and parts of Central Asia, levying a 10 per cent death toll on a population of fifty or sixty millions. This climax in the human tragedy of the peasantry, this

low point in the Soviet agrarian situation, has been followed
by a fair measure of recovery, as a result of the more favorable harvest of 1933.   But much reconstruction remains to
be done, especially in the field of animal husbandry, before
Russian agricultural production can be regarded as normal
and satisfactory.

Although the peasantry, in the official phraseology, is
characterized as the faithful ally of the sovereign proletariat,
it has always, in practice, represented a tough nut for the
Soviet rulers to crack.   The peasant, with his instinctive sense
of private property, his desire for self-enrichment, was an
anachronism in a socialist state.   In 1921 the passive resistance of the peasantry, expressed in a systematic curtailment
of the planted acreage, was the main factor in forcing the
Soviet Government to carry out the strategic retreat which
was known as the New Economic Policy, with its substitution
of fixed taxes for irregular requisitions, and its toleration
of free trade within the country, small privately owned factories, and handicraft enterprises.

By 1928, Stalin felt strong enough to launch a new drive
against the individualist peasants.   Convinced that the country could not go on half socialist and half capitalist, he
decided to make a thoroughgoing reorganization of agriculture a part of the new system of planned economy.   Since
that time Soviet agrarian policy, while it has performed
occasional zigzags under the pressure of food shortage, has
remained mercilessly true to its two main objectives, which
may be summed up in the polysyllabic words "mechanization" and "collectivization."

Changes of method and of detail there have been from
year to year.   The margin of private property which has
been left to the peasant has been narrowed at some times,

widened at others.   But there has been no wavering in the pursuit of the main goal: the nationalization of the peasants' land, working animals, and machinery, and the substitution of state and collective for individual farming.

Whatever one may think of the methods by which this enormous experiment in the transformation of agriculture was carried out, however one may judge its practical results and future prospects, it has, to a very large extent, been carried irrevocably into effect.   According to the latest official figures,[1] 15,200,000 peasant households, 65 per cent of the total number, are now organized in 224,500 collective farms; and the remaining 35 per cent of individual peasants account for only 15.5 per cent of the acreage sown to grain. Collective farms sowed 73.9 per cent of this area in 1933, state farms 10.6 per cent.   Crushed under a variety of discriminatory taxes and other burdens, denied opportunity to purchase new machinery, the individual peasants seem doomed to economic extinction; their complete elimination and inclusion in collective farms is one of the objectives of the second five-year plan.

The overwhelming majority of the collective farms are of the artel type, where the peasant keeps as his own property house and garden, a cow and a pig and a few chickens, if he is lucky enough to own them.   The main field crops, together with all working animals and machinery, on the other hand, are the property of the collective farm as a whole.   The members of the collective farm are paid in a theoretical unit known as "the work-day," the value of which, in money and in kind, is calculated after the harvest is gathered in and the accounts of the farm have been cast up.

[1] *Cf.* Stalin's report at the Seventeenth Congress of the All-Union Communist Party published in *Pravda* for January 28, 1934.

Payment is according to quantity and quality of work; a tractor driver would receive several times as many "workdays" for the same period of work as an unskilled woman field hand. The collective farm members receive some payment in money, some in grain and other products.

A few of the collective farms are of the "commune" type. Here there is no individual ownership of animals or gardens — the members put everything into the common pool and eat at a common table. Very often, although not invariably, members of communes live in dormitories, not in individual houses. Originally many communes established the rule that all members should be paid equally; but this has been discarded because of the rigorous insistence of the Soviet leaders that payment must be unequal, so as to stimulate greater productivity of labor. One usually finds more sympathy with the Soviet régime, more sense of voluntariness, in a commune than in an artel. The communes were in many cases formed when there was no special state pressure to force the peasants to give up individual farming. Their members were often recruited from the very poorest peasants, who had nothing promising to expect under the individualist system; a few communes were established by returned Russian emigrants or by political refugees from other countries with Communist sympathies.

Along with the collective farms, which have swallowed up the former individual holdings of the peasants, are state farms, which have mostly been established on previously unused land. A state farm is managed by a director who is appointed by the government and pays its laborers fixed wages. The chief grain farms are under the management of the Grain Trust, which has over 200 large farms with a total area of more than 30,000,000 acres.

State farming has proved far from successful. The Grain Trust in the early years of its existence suffered acutely from "giant-mania" and built up farms with hundreds of thousands of acres which proved unmanageably large. Moreover, it established many of its wheat farms in arid regions of the southeastern steppe, which were subject to drought. The elementary teachings of agricultural science about the necessity of crop rotations were ignored in an effort to create huge "grain factories" which would produce wheat every year. Whereas all practical considerations in the Soviet Union, with its shortage of materials and transportation, demand the organization of a large farm as a self-contained unit, capable of supplying its own needs as far as possible, the organizers of the state farms yielded to the theoretical arguments in favor of extreme specialization and only recently have made some effort to supplement their grain production with vegetable gardens and animal husbandry.

Inefficient management and the difficulties of recruiting an efficient force of farm laborers for the short harvest season have added to the difficulties of the state farms. There have been ironical instances when tractors and threshing machines on the big state farms, which were supposed, in the popular Soviet phrase, "to be mechanized according to the last word of technique," simply could not function amid the sea of luxuriant weeds which had grown up, and when peasants from the neighborhood had to be called in with primitive sickles in order to clear the fields.

Efforts are being made to reform the state farms, to correct the cruder blunders of their first period of organization. They exist in other fields besides grain: there are state livestock ranches, cotton plantations, flax and sugar-beet farms. Their rôle in the future of Soviet agriculture seems destined to be a minor and subordinate one, however; much more important are the collective farms, in which the overwhelming majority of the peasants are employed.

The Soviet leaders have always regarded mechanization as an integral part of their programme of shifting farming from an individual to a collective basis. Tractors, harvesting combines, threshing machines, and other large-scale implements were to furnish the cement which would hold the new collective farms together and increase their productivity. Three huge tractor plants (of which two are in full operation) were constructed during the five-year plan; the largest agricultural machinery works in Europe was set up at Rostov-on-the-Don; and there have been an enlargement of old factories and a building of new ones for the manufacture of combines.

It is significant of the spirit of the new Soviet agriculture that collective farms are not permitted to acquire, even in common ownership, tractors and other large machines. These are concentrated in the nerve centres of the country's agriculture, the so-called machine-tractor stations. (A considerable number of the large machines are also used on the state farms.) There are between 2500 and 3000 machine-tractor stations all over the Soviet Union; and they dispatch their machines in the planting and harvesting seasons to all the collective farms within a convenient radius, exacting, in return for their services, a fee in kind that may run as high as 20 per cent of the crop. There are now about 200,000 tractors on the Soviet fields.

The massing of equipment in state-operated machine-tractor stations serves a double purpose, at once technical and political. Provided that the station is efficiently managed and keeps its machines in reasonable repair, it is able to

TRACTORS AT WORK ON A COLLECTIVE FARM

ensure a more continuous use and a more even spread of mechanical power than would be possible if every collective farm had its own share, large or small, of machinery. On the political side, this system is calculated to keep the collective farmers in submission by depriving them of any possession of their means of production. Apart from such cruder methods as arrests and deportations, the state could bring very strong pressure on a collective farm that failed to make the prescribed grain deliveries by simply cutting off its supply of mechanical power. I once spent several days in a machine-tractor station in the Odessa district and felt that here was something like a modernized feudal castle, created for the purpose of holding the surrounding countryside in subjection.

This reorganization of Soviet agriculture has been brought about only at the expense of a most ferocious internal struggle, which at certain times almost assumed the aspect of a very one-sided civil war, and resulted in tremendous human and material losses. The difficulties of the Iowa farmer or the Balkan peasant, serious though they undoubtedly are, seem slight by comparison with the ordeal of the Russian peasantry. The official figures of live stock alone bear witness to a process of devastation that would normally have indicated the invasion of a hostile army. If the figures of the human victims of collectivization, of the kulak children who died like flies in the northern timber camps, of the unnumbered peasants who swelled up and died of outright hunger or of diseases originating in hunger, should be published, the picture would be still more impressive in its tragedy. Let us take the live-stock statistics, computed by the million head, as printed in Stalin's report in *Pravda* for January 28, 1934: —

	1916	1929	1930	1931	1932	1933
Horses	35.1	34.0	30.2	26.2	19.6	16.6
Big-horned cattle	58.9	68.1	52.5	47.9	40.7	38.6
Sheep and goats	115.2	147.2	108.8	77.7	52.1	50.6
Pigs	20.3	20.9	13.6	14.4	11.6	12.2

In other words, the Soviet Union, during the period of violent and forcible collectivization of its agriculture, lost over half of its horses, almost half of its big-horned cattle, almost two thirds of its sheep and goats, and over 40 per cent of its pigs. The disastrous effect of this on the supply of meat and dairy products and such raw materials as wool and hides is obvious. The live-stock catastrophe has up to the present time more than nullified the new mechanical power which has been poured into Soviet agriculture. It is officially computed [2] that the Soviet Union's approximately 200,000 tractors represent 3,100,000 horsepower. But meanwhile over 17,000,000 live horses have been lost. Far from becoming easier, the peasant's labor has become harder. In a recent trip through Ukraina, I more than once found men and women staggering under loads which formerly have been placed on horses.

What of the acreage planted and the crop yields under the new system? Substantial gains in 1930 and 1931 were followed by slighter retrogressions in 1932 and 1933, as is evident from the following table, computed in millions of hectares, a hectare equaling 2.5 acres.

ACREAGE PLANTED

1913	1929	1930	1931	1932	1933
105.0	118.0	127.2	136.3	134.4	129.7

The Soviet grain crops for the last five years are officially stated as follows: 1929, 71,740,000 tons; 1930, 83,540,000

[2] *Cf.* Stalin's report in *Pravda* for January 28, 1934.

tons; 1931, 69,480,000 tons; 1932, 69,870,000 tons; 1933, 89,800,000 tons. The figure for 1933, incidentally, seems open to grave question.[3] In the five-year period from 1909 until 1913 that part of the Russian Empire now included in the Soviet Union reaped an average crop of 70,000,000 tons of the main kinds of grain. These comparative figures, incidentally, furnish a conclusive answer to the question whether the masses of the people were eating more in Tsarist days or under the five-year plan. In 1931 and 1932 the Soviet Union, with a population of over 160,000,000, realized less grain than the same territory in pre-war days, with a population of 138,000,000. True, the average annual export of Tsarist Russia was 9,400,000 tons as against 4,600,000 tons in 1931 and 1,819,914 tons in 1932. But, after allowance is made for this, the *per capita* grain consumption is less under the Soviet régime than in Tsarist times, when the chronic undernourishment of the rural population

[3] Ordinarily I accept Soviet official statistics, sometimes with mental misgivings, because it is impossible for an outsider to obtain alternative figures of real credibility. In the case of the 1933 harvest, however, the head of the State Statistical Department, Mr. Ossinsky, in an article in *Izvestia* of September 21, 1933, described methods of computing the crop which would seem to be at once highly original and decidedly untrustworthy. According to Mr. Ossinsky, the yield was obtained by deducting 10 per cent from the estimate of what the crop would have been if it had been brought from the fields to the granaries without any loss. Russian losses in harvesting have always been notoriously high; and in the same article Mr. Ossinsky makes the significant admission that "in most cases the threshings proved to be 30, 40, or 50 per cent lower than the estimated 'biological crop.'" (The "biological crop" was the theoretical yield without losses.) In view of Mr. Ossinsky's admissions it would seem necessary to suspend judgment on the real amount of the 1933 harvest, especially as it would tax one's credulity to believe that the Soviet Union, which comfortably fed its population from 1925 until 1928 without rationing restrictions on crops that averaged 75,000,000 tons, would find it necessary to preserve those restrictions if it had really produced a crop of almost 90,000,000 tons.

was a favorite theme of radical and liberal publicists. The comparative food situation becomes still less favorable to the Soviet régime when one considers the immense diminution in the supply of meat, milk, and dairy products.

Cotton, of which pre-war Russia produced 740,000 tons, had been driven up to 1,320,000 tons in 1933. This was done to some extent at the expense of the stomachs of the Central Asians, who were compelled to give up growing rice and sometimes failed to receive in adequate amount bread or other food substitutes in exchange for the cotton which they were forced to plant. The output of flax, which was 330,000 tons in 1913, was 560,000 tons in 1933. In the case of sugar beets, on the other hand, a crop of 10,900,000 tons in 1913 compares with one of 6,560,000 tons in 1932 and of 9,000,000 tons in 1933 — a sufficient explanation of why Russians have little sugar for their tea in the large cities and sometimes none at all in small towns and country districts.

There were several reasons why the Soviet programme of collectivization turned the vast Russian countryside into an arena of desperate struggle, many of the scars of which are still very evident. I do not agree with the facile suggestion put forward sometimes by Soviet apologists that the explanation of the initial difficulties of collectivization is to be found in the "backwardness" of the peasants. The best disproof of this idea is the unquestionable fact that collectivization wrought greatest havoc, in the main, just where the peasants were more intelligent, more progressive in farming methods, where the pre-war standard of living was highest. It is not in the primitive Caucasian *aul* (mountain village) or in the forest hamlet of the North that one finds the clearest signs of devastation. The worst famine regions in

1932–1933 were in many cases the most fertile and prosperous farming districts of pre-war Russia: the rich North Caucasus; the German colonies on the Volga and in Ukraina, where the people were always noted for their good farming; the fertile "black-earth" Ukrainian provinces of Kiev and Poltava.   It was not the more backward peasants, but the more progressive and well-to-do, who usually showed the greatest resistance to collectivization, and this not because they did not understand what the new policy would portend, but because they understood too well.

Broadly speaking, the widespread peasant objection to the collective farms was rooted in two sets of causes, one psychological and the other material.   It implied a vast wrench from old habits and instincts for a peasant who had been used to taking care of his own little homestead to cast horse, farm implements, and land into a melting pot; to place himself under the orders of a collective-farm manager, who might, incidentally, be an ignoramus on matters of practical farming; to take a chance that he would receive a satisfactory share of grain when the payments were made after the harvest.

The average peasant's desire for a sense of personal ownership, which to him meant freedom and independence, his deep distrust even of his own neighbors, to say nothing of alien city Communists who came to tell him how farming ought to be carried on, could have been overcome only if collective farming had meant a swift and marked rise in the peasants' standard of living.   But just the reverse occurred. Determined to achieve the maximum amount of industrialization within the shortest possible time, the Soviet leaders found themselves obliged to place heavier and heavier burdens on the peasants.   The state needed more grain, more meat, more milk, more cotton, flax, wool, and sugar beets, both for the needs of the city population and for purposes of export. Concentrating on the heavy industries, it did not possess sufficient stocks of manufactured goods to offer the peasants a fair equivalent for their produce.

The result was that a system of virtual requisitioning of the peasants' products at fixed prices in paper rubles grew up. During the last few years no words have been so hated on the Soviet countryside as *khlebozagotovki* (grain collections) and *kontraktatsia* (contracting). The former stood for the ruthless squeezing out of the last bushel of the peasants' surplus grain which became one of the most important functions of Communist local officials; the latter for a system, highly unfair in the eyes of the peasants, under which they were obliged to deliver up all the surplus of their more important crops for paper rubles and a doubtful chance of buying manufactured goods. I remember a meeting in a collective farm which I visited on the lower Volga in the fall of 1930. A local Communist orator, sent from a neighboring town, harangued the peasants on the international situation and then explained a scheme of exchange of grain for manufactured goods under which the peasants would receive thirty-five kopecks' worth of manufactured goods for every ruble's worth of grain which they sold to the state. This aroused a tumult of protest; and the collective-farm blacksmith, who was sitting near me, shouted in disgust: "Thirty-five kopecks for a ruble is n't a fair deal! Could n't they give us all at least one shirt?"

I traveled widely in the Soviet Union during the years of the first five-year plan; and everywhere, from the timber camps of Karelia, the northern country of lakes and forests, to the hot steppes of the lower Volga, the peasants had one keenly defined sense of grievance: that more was being extracted from them, in the form of products and labor, than they were getting in the form of clothes and boots, tea and sugar and soap. Indeed, these last commodities were often completely lacking in the rural districts; the peasants brewed unsweetened tea substitute out of berries and used a preparation of ashes as a substitute for soap.

All this furnished a striking practical exemplification of the heretical Communist Preobrazhensky's theory that the peasants represent a colony which the socialist state must exploit — a theory which Preobrazhensky has duly recanted. The increasing tendency to substitute deliveries in kind — so much grain, so much meat, so much milk, and so forth — for the former money taxes has a flavor of feudal times and lends point to another assertion, which has also been recanted, by the Communist theoretician, Nikolai Bukharin, that what was going on in the villages was equivalent to "military feudal exploitation of the peasantry." And one of the bitter "anecdotes," or satirical jokes, of recent years was that the Russian initials for All-Union Communist Party, V K P, really stand for *vtoroe krepostnoe pravo* (second serfdom). A parallel "anecdote" is to the effect that Russia, after the five-year plan, needed three Tsars: Peter the Great to clear up the unfinished building, Alexander II to free the peasants from serfdom, and Nicholas II to raise enough food to make up for the shortage.

Up to 1929 the collective farms were tiny islands in the sea of individual homesteads. The big inrush of peasants into the collective farms in the fall of 1929 and the winter of 1929–1930 closely coincided with a process that was euphemistically characterized as "the liquidation of the kulaks as a class." The Soviets, it should be noted, have given the term "kulak" a different meaning from what it possessed before the Revolution. In Tsarist days the "kulak," or "fist," was a thoroughgoing exploiter, a man who perhaps had half the village in his "fist" through money loaned at usurious rates of interest. With their usual capacity for fastening opprobrious epithets on their opponents, the Communists began to apply the term "kulak" to every peasant who rose conspicuously above the low average living standard of the village, regardless of whether or not he was a money lender. So, while the pre-war kulaks were a small number of village Shylocks, the Soviet kulaks constituted 4 or 5 per cent of the whole peasant population and included all the peasant families that owned mills or other little enterprises, or possessed much in excess of the average amount of cattle and machinery.

One would search the voluminous collections of Soviet decrees in vain for a precise definition of what constitutes a kulak. It was to the advantage of the Communists to keep the term loose and elastic. As the struggle over collectivization became more intense, any peasant who spoke out strongly against the new system was likely to be denounced as a kulak if he possessed any property; if he was too hopelessly poor to make the epithet plausible, he could be disposed of as a "kulak agent."

The "liquidation of the kulaks as a class" in regions where collectivization was fairly complete was announced by Stalin as a policy and was legally authorized and carried into effect in the winter of 1929–1930. Under this system the kulak families were driven from their homes, with few possessions except the clothes on their backs, and were either deported in freight cars to the northern forests and other places of forced labor or obliged to live in dugouts and shanties on

the outskirts of the village. The measure was often executed with great brutality, men, women, and children being
driven out in the bitter cold of the Russian winter; and its
toll of death, especially among young children and old men,
was very great. It was quite in the spirit of the Iron Age;
it showed that the Communist leaders would spare no weapon
of ruthlessness in breaking the recalcitrant peasantry to
their will.

Some relaxation of pressure on the peasantry took place
in the spring of 1930, when the authorities realized that an
enormous destruction of cattle had taken place as a result
of the prevalent policy of forcing the peasants to surrender
all their animals to the possession of the collective farm.
Stalin at this time published his famous "Giddiness from
Success" instructions, in which he conveniently threw all
the blame for excesses on local officials and laid down as a
general rule that the peasant in the collective farm should
keep house and garden, cow and chickens. At the same
time, peasants in parts of the country which were not considered technically prepared for collectivization were permitted to leave the new farms if they desired; and the percentage of collectivization fell rapidly from 55 to 21.

Nature was kind to the Communists in 1930; a bountiful
harvest covered up much inefficient work in the new collective farms and gave the Communists the impression that
the major part of the agricultural transformation was over.
Pressure was again applied to the peasants, and the percentage of collectivized homesteads began to mount upward. The most convincing argument to the average peasant was the fate of his kulak neighbors. This was a plain
enough intimation that if he persisted in his individual farming and had any degree of prosperity he would also be

eligible for "liquidation." Moreover, any peasant who talked loudly against the government measures at a public meeting was likely to be regarded as a kulak and treated accordingly. Very powerful economic pressure was brought to bear on the peasants by giving the collective farms preferential treatment in everything, from taxes to social benefits and occasional itinerant moving-picture performances.

But the worst of Russia's agrarian crisis was not over. As a result of poor climatic conditions, the crop of 1931 was substantially inferior to that of 1930. The state exactions from the peasantry, on the other hand, were not relaxed, but intensified. In 1932, climatic conditions were better; but the peasants, discouraged and in many cases already suffering from undernourishment, showed little interest in reaping the crops which, as they felt, would be taken away from them anyway. The stage was set for a climatic catastrophe. The government had in reserve and was prepared to employ the last and sharpest weapon in the armory of class warfare: organized famine.

Rumors of wholesale starvation in the villages, especially in the southern and southeastern provinces of European Russia and in Central Asia, began to filter into Moscow in the early spring. A clear intimation that things were happening in the country districts which the Soviet censors very definitely wished to conceal from the outside world was the unprecedented action of the authorities in forbidding several foreign correspondents to leave Moscow, and the establishment of a new ruling to the effect that no foreign correspondent could travel in the countryside without submitting a definite itinerary and obtaining permission to make the trip from the Commissariat for Foreign Affairs.

No such permissions were granted until September, when

the new harvest was largely gathered in, the corpses had all been buried, the trucks which, during late winter and early spring, made regular rounds in Poltava, Kiev, and other centres of the famine region, picking up the corpses of refugees from the country districts, had ceased to function, and conditions were generally more normal. After the prohibition had been lifted, I visited three widely separated districts of the Soviet Union — Kropotkin, in the North Caucasus, and Poltava and Byelaya Tserkov, in Ukraina. I talked at railroad stations with peasants ranging from the southeast corner of Ukraina, in the Donetz Basin, to the northwestern part of Chernigov Province. On the basis of talks with peasants and figures supplied not by peasants, who were often prone to exaggeration, but by local Soviet officials and collective-farm presidents, whose interest was rather to minimize what had taken place, I have no hesitation in saying that the southern and southeastern section of European Russia during the first six months of 1933 experienced a major famine, far more destructive than the local famines which occurred, mostly on the Volga, in exceptionally bad drought years under Tsarism, second in the number of its victims probably only to the famine of 1921–1922.

The first thing that struck me when I began to walk about in the Cossack villages in the neighborhood of Kropotkin was the extraordinary deterioration in the physical condition of what had once been an extremely fertile region. Enormous weeds, of striking height and toughness, filled up many of the gardens and could be seen waving in the fields of wheat, corn, and sunflower seeds. Gone were the wheaten loaves, the succulent slices of lamb that had been offered for sale everywhere when I visited the Kuban Valley in 1924.

At that time every Cossack settlement had its large number of fierce, snapping dogs, trained to guard sheep and cattle; now there was an almost ghostly quiet; the bark of a dog was never heard. "The dogs all died or were eaten up during the famine," was the general explanation of their disappearance.

In the first house which I entered, quite at random, in the *stanitsa*, or Cossack settlement, Laduzhskaya, southwest of Kropotkin (the Cossack *stanitsa* is usually much larger than the typical peasant village), I encountered a grim episode of what would officially be called "class struggle on the agrarian front." A handsome young Cossack woman, who had just given birth to a baby and who lived in the house with her mother, her husband being away on military service, told me how her brother, with some companions, had beaten a grain collector so badly that he died; and how he returned from serving a term in prison, where he received nothing but water and very little bread, so weakened that he, with his wife and five children, had all died of hunger and exhaustion in the spring. An optimist would perhaps see a sign of the amazing toughness and vitality of the Russian peasantry in the fact that the woman who told this story had not only lived through the famine herself, but had given birth to a child and was already claiming her share of "work-days" from the local collective farm.

In another *stanitsa*, Kazanskaya, which is picturesquely situated on a high bluff above the Kuban River, I called on the president of the local Soviet, Mr. Nemov, in an effort to obtain some official information about the mortality rate during the preceding winter and spring. Nemov scouted the stories of the peasants that a third or a half of the inhabitants had perished. "The population declined from

about 8000 to about 7000," he declared. "About 850 died
and another 150 were deported because they sabotaged the
government's programme of grain collection."   Mr. Nemov
showed me mortality statistics for four months — January,
February, March, and April.   They indicated how the curve
of death mounted upward as the peasants' last reserves of
grain were exhausted toward spring.   Thus 21 persons died
in January, 34 in February, 79 in March, and 155 in April.
This upward tendency most probably continued during May
and early June, until early vegetables provided some relief.

Regarding the causes of the famine, the accounts of
Mr. Nemov and of the peasants tallied fairly closely, if
one made allowance for differences of point of view and interpretation.   Hot dry winds had blighted some of the
crops in 1932, and there had been a good deal of neglect in
cultivation, as a result of apathy and discouragement.   The
huge weed crop choked out much of the grain, and in some
cases a considerable part of the crop remained unharvested.
Still it was the general testimony of the peasants that they
could have pulled through if the local authorities had not
swooped down with heavy requisitions.   The last reserves
of grain, which had been buried in the ground by the
desperate peasants, were dug up and confiscated.   A man
named Sheboldaev, with a reputation for cruelty in "liquidating" kulaks in the lower Volga district, was made President
of the North Caucasus, where the passive resistance was
doubtless stiffer than in other sections of the country, because
a considerable part of the population consisted of Cossacks,
who had enjoyed a higher standard of living than the mass
of the peasants before the Revolution and who had mostly
fought on the side of the Whites during the civil war.
Under Sheboldaev's orders whole communities, such as

Poltavskaya, in the Western Kuban, were deported *en masse* to the frozen regions of the north in the dead of winter. Other villages which did not fill out the grain quotas that were demanded from them were "blockaded," in the sense that no city products were allowed to reach them. Local officials who protested against the pitiless repression were deposed, arrested, in a few cases shot.

Sheboldaev's methods, which were, of course, applied with the knowledge and approval of the central authorities in Moscow, squeezed out of the North Caucasus the full amount of grain which Moscow demanded.[4] But they turned what would otherwise perhaps have been a hunger into a famine, and they left a diseased and weakened population (there was a tremendous epidemic of malignant malaria in the Kuban Valley in 1933) and a ravaged and devastated countryside which will require years of reconstruction before it can hope to regain its former prosperity.

In the villages around Poltava, a charming Ukrainian town built on a hillside with an abundance of leafy trees along its streets, and in the vicinity of Byelaya Tserkov, a small town southwest of Kiev, largely inhabited by Jews, I found much the same situation as in the North Caucasus. These Ukrainian regions showed greater evidences of recovery, because the 1933 harvest was well above average in

---

[4] How ruthlessly the fertile North Caucasus was plundered under the régime of collectivization is evident from the following figures, which Sheboldaev cited at the last Party Congress. The amount of grain realized by the state in the North Caucasus was as follows: 1928, 56,000,-000 poods (a pood is about three fifths of a bushel); 1929, 92,000,000 poods; 1930, 123,000,000 poods; 1931, 187,000,000 poods; 1932, 112,000,000 poods; 1933, 133,000,000 poods. In other words, the state, during the last three hungry years, has been regularly taking from the North Caucasian peasants two or three times as much as the peasants gave up in 1928, when the situation with meat and dairy products was vastly better.

Ukraina and substantially better than it was in the North Caucasus. But people often broke down and wept when they described what they and their relatives and friends had experienced during the preceding winter and spring. "No war ever took from us so many people," exclaimed one woman with whom I talked in Poltava. And in one veritable Village of Death (its name was Cherkass), some eight miles south of Byelaya Tserkov, I had it on the authority of the secretary of the local Soviet, Mr. Fishenko, that about 600 of the village's former 2000 inhabitants had perished. Hundreds of others had fled. Fishenko's figure found abundant confirmation in the stories of the famine survivors and in the grim mute evidence of the numerous abandoned houses, with their weed-grown gardens and gaping doors and windows.

Two noteworthy features of the famine were that far more men died than women and far more *edinolichniki* (individual peasants) than members of collective farms. If in many districts 10 per cent of the collective farmers died, the percentage of mortality among the individual peasants was sometimes as high as 25. Of course not all who died passed through the typical stages of death from outright hunger, abnormal swellings under the eyes and of the stomach, followed in the last stages by swollen legs and cracking bones. The majority died of slight colds which they could not withstand in their weakened condition; of typhus, the familiar accompaniment of famine; of "exhaustion," to use the familiar euphemistic word in the death reports. Here and there one heard dark stories of cannibalism; in Poltava it was said that a trade in human flesh had been going on until the authorities discovered it and shot the participants. But apparently cannibalism had not been widespread. The famine area, so far as I could observe and learn from reliable information, included Ukraina, the North Caucasus, a number of districts in the middle and lower Volga, and considerable sections of remote Kazakstan, in Central Asia. Northern and Central Russia and Siberia suffered a good deal of hardship and under-nourishment, but not actual famine. The number of people who lived in famine areas was in the neighborhood of sixty million; the excess of deaths over a normal mortality rate can scarcely have been less than three or four million.[5]

There is something epically and indescribably tragic in this enormous dying out of millions of people, sacrifices on the altar of a policy which many of them did not even understand. The horror of this last act in the tragedy of the individual peasantry is perhaps intensified by the fact that the victims died so passively, so quietly, without arousing any stir of sympathy in the outside world. The Soviet censorship saw to that.

Of the historic responsibility of the Soviet Government for the famine of 1932–1933 there can be no reasonable doubt. In contrast to its policy in 1921–1922, it stifled any appeal for foreign aid by denying the very fact of the famine and by refusing to foreign journalists the right to travel in the famine regions until it was all over. Famine was quite deliberately employed as an instrument of national policy, as the last means of breaking the resistance of the peasantry to the new system where they are divorced from personal ownership of the land and obliged to work on the conditions

---

[5] The average mortality rate which I found with monotonous regularity in the districts I personally visited was about 10 per cent. If one makes allowance for normal mortality and also for the fact that the towns suffered much less than the country districts, the excess of three or four million still remains.

which the state may dictate to them and deliver up whatever the state may demand from them.

"The collective farmers this year have passed through a good school. For some this school was quite ruthless." In this cryptic understatement President Kalinin summed up the situation in Ukraina and the North Caucasus, from the Soviet standpoint. The unnumbered new graves in the richest Soviet agricultural regions mark the passing of those who did not survive the ordeal, who were victims of this "ruthless school." [6]

There can be no doubt that famine, which brings death in its most painful forms, was an effective means of breaking any tendency on the part of the peasants to indulge in passive resistance or "sabotage." There was general testimony that work in the collective farms proceeded at a much faster pace in 1933 than in preceding years, even when the collective-farm members were weakened by hunger.

There were other factors which helped to overcome or at least to relieve the agrarian crisis which reached its high point at the end of 1932. The good harvest of 1933 marked a definite turn for the better. The Soviet Government completely changed its method of making levies in kind early in 1933 and promulgated a new decree, under which the peasants are obliged to deliver up (for a nominal payment in paper rubles, but actually as a tax) hard-and-fast quantities

[6] The Soviet Government could easily have averted the famine from its own resources if it had desired to do so. A complete cessation of the export of foodstuffs in 1932 or the diversion of a small amount of foreign currency to the purchase of grain and provisions would have achieved this end. The Soviet attitude was pretty adequately summed up by Mr. Mezhuev, President of the Poltava Soviet, who said to me: "To have imported grain would have been injurious to our prestige. To have let the peasants keep their grain would have encouraged them to go on producing little."

of grain, the amounts varying with the normal fertility of the soil. At its highest, in the fertile regions of the south and the southeast, the levy works out at about five bushels an acre. Once this has been paid, the peasant is legally guaranteed against further exactions and may consume the remainder of his produce, or sell it as he sees fit, although the existing virtual prohibition of private trade makes it almost impossible for the peasant to sell except to state or coöperative organizations. A similar system has been introduced with regard to meat, milk, and other products. While these levies in kind are quite heavy (the grain tax of 1933 is supposed to yield a little more than the compulsory purchases at fixed prices in previous years), they possess the merit of fixed regularity and they put a stop to the formerly all-too-frequent practice of making repeated levies on the same collective farm.

The establishment in the machine-tractor stations of so-called political departments, led by Communists of administrative experience, has strengthened Party leadership and control in the rural districts. The leaders of the political departments have given a considerable impetus to propaganda work in the collective farms. They have also from time to time corrected abuses and mistakes of local officials.

Organization and discipline in the collective farms have improved. The mismanagement in the first years was colossal. The enormous losses in live stock are attributable not only to the wholesale slaughtering of cattle by kulaks and other peasants who feared that they would be confiscated or bought under compulsion, but also to gross mistakes in the feeding and treatment of horses and cows, chickens and pigs. Indeed, the sufferings of animals which were maltreated rivaled those of human beings. Now there is more order, and more intelligent management, although much progress certainly remains to be made. The collective-farm member is more regular in coming to work, is attached more definitely to a single job, for the execution of which he is held responsible.

The Soviet leaders seem to have given up the former ill-judged efforts to force the socialization of live stock in the collective farms, and now the collective-farm member is encouraged to have his own cow and pig. There is a good deal of ultimate significance, if not much immediate practical reality, in the enunciation of the slogan: "All collective-farm peasants should be *zazhitochni* (well-to-do)." [7] One does not leap immediately from famine to a state of being well-to-do, but the official announcement of such a slogan means a breach with the dreary traditional Soviet agrarian policy of inciting the poorest peasants against their neighbors who were a little less poor.

In some ways, time is on the side of the new system. A younger generation of peasants, brought up in Soviet schools and receiving further intensive propaganda in the Red Army, may come to forget that there ever was an individualist system of farming. Every year means an accretion of tractors and large agricultural machines for the Soviet fields, although up to the present time the productive effect of this has been neutralized by the huge loss of live stock and the frequent bungling in the operation of the machines,

[7] During my trip in the fall of 1933, I asked three peasants, all members of collective farms, what they thought of Stalin's statement that all collective farmers should be well-to-do. The first one observed: "These are words that don't agree with the actual facts." The second one commented: "It doesn't look that way." And the third, a bronzed, bare-legged woman who was digging out her allotted share of sugar beets near Byelaya Tserkov, declared, in a burst of lese majesty: "Oh, they're always telling us a bunch of lies."

which, if they come from Soviet factories, are often not of the best quality.

So it seems reasonable to believe that the famine marked the low point in the Soviet agrarian crisis and that a process of recovery has set in. At the same time, one cannot lose sight of two negative factors: the elimination from agriculture of great numbers of just those peasants, the so-called kulaks, who were often most capable and industrious; and the terrific decimation of the country's live stock.[8]

Over and above these considerations, there is a more fundamental objection to the new system. It is not free. The peasant must do precisely what the state tells him to do and, under the present Soviet political and economic régime, has no effective means of determining the conditions under which he labors, the crops which he would like to plant, the levies to which he may be subjected. Collectivization is a grim caricature of the utopian dream of free, voluntary peasant coöperation and mutual aid which was cherished by a whole school of pre-war radical Russian intellectuals. It is a gigantic system of state landlordism, clamped down on the peasants with the same methods of terroristic repression with which the Tsarist state gradually forged the chains of serfdom for the peasants in the seventeenth and eighteenth centuries. It can only lose this character if and when the present absolute dictatorship of the state over the peasantry gives way to a system under which the peasant possesses an equal voice in determining what disposition is to be made of the fruits of his labor.

[8] The second five-year plan estimates that even by 1937 Russia will be considerably short of its 1929 supply of horses, big-horned cattle, sheep, and goats. The country's supply of meat and dairy products is, therefore, likely to be straitened for many years to come. Moreover, such live stock as the Soviet Union now possesses is generally in poor physical condition.

V

THE FRUITS OF PLANNED ECONOMY

AMONG all the characteristics of the modern Soviet régime the idea of a planned economy has probably made the strongest and most favorable impression abroad. By a striking coincidence, the effort of the Soviet Union to plan its national economic and social development coincided with a world crisis of unusual severity, which some observers were inclined to attribute to the planless character of private capitalist production.

Apart from this coincidence, which was calculated to intensify foreign interest in the outcome of the Soviet experiment, the attempt to foresee and project every step in the development of a country of Russia's size and population was of the highest fascination and interest. Every kind of fate was predicted for the five-year plan, from complete fiasco to the emergence of the Soviet Union as one of the world's richest and strongest countries.

Now Russia is an immense panorama with many lights and shadows, and one's judgment of it is inevitably determined to a considerable degree by those aspects which impress one as most significant and most permanent. An enthusiastic Communist can make out a robust case for the achievements of planned economy. Some characteristic traits of the crisis in other countries have been entirely absent in the Soviet Union. The volume of industrial production has been expanding from year to year, and along with this has gone an impressive amount of new building. At a time when some other countries tend to restrict admission to their higher schools, on the ground that the professions are over-crowded, the Soviet Union has extended very considerably its network of universities, technical schools, and high schools and has introduced universal compulsory elementary educa-tion. Unemployment has disappeared, at least in the sense that anyone who registers as unemployed can get some kind of work.

The Soviet newspapers make the most of these facts in strident comparative columns under the heading, "With Us and With Them." Under "With Us" one reads edifying items about the opening of new factories, the numbers of students who are being educated, new scientific discoveries. Under "With Them" is a dreary chronicle of unemployment statistics, currency disasters, closed factories, and wheat, milk, coffee, and other valuable products deliberately destroyed in desperate attempts to raise prices.

These didactic "With Them and With Us" columns un-questionably contain a good deal of food for wholesome re-flection on the part of adherents of the individualist economic system. But, while they present a certain amount of truth, they are very far, like most propagandist efforts, from pre-senting the whole truth. A foreigner in Moscow once passed a well-stocked Torgsin shop, open only to foreigners and to the few Russians who are lucky enough to possess gold, silver, or foreign currency, and shortly afterwards noticed the uninviting bare shelves of an ordinary coöperative shop. "The Torgsin store ought to be labeled 'With Them' and the coöperative store 'With Us,' " he dryly remarked.

And it is significant that the abolition of unemployment

in the Soviet Union has attracted singularly few unemployed
workers or professional men from other countries. A few
thousand Americans, mostly of Russian or Finnish origin,
have come to the Soviet Union as immigrants during
recent years. Some have adjusted themselves fairly satisfactorily; others bitterly regret the move. The same observation would hold true for a smaller number of German work-
men, including a number of Ruhr miners, who came to Russia as permanent settlers. It is noteworthy that extremely
few of the many intellectuals and professional men who were
displaced in Germany on racial grounds after the advent of
National Socialism have sought a haven in Russia, although
the Soviet Union needs trained men in all fields and prides
itself on its absence of racial and national prejudice.

It is doubtful whether the number of immigrants into the
Soviet Union in recent years exceeds to any considerable
extent the number of people who have left the country. And
this comparison is a very inadequate one. The unemployed
American or Englishman who wants to go to Russia en-
counters no objection on the part of his own government.
The Soviet Government, on the other hand, is most rigorous
in holding its own citizens within the country, especially if it
suspects that their sentiments are not enthusiastic. And of
course it is just the people who are not enthusiastic who are
most anxious to emigrate. Permission to leave Russia permanently is usually granted only to persons who are able,
sometimes with the help of friends or relatives abroad, to pay
a fee of several hundred gold dollars in foreign currency.
In some cases the permission is refused even if the fee is
offered. If it were not for these abnormal restrictions on
free emigration, it is safe to say that the number of people
who would have left Russia during recent years would have

enormously exceeded the number of those who have come there with the intention of making it their permanent home.

While it may be technically true to say that the Soviet Union has abolished unemployment, this statement is extremely misleading unless it is accompanied by a qualification to the effect that the standard of living of the Russian worker or employee has fallen far below the very modest level which had been attained in 1927 and 1928, and is, therefore, immensely lower than that of workers and employees in America and Western Europe in such bread-and-butter things as food and clothing, housing and transportation. Indeed, the "abolition of unemployment" might be just as plausibly, although less pleasantly, described as a mass conscription of labor. An unemployed Russian must accept work which is offered him by the state, even if it is in some far-away place. His readiness to accept such work is promoted by the fact that he automatically loses his food card as soon as he becomes unemployed.

The Soviet method of abolishing unemployment could easily be imitated by any government which endeavored to exercise absolute power in disposing of the labor power of its citizens. In America, for instance, President Roosevelt could "abolish unemployment" immediately if he should assume dictatorial powers and declare that every unemployed person should do some prescribed work in exchange for the food and clothing which he receives in the form of relief.[1] Such action would, of course, elicit the most

---

[1] The British unemployed and American unemployed in communities where relief is well organized are often materially better off, especially as regards food supply, than are employed workers in Soviet provincial towns. When I returned to the Soviet Union from America and read to some Russian friends a list of the rations which unemployed families in Milwaukee received, the Russians exclaimed: "That sounds more like

strenuous opposition on the part of the unemployed them-selves and would scarcely be conceivable in a democratic country.

If one runs down the familiar line of the "With Them and With Us" contrasts and examines the facts on both sides, one is apt to find that what the Soviet Union usually has to offer in exchange for the unquestionable defects of the individualist system of production are not solutions, but rather alternative defects. There is certainly no more obvious and justified target for satire and denunciation than such practices as dumping milk in rivers, throwing coffee into the ocean, burning grain, and ploughing up cotton, all at a time when there are undernourished and underclothed people. When the Communists characterize such things as barbarous and irrational it is difficult to disagree with them. But there are debit items on the other side of the ledger. If one could theoretically set up, as a monument to the follies

---

the ration of a 'responsible worker' [a Soviet official of fairly high grade] than of our ordinary worker or employee." They were especially amazed at the variety of fruit, vegetables, and canned goods. The average Rus-sian worker's monthly wage (125 rubles), reckoned in gold rubles at the general current unofficial rate of exchange (forty paper rubles to one gold ruble), would not buy three dollars' worth of provisions in a Torgsin shop. Of course the worker has his factory dinner (a meal of somewhat variable quality) at moderate cost, his low rent, his free medical service, and many social and educational benefits which cannot be reckoned in terms of currency. The mere fact that he is at work gives him some psychological advantage over the unemployed man in another country. And of course no comparison between the position of the Soviet workers and employees and the unemployed in Great Britain and America could fairly overlook the fact that Russians have always been accustomed to a much lower standard of living. But, when every allowance has been made for the favorable sides of the Russian worker's life, there can be no doubt that the American or West European worker, suddenly transplanted to Russia, would be conscious of a sharply lower standard of living, which he would require a good deal of strength in the Communist faith to bear with patience and hope for the future.

and weaknesses of capitalism, a vast mountain of destroyed wheat and coffee and cotton, one could easily build a rival mountain out of the spoiled and wasted food products in the Soviet Union which have been destroyed not deliberately, but as a result of carelessness and inefficiency, and at a time when food shortage has been most acute. How many potatoes, wrested by ruthless requisitioning from the reluctant peasants, have rotted in damp and unsuitable cellars! How many tomatoes and other vegetables have spoiled from poor packing and dilatory shipment! How much meat has been wasted for lack of proper refrigeration! One can invoke as testimony on this question such picturesque headlines as one regularly finds in the Soviet newspapers in the summer months: "On the Vegetable Front — Breach after Breach — Cars with Decayed Vegetables Arrive Daily in Moscow — Carloads of Rotting Vegetables Advance on Leningrad."

If private capitalism cannot escape the responsibility for the wanton destruction of foodstuffs in New York and Brazil, the Soviet system is equally responsible for the abnormally large losses in Moscow and in the Soviet provinces, which are attributable to poor management, inefficiency, and carelessness. The wasting of perishable fruits and vegetables in the summer months has become so chronic that the Commission on Execution, a permanent investigating body attached to the Soviet Cabinet, on one occasion ordered a detailed investigation into the causes of the breakdown of Moscow's vegetable supply. The report revealed one leak after another in the flow of vegetables from producer to consumer, with the result that what might have seemed a torrent of beets and carrots, cabbages and spinach, when it was sowed, became a thin trickle before it reached the Muscovite consumer.

Leak No. 1. About 5000 acres of state truck gardens in the vicinity of Moscow were so incompetently managed that weeds proved the most plentiful crop. The crop was lost entirely on about 500 acres and was only half of normal on the remaining 4500. There were similar difficulties in other state and collective farms.

Leak No. 2. An abnormally large proportion of the vegetables became spoiled in transport, partly because they were poorly packed, without proper ventilating holes, partly because even short-distance shipments sometimes required several days for completion.

Leak No. 3. More vegetables were lost because of poor handling and long delay between the arrival at the central warehouse and dispatch to the stores. For this leakage sheer incompetence and bungling, lack of labor and transport, seem to have been about equally responsible.

Some economists have been so fascinated by the theoretical advantages of planned economy that they have looked on it as a sort of magician's wand which would almost automatically bring order out of chaos and plenty out of want. The experience of the Soviet Union, which has been able to institute a very complete type of planned economy because the state monopolizes every branch of economic activity, has not borne out this pleasing dream.

There is perhaps no problem in the world so difficult and responsible as the accurate and efficient planning of a nation's economic development over a fairly long term of years. What provision is to be made for new inventions, for discoveries of new natural resources which may alter entirely what would have seemed at first a logical and rational programme of development? What of such incalculable factors as weather and abrupt unpredictable changes in world markets and world price levels? How are the conflicting claims of various classes of the population for a share of the national income to be adjusted? How far can a state, even when it is endowed with very sweeping powers, combat the familiar law of supply and demand and enforce a desired level of prices?

These are only a few of the insistent questions which have confronted the directors of the Soviet planned economy; and to some of them, at least, no satisfactory answers have been found. The Russian experience has demonstrated very clearly that planned economy is no automatic panacea, that mistakes in the operation of a closely centralized, state-controlled economic system may be quite as disastrous as the failures and breakdowns of a system that operates without benefit of central plan.

The failure of the makers of Russia's first five-year plan to foresee the necessary measure of expansion of transportation facilities has led to a chronic crisis of the Soviet railroad system, accompanied by immense losses of perishable freight and delays in important building projects. Still more serious were some of the mistakes in the application of planned economy to Soviet agriculture. Leaving aside the question whether collectivization itself was a desirable economic policy, one can scarcely fail to recognize, in retrospect, two major blunders which increased enormously the human and material losses of carrying out this gigantic agrarian transformation. The first of these was the attempt in 1929 to socialize most of the peasants' live stock without giving them any compensation. By the time Stalin had realized the harmfulness of this policy and published his "Giddiness from Success" letter the damage was done; a large part of Russia's cattle had been destroyed by the peasants, whose desperate slaughtering of their beasts somehow suggested the tactics of the Russian generals who laid waste their country before Napoleon's invasion. The other major agrarian mistake was in making, year after year, irregular requisitions on the peasants, forcing them to sell an undefined "surplus" of their crops at arbitrary fixed prices in increasingly valueless paper rubles. This mistake seems all the more inexcusable because a similar requisitioning policy, made necessary to some extent by the exigencies of civil war, led to a steady contraction of peasant production and to the ultimate crisis of food supply which brought about the adoption of the New Economic Policy in 1921. One would have thought that lessons could have been learned from this experience.

Now the more reasonable system of a fixed tax in kind has been introduced. But this occurred only after the former system (under which the peasant had to give up an unspecified amount of products and therefore came to feel that the more he raised the more would be taken away from him) had led to the widespread neglect of the fields in 1932, and the subsequent famine.

All the calculations of the first five-year plan in the sphere of currency issue, wages, prices, and costs went completely awry. Indeed, the most indubitable overfulfillment of the plan was in the matter of printing paper money. The maximum issue which the plan had prescribed for 1933 was 3,200,000,000 rubles. The actual amount in circulation in that year was in the neighborhood of 6,800,000,000 rubles. Inasmuch as this heavy overissue of currency coincided with an acute shortage of foodstuffs and a scarcely less severe lack of manufactured goods, all the minute calculations about how much real wages would increase as a result of the reduction in the cost of living became grotesquely unreal, and people began to repeat such jokes as "The Russians are the richest people in the world, because they don't know what to do with their money," and "Soviet money is the jolliest with which to travel, because every foreigner laughs when he sees it." An elaborate system of surreptitious bartering between institutions and between individuals, which represented the very antithesis of planned exchange and distribution, also grew up, despite all the efforts of the government to suppress it. A factory which produced nails (a scarce and highly prized commodity in Russia) would try to trade them off for jam and macaroni to eke out its food supply; a textile mill would try to secure shoes or biscuits in exchange for its wares.

Any observer of the Soviet Union during recent years must have been struck by the many similarities between its economic problems and those which confront a country in time of war. Instead of the problems of "overproduction," of underconsumption, which have been tormenting statesmen and economists in other countries, Russia has had the familiar war-time problem of shortage: shortage of food, shortage of transport, shortage of raw materials, shortage of working hands.

Some of the most interesting tests of the effectiveness of the Soviet planned economy lie in the future. There are already signs of an abatement of the terrific pace of new building, which was at its height in 1931 and 1932, when everyone had work, but at low real wages that would scarcely buy the equivalent of a soldier's war-time rations. Will the Soviet system make possible a permanent elimination of unemployment, together with a gradual rise in the popular standard of living as the worst phases of the agrarian crisis are overcome? Or was the elimination of unemployment a temporary "war-time" accompaniment of an orgy of new construction at a pace which cannot be indefinitely sustained? General employment in the Soviet Union to-day is certainly a result, in part, of the low productivity of city worker and peasant alike, with the result that several men are often required to do the job which a single skilled mechanic could perform in Western Europe or America.

A serious problem of "technological unemployment" might arise in time in the country districts as a result of the intensified mechanization of agriculture. One habitually finds scores of peasant families employed on a collective farm the area of which would be perhaps equivalent to half a dozen middle-sized American Mid-Western farms. At the moment there is an acute lack of draft animals and Russian agriculture still possesses only a small fraction of the number of tractors, combines, harvesting machines, and so forth, which would be required for complete mechanization. But after the Soviet factories have been pouring out a stream of tractors and other agricultural machines for another five or ten years a great many working hands may become superfluous. It will then be very interesting to see how effectively and painlessly readjustments can be made under the system of planned economy, whether the slack of superfluous agricultural labor can be taken up in the towns or in more intensive cultivation of the soil.

One insuperable objection to the imitation of the Soviet system of planned economy in Western countries is the enormous curtailment of individual liberty which it has brought about. It is no accident that just during the period when planned economy was going into effect repression and regimentation of every kind became vastly more intense, that executions for political reasons became much more numerous, that the population of concentration camps swelled enormously, that a whole new system of forced labor grew up. In many other ways the freedom of the Soviet citizen was circumscribed: he was placed on rations; his chances of traveling abroad greatly diminished; the range of books and magazines which he could read was more narrowly controlled.

It is perhaps not generally realized that the individuals who make the decisions under a system of planned economy are wielding enormous power and are invested with corresponding responsibility. To take an extreme case, the decision of the highest Soviet authorities as to how much grain should be taken from the peasants in the fall and winter of 1932 had a very direct effect on the number of peasants who were doomed to die of hunger. This was, to be sure, an exceptional situation. But that it could arise at all shows what a formidable weapon planned economy may become, when it is unaccompanied by any effective popular control of the planners.

The world significance of Russia's plunge into centralized economic planning is not diminished, of course, by the fact that it has not as yet raised the standard of popular well-being and that it has given not so much solutions as new problems in exchange for the old ones which it has endeavored to solve. So one has a rationed low standard of living and, for the more unfortunate Soviet citizens, compulsory employment by the Gay-Pay-Oo as a set-off to unemployment in other countries; wastes of bureaucracy and inefficiency to compare with the wastes which elsewhere may be set down to the fact that the general pursuit of individual profit has not worked out so smoothly to everyone's benefit as utilitarian philosophers imagined it would.

So strong and varied are the present-day trends toward state intervention in what would have been regarded as the untouchable domains of private business in pre-war days that the problem of planned versus *laissez faire* economy scarcely seems real to-day. It is rather a question of who should do the planning, what kind of planning should prevail, and how much. While the technical details of the annual and five-year economic plans of the Soviet Union are left to the State Planning Commission, — a body which includes in its membership a number of Communist executives, with a sprinkling of non-Party technical advisors, — the big decisions are taken by the government, or, more concretely, by Stalin and his associates in the Political Bureau.

Perhaps the fundamental issue that has been raised by the Soviet venture and by the unmistakable trend toward planned economy in other parts of the world — which finds such varied forms of expression as currency manipulation, artificial aids to domestic industries and agriculture, import quotas, manœuvres for the achievement of specific price levels, state control of credit and hence of industrial development, and so forth — is whether planning can be carried out with the consent of the people whose livelihoods and destinies are being planned. To put the question in another way, is it possible to combine an increased measure of public control over economic life, calculated to curb the excesses of the speculative spirit and to avert or at least mitigate economic crises, with a reasonable degree of personal independence and of the civil liberties which are part of the essence of civilization, and without which planned economy, even if it is successful on the productive side, may easily degenerate into a kind of barracks-room tyranny? The whole temper and quality of Western civilization will be profoundly affected by the answer which history gives to this question.

The Soviet Union has struck out on a path which no other country is likely to follow. If economic distress should lead to new efforts to seek salvation through the dubious remedy of dictatorship in Europe or in America, the odds are overwhelmingly that the dictatorship will be on the Fascist, not on the Communist, model. The balance of class forces in Great Britain, France, and America is much more similar to what it was in Germany than to what it was in Russia when the Bolsheviki seized power.

Russia's experience during the last few years of socialist planned economy has led to varied results. Industrialization has certainly made substantial progress, even if the goals which were set by the first five-year plan were not always reached. On the other hand, the complicated mechanism of industrial costs, prices, and real wages failed definitely to function as the plan had foreseen; and there was an enormous discrepancy between the figures of the plan and the actual results in agricultural production, the figures of live stock and the food supply of the population. For the town dwellers of the Soviet Union the first years of planned economy brought more sustained and widespread deprivation than one would have found in other countries during the world crisis. As against this undeniable fact one must recognize that the deprivation was not aggravated by ostentatious contrasts of wealth and poverty; almost everyone had work, so that the psychological hopelessness which comes from unemployment was spared; and a portion of the population, more especially the Soviet-minded youth, found compensation for short commons and hard living conditions in an exhilarating sense of being a part of a country in a process of upbuilding, possessing wider opportunities for education and promotion. So far as the country districts are concerned, nothing that European peasants or American farmers suffered as a result of price maladjustments can reasonably be compared with the famine that marked the climax of Russia's agrarian crisis. How the future lot of Russia's forcibly collectivized peasant and of the individualist farm owner of other lands will compare is, of course, a matter of opinion and conjecture.

VI

SOVIET DAILY LIFE

Russia's five-year plan was very far from being a mere collection of maps and diagrams, blueprints and statistics. It was an immense dynamic force which laid a heavy transforming hand on every phase of Soviet daily life. The strongest impression which the Soviet Union conveyed during the first years of its Iron Age (there is now a slight relaxation of the strain and the deprivations) is that of a nation that had stripped itself to the very barest essentials in its struggle to achieve huge industrial projects. As has been aptly said, Russia was endeavoring to starve itself great.

All sorts of things that add to the amenities and comforts of life, from food and manufactured goods to foreign magazines and newspapers, were ruthlessly struck off the list of permitted imports or confined to the smallest possible limits. Foreign currency had to be conserved at all costs, in order to pay the expensive bills for equipping new factories with machinery that could not be produced in Russia, and to import indispensable metals and raw materials. At the same time the Soviet Government forced its exports as hard as possible, selling on foreign markets at low prices grain and butter, meat and eggs, poultry and sugar, when there was a most acute shortage of these products in the Soviet Union. Here again the justification was the same: the people were supposed to tighten their belts uncomplainingly for the sake of the grandiose industrial structure which was in process of building.

The greatest change in the daily life of the Soviet citizen during recent years has been in the matter of food supply. From 1921, when the New Economic Policy came into effect, until 1928, there was no trace of rationing in the Soviet system. Foodstuffs were bought, without limitation as to quantity, in stores, just as in other countries, the only difference being that under the Soviet system there were fewer private shops and more state and coöperative stores.

The first pinch of food shortage was felt in 1928, and by the end of 1929 a widespread rationing system was in operation. At the same time a merciless drive of expropriation and confiscation was launched against the private traders. At the present time there is not a private store or a privately owned restaurant or a private business enterprise of any size and consequence throughout the length and breadth of the Soviet Union. The only private "traders" who remain are old ladies of the former régime who maintain a miserable existence by disposing of brooches, bits of lace, and other finery; individual peasants who bring a few carrots or a pat of butter to the market; and street hawkers of such commodities as worm-eaten apples and children's toy balloons.

The Soviet rationing system has undergone several modifications. It was never absolutely hard and fast in the sense that it was illegal to procure foodstuffs except on the ration booklets which were given to trade-union members and their dependents. There is now a tendency to loosen it, and by the end of the second five-year plan it may be possible to dispense with it altogether. At the same time it has been extremely difficult for the average Soviet worker or employee, earning between a hundred and two hundred rubles a month, to buy butter at twenty rubles a pound or meat at seven rubles a pound on the private market or in the "commercial" shops which have been opened by the state in increasing numbers during the last year or two, and which afford some relief to the more well-to-do classes of Soviet society, to highly qualified engineers and technical experts, successful authors and playwrights, prominent actors and singers, and the like.

In the beginning there was an attempt to sell to the holders of ration booklets, at moderate fixed prices, an adequate allotment of bread (two pounds a day for manual workers and one pound a day for others) and limited but fixed amounts of meat, fish, eggs, butter, and other products. Only the bread ration has remained constant, and this only in Moscow and a few main industrial centres; in provincial towns bread rations have been curtailed in times of stringency. With other food products the tendency has been to dispense less by the ration booklets and to shift the emphasis to so-called "public feeding." Almost every factory and public institution now has its own dining room, where workers or employees may get one or two meals of variable quality at fairly moderate prices. Children receive hot lunches in the schools. This system leaves out some classes of the population, such as persons who work at home or housewives who have no other occupation, and has been a big factor in impelling housewives to seek occupation outside the home.

On a visit to the well-known textile town of Ivanovo (formerly Ivanovo-Voznesensk) early in 1934, I found that the workers received monthly,[1] apart from the meals in factory dining rooms, a little over two pounds of meat, a little less than two pounds of sugar, and about three pounds of *kasha* (a Russian cereal prepared out of millet) on their ration booklets. There were smaller allowances for the members of their families.

The diet which the Soviet citizen can enjoy on the fruits of his rationing system, even supplemented by meals in the factory or office dining room,[2] is a meagre one, and is especially lacking in fats. There are three means by which he can supplement it: the private markets, which are still permitted to exist; the commercial shops; and the extraordinarily numerous and well-stocked Torgsin stores, which take only foreign currency, gold, silver, and jewels in payment.

The commercial shops and the private markets are an aid to people whose pockets are well filled with rubles. In order to make purchases in a Torgsin store, on the other hand, the Soviet citizen must either be receiving help from abroad, or possess a stock of foreign currency, or bring in some gold or silver ornament. As a means of extracting hidden gold and foreign currency from a hungry population, the Torgsin shops — with their tempting display of such "luxuries," from the Soviet standpoint, as ham and sausage, butter and eggs, oranges and lemons — have been very successful; in some cases individuals have had gold fillings removed from their teeth and replaced with baser metal in order to be

---

[1] That is, they were permitted to buy this food in the coöperative shops at fixed prices which were moderate by comparison with those of the free market or the commercial stores, although they have been substantially increased by comparison with 1928.

[2] During recent years a network of factory and office dining rooms, open only to workers and employees of the given factory or office, has grown up all over the country.

able to satisfy their longing for some delicacy which was unobtainable for Soviet currency. The Torgsin system has been more effective in filling the state coffers than the cruder Gay-Pay-Oo method of occasionally arresting Soviet citizens who were suspected of possessing hidden stores of foreign currency and making them stand up to the point of exhaustion in suffocatingly crowded rooms and subjecting them to other forms of "third-degree" pressure in order to make them disgorge their actual or supposed treasures.

Rationing usually implies leveling. Since 1931, however, the Soviet policy has been to discourage very strongly any leveling tendencies in wage and salary payments, on the ground that productivity of labor depends on payment according to merit. So, when rationing destroyed to some extent the effectiveness of differential wage and salary scales, new forms of inequality were created in the form of the "closed store" and the "closed dining room." [3] When I visited Magnitogorsk I found a whole hierarchy of dining rooms in operation. There were eating places of at least five different grades, with perhaps others of which I did not learn. The distinction between them was not one of price so much as of the class of diners who were qualified to eat in each one.

At the top of this Magnitogorsk dining-room hierarchy was the eating place reserved for high officials of the plant and famous foreign specialists. The food here, while it was a trifle monotonous, was substantial, with an abundance of meat. Somewhat lower in the scale was a dining room for Russian engineers and technicians. Then came the eating place for *udarniki*, workers who had distinguished themselves by their labor. There was a big drop from the

[3] "Closed" in the sense of being reserved for a certain class of patrons.

udarniki to the ordinary laborers, who were fed in crowded canteens, mainly on bread, cabbage soup, and *kasha,* with meat as a rare luxury. And lowest of all in the scale was the place assigned to the unfortunate kulaks. In this careful apportionment of dining-room facilities one seemed to see, on a small scale, the class or caste stratification of Soviet society.

The same system applies in the case of manufactured goods, where the supply for high Soviet officials and Red Army officers is considerably more abundant than that for the average citizen. In hospital service, too, shortage brings a more or less inevitable discrimination. Diplomats and other foreign residents in Moscow are sometimes referred to the Kremlin Hospital for medicines and drugs which cannot be found in any ordinary Soviet drug store. The number of Soviet citizens who are eligible for treatment in the Kremlin Hospital is, of course, very limited.

Along with rationing, queues have come to play a large part in the life of the man, or still more of the woman, in the street in Moscow. It would be difficult to think of anything for which queues have not been formed at some time or another: for meat, for shoes, for textiles, for feathers; for bread, when it is sold in unlimited quantity at high "commercial" prices; for buses and street cars, which are almost always overcrowded; for vodka, the fiery national drink; for newspapers, of which the supply falls short of the demand because of the lack of print paper; for railroad tickets. The right of place in the *ochered,* or queue, is most jealously guarded; and anyone violates it at the risk of a storm of abuse, if not of physical violence, on the part of the harassed, nervous people who have been standing in the line.

On one occasion I was in a questionable, or at least in a questioned, position in one of the unusually long queues that form for hats and coats after every theatre or concert performance. The right of my predecessor in the line to be there had been fiercely disputed by a woman who had even threatened to invoke the public prosecutor against the hapless cloakroom attendant. Expecting a similar fate myself, I casually remarked in English to my companion: "Nature in the raw is seldom mild." The effect, not of the well-worn advertising slogan, but of the foreign language, was electrical and I received my belongings without the slightest dispute or protest.

This very general attitude of willingness to defer to the foreigner and to grant him special favors is a trait of Russian character which I have never been fully able to understand. Almost any other people, subjected to the hardships which have been the lot of the Russians during recent years, could scarcely have failed to develop an attitude of bitter antagonism to foreign permanent residents and tourists who are so obviously living on a much better scale, getting the main benefit of the Torgsin stores and of the hotels which are open only to possessors of foreign currency. Yet nothing of the kind has been noticeable in Russia; a few words in a foreign language or in obviously imperfect Russian are the best means of securing redress and attention; and I have a friend, who speaks excellent Russian, who consistently resorts to a jargon of German, English, and deliberately broken Russian in the Torgsin stores in the belief that this ensures prompt and efficient service.

Some of the fiercest battles of the queue are fought over the obtaining of a railroad ticket. With about the pre-war amount of rolling stock, the Soviet railroads are now carrying about four times as many passengers as in pre-war times. What this means to the ordinary Soviet citizen who wishes to board a train was vividly brought home to me on one occasion when I was trying to leave Sverdlovsk, the capital of the Ural territory. I was armed with a note of recommendation from the local Soviet and with a journalist's credentials, so that my advantage over the average applicant for a ticket was considerable. Even so, the getting of the ticket required the expenditure of three or four hours of nervous and physical energy, with visits to half a dozen worried and overworked railroad officials, each of whom was eager to pass me on to his neighbor, and standing in several disorderly queues of pushing, struggling, quarreling, fuming people, some of whom had been involuntarily detained in Sverdlovsk for days.

The last decisive queue was formed, not in accordance with the amount of time which the traveler might have waited, but according to the importance of the "document," or credentials, with which he was equipped. There were seven categories of preference in this connection, and I wrote them down as follows: (1) military officers and Gay-Pay-Oo officials; (2) persons with cards of admission to rest homes and sanatoria; (3) persons employed in the "campaign" to stimulate harvesting; (4) passengers in transit with proof that they were on a mission for a state or public organization; (5) passengers in transit; (6) all others.

I was hospitably assigned to a place between categories 1 and 2, and even so obtained my ticket by a narrow margin. One wondered when and how the people in category 6 ever got on a train.

In connection with this tremendous congestion on the railroads the experience of another foreigner at a provincial station was amusing and instructive. He received from the local authorities an authorization to buy his ticket without waiting in line. Noticing two queues of about equal length, he tried to approach the window without waiting his turn and aroused shouts of indignant protest. "But I have a permit to buy my ticket without standing in a queue," he explained. "But we all have such permits!" came the chorus in response. "This is the queue for persons who have the right to buy tickets without standing in a queue."

There were several causes for the terrific overcrowding of the Soviet trains, which perhaps reached its height in 1932 and has now been slightly but very inadequately relieved. Money means less in Russia than in most countries, and people are readier to assume the expense of a trip. Then, the Russian who finds his local food and housing conditions unsatisfactory seems to have an incurable streak of optimism in believing that he can improve them somewhere else. During my trip to the Ural industrial centres I was struck by the vast numbers of unskilled and semi-skilled laborers who were drifting from Cheliabinsk to Magnitogorsk, from Magnitogorsk to Berezniki, from Berezniki to Stalingrad, although to a casual observer each one of these new centres looked just about as bleak and unpromising as the next.

The Soviet economic system calls for more investigating commissions than one would find in other countries. This results in travel. The springing up of new cities around the industrial plants, the habit of "mobilizing" students and Young Communists and sending them wherever an urgent piece of industrial or agricultural work remains to be done, the large number of workers and employees who spend their vacations in distant rest homes or in walking trips in the Caucasus and the Crimea — all this tends to increase the burden under which the transportation system is groaning.

Many things have changed greatly and fundamentally since I arrived in Russia in 1922. But two points on which there has been little if any improvement are housing facilities and the sanitary habits of the people. Not that there has been no building of new houses. On the contrary, one can see impressive new settlements of brick houses, especially in the industrial quarters of every large town. The quantity of new building, especially during the last few years, has been impressively large. Its quality has often been admittedly bad. The new houses were often thrown together hastily and poor building materials were used, with the result that painting and plastering were unsatisfactory, roofs leaked and floors showed cracks, while ceilings were often low and staircases narrow, and the planting of trees and grass was entirely neglected. A number of outspoken articles on this subject appeared in the Soviet press in the spring of 1933, an engineer named Kozmenko being especially critical in an article published in the trade-union newspaper, *Trud*.

But the population of the Soviet towns has been growing at such an abnormal rate that the new housing has failed to keep up with it. Up to 1933, Moscow and Leningrad had been adding to their population at the rate of half a million a year. Smaller towns where large factories were built (Sverdlovsk, Stalingrad, Gorky, Cheliabinsk) had been growing at an even faster pace proportionately. The food shortage in the villages and the inauguration of many large construction projects in the cities both stimulated an extraordinarily rapid swelling of the town population. Early in 1933 there was an effort to offset this process by the introduction of a severe passport system under which persons who were regarded as undesirable could be summarily banished from large cities and industrial centres and sent to live in smaller places. But this measure did not free any very large amount of housing space. Moreover, the building of new houses in Moscow has been checked to a considerable extent because of the diversion of most available building materials to the construction of the city's subway.

So a condition of extraordinary congestion prevails in the Soviet capital — an observation, incidentally, which would have been equally true at any time since 1922. Thousands of Communists in important administrative posts, to say nothing of the common run of mortals, are on the Moscow Soviet's long waiting list for new apartments, when and if they are built, and even the payment of a substantial rental in highly prized foreign currency does not assure a newly arrived foreigner the quick occupancy of a new apartment.

A cynic might suggest that Russia preaches sanitation more and practises it less than almost any other country. Russian personal habits have never been very cleanly; Macaulay, in typically sonorous prose, intimates as strongly as the delicacy of his times would permit that Peter the Great and his attendants behaved very badly indeed in rooms which were assigned to them on the occasion of Peter's visit to England, toward the end of the seventeenth century. And the condition of lavatories in present-day Russia often suggests even to the most dyed-in-the-wool "friend of the Soviet Union" that something may be amiss in the Soviet régime.

To be sure, there is a vigorous effort to promote public and personal cleanliness: hygienic habits are inculcated in Young Communists and Young Pioneers; the streets in Moscow and other large cities are swept and sprinkled in summer and cleared of snow in winter with commendable regularity. But some of the deprivations which are imposed by the exclusive concentration on industrialization militate against the carrying into practice of the most admirable theories of hygiene and prophylactic medicine. Tissue paper, for instance, has completely disappeared from the Soviet horizon since the five-year plan went into effect. Soap has also become extremely scarce and is often of poor quality, and this accounts for the suspiciously greenish hue which one sometimes detects in the sheets of Russian provincial hotels.

In the same way, while a devoted staff of physicians, now all enrolled in the state service, does what it can to maintain public health on a high level, efforts in this direction are bound to be hampered by the shortage of medicines and by the overcrowding of houses and schools, which make for the rapid spread of any contagious disease. An acquaintance who went to Sochi, on the notoriously malarial coast of the Black Sea, asked for quinine, which is the surest preventive of malaria. He was told that the shortage of quinine was so great that it could be sold only to people who were already suffering from the disease; this is typical of the breakdown in the field of medicine.

There is something bleak and austere about Moscow, and still more about the typical Russian provincial town, for Moscow is relatively much better provided with food and clothing and its shops, after those of Armavir or Poltava, seem positively glittering and brilliant.

Somehow my strongest impression of the strain and bleakness that have been perhaps an inevitable accompaniment of Russia's terrific effort in the sphere of industrial building was derived from a brief visit to the Ural capital, Sverdlovsk.

Whereas the pre-war Ekaterinburg had a population of about 75,000, Sverdlovsk (renamed in honor of the first president of the Soviet Executive Committee) claims 500,000 residents. Now a Soviet city in process of rapid growth may be an impressive spectacle to lovers of change and bigness for their own sakes, but it is emphatically not a comfortable place of residence, either for its inhabitants or for the casual traveler. The inevitable jobs of municipal reconstruction — the laying of pipes, erection of buildings, and so forth — involved a vast amount of clutter in the shape of disorderly heaps of dirt, sand, bricks, and other materials; the housing shortage was so acute that, according to the local newspaper, the chief engineer of one of the most important of the new factories under construction, Mr. Grabovetzky, had been hurled out of his room in a hotel and left stranded with no place in which to live; and the food stringency, which was especially severe in the Ural territory, added to the generally bleak and raw atmosphere.

One could have ransacked this city at the time of my visit without finding an orange or a lemon, or candy or pastry worthy of the name, or a comfortable tea shop. The most expensive dish on the menu of the chief restaurant consisted of sour black bread, burned potatoes, and an incredibly tough piece of meat that passed as lamb. All the things that soften and beautify a European city — parks and monuments and well-laid boulevards and specimens of old architecture, civil and ecclesiastical — were conspicuously absent in this Ural capital, whose chief historical association is the slaughter of the last Russian Tsar, his wife, and the members of his family in the summer of 1918, and whose outstanding landmarks are the new six-, eight-, and ten-story buildings which are rising as the headquarters of government institutions and state trusts.

An enthusiastic local official recited a long list of Ural industrial projects, under construction and planned for the future, and triumphantly ended: "Sverdlovsk will have 1,200,000 inhabitants by the end of the second five-year plan." Perhaps it will; but I should regard this development as a curse rather than a blessing unless the city can give its prospective 1,200,000 dwellers a more civilized life than its 500,000 were able to lead in 1932.

The Soviet Union in Construction, to borrow the title of an illustrated Soviet magazine, has been no place for lovers of a soft and easy life. To get on or off a Moscow street car not infrequently requires an outlay of physical energy that vaguely recalls a combination of the undergraduate cane-rush and the football manœuvre known as a plunge through centre. The inconveniences of Soviet housekeeping are suggested by the fact that for a long time we used a raw potato as a replacement for a missing bathtub plug, since no substitute could be found in Moscow.

At the same time there are brighter and more cheerful sides of Soviet life. Most Russians possess not only an exasperating capacity for causing, but a stoical capacity for enduring, discomfort and inconvenience; they are able to work and even to study amid physical conditions that would seem impossibly hard and overcrowded to softer peoples. This iron endurance impressed me very strongly during a five-day walking trip which I took, partly in company with a group of Russian vacationists, over the Sukhum Military Road in the Caucasus. The trip included the crossing of a ten-thousand-foot mountain pass; and during the first days the going was fairly rough, involving a good deal of ploughing through snow, wading across mountain streams, and tramping across flinty rocks. A good pair of shoes might have been considered essential on such a trip. But the footwear of my companions reminded one of Washington's soldiers at Valley Forge. In the whole group there was scarcely a single stout or sound pair of shoes; at every stopping point one saw several of the wayfarers tying up loose soles with bits of string or carrying out other amateur repairs. Some made the whole journey in sandals or tennis shoes; some found it more comfortable to walk barefoot over considerable stretches. Accommodations were extremely bad, not only in the wilder places where nothing but bare shelter could reasonably have been expected, but also in Sukhum, the Black Sea town where the walk ended, where the tourist "base" to which we were assigned proved to be an extremely overcrowded barracks, so inadequately and incompetently staffed that it took from half to three quarters of an hour of standing in line to get a slip entitling one to take breakfast or to leave the base.

Yet the morale of the "tourists," as vacation travelers are called in Russia, remained surprisingly good. Every night there would be lusty singing at the camps and shelters; on one occasion some of the party developed enough energy, after a rough twenty-five-mile walk, to start a game which seemed to be a Russian form of hide-and-seek. Tempers did become frayed in the Sukhum base, and there were mutterings about sabotage and suggestions of turning to the local public prosecutor for redress. But in the main the walkers did not let the numerous hardships interfere with their enjoyment of the magnificent Caucasian scenery, and doubtless returned to Moscow, and to the other cities from which they had come, somewhat refreshed.

The Dining Room of a Sanatorium for Tubercular Workers

Outdoor life and sport have developed very greatly in Russia; and, in view of the prolonged food stringency, it is surprising how fit the participants in physical-culture parades which are sometimes held in Moscow look. To be sure, an investigator of poverty and unemployment in Germany found that a champion local soccer player had been living on a diet of bread and potatoes for two years.

Soccer is the most widely played game in the Soviet Union; baseball remains an exotic innovation, despite the attempts of Americans to introduce it; and if there is a golf course in the Soviet Union, I do not know of its whereabouts. Tennis, on the other hand, is becoming increasingly popular, and this is also true of handball and volley ball. The traditional Russian winter sports, skating and skiing, attract masses of enthusiasts in winter; and the Moscow River has its full quota of swimmers and boaters on hot summer days. The practice of bathing in the nude, which excites so much interest among some foreigners, is not a revolutionary innovation, incidentally, but an old Russian custom which is going out of style. The typical Young Communist prefers a bathing suit.

Soccer games between teams representing different cities and different parts of the country attract large crowds to the Moscow stadiums, and occasionally a visiting team from Turkey or some other country adds the flavor of an international competition. The rigid application of Communist principles, however, is a handicap to the development of international competition, because it is considered improper to play with "bourgeois" athletic bodies * and most

* Turkey is exempted from a rigorous application of this rule, partly perhaps because the Soviet Government, for strategic reasons, wishes to remain on especially good terms with that country, partly because it possesses a very small "proletariat."

of the sport organizations which qualify as "proletarian" are pitifully weak and unable to furnish equal competition.

The ideal of Soviet sport is not to set up individual records, but to stimulate all-round physical development. A badge with the inscription "Ready for Labor and Defense" is awarded to athletes who pass an all-round test in swimming, running, jumping, shooting, and one or two other exercises. Every large factory has its teams and sport groups, and the rest homes where many workers and employees spend their annual two weeks' vacation encourage organized games.

The Soviet Union is a country of rapidly vanishing land-marks. Anyone who should visit Moscow at the present time after an absence of a number of years would be struck by the many changes in the physical aspect of the city. Gone is the solid Cathedral of the Redeemer, Russia's memorial to the victory over Napoleon; gone is the chapel of the Iberian Virgin, where the Tsars paid their devotion at the time of their coronation; gone are the Red Gates, the arch at the entrance to the Red Square, and scores of churches, large and small, in all parts of the city. The most prominent new feature of Moscow is the subway now under construction; its shafts protrude at many street corners; in some cases whole streets are blocked off as a result of the digging; on free days one can see squads of Young Communists and other Soviet workers and employees marching through the streets on the way to places where they are to perform extra work in order to hasten the completion of the subway. The appearance of many Moscow houses has been changed by the practice of tacking on one or more extra stories, with a view to providing more rooms with the smallest ex-penditure of building materials. One can see the beginnings

of a new central boulevard, flanked on each side by public
buildings and hotels, which is to run to the former site of the
Cathedral, where the Palace of Soviets will ultimately be
constructed. And the Bolsheviki may boast that they found
the streets of Moscow cobblestone and left them asphalt; the
rough inconvenient cobbles are now to be found only on
obscure side streets.

This rapid vanishing of old landmarks and the substitution of new ones are symbolic of the rapidly changing life
which the typical Soviet citizen leads. Old posts are exchanged for new ones in the Soviet Union with mercurial
rapidity. I have a Communist acquaintance who in less
than a decade has held posts in the Commissariat for Foreign
Affairs, in a Soviet Embassy abroad, in the concessions committee, in a trust for the production of medicinal herbs,
and in the Intourist, or State Tourist Organization, and who
is uncertain whether the future will take him to Uruguay, to
Japan, or to a political department in some Soviet country
district.

This continual shifting from one kind of employment to
another is very characteristic of a system under which the
Communist is somewhat in the position of a soldier, liable to
be sent wherever the Party may order him. It tends to
make Communists Jacks-of-all-trades and may conceivably
give way to greater specialization in the future. Non-
Party Russians also tend to change employment and move
about more frequently than people in other countries; the
creation of new industries, new professions, new centres of
population, tends to strengthen the old nomadic instinct of
the Russian; and the very difficult food situation in various
parts of the country has stimulated permanent or tempo-

rary migratory movements. When people remain stationary for some time it is often the result of external compulsion, which may assume the form of Party discipline for
a Communist engineer or executive and of cruder forms of
restraint for the people who have been condemned to forced
labor.

The unique quality of Soviet life can only be appreciated
if one visits America or Western Europe after a prolonged
period of residence in Russia. So different are the problems and difficulties that one feels as if the world were suddenly standing on its head. Among my first surprises when
I visited America after more than a decade in the Soviet
Union I noted these items: express elevators rushing up
and down skyscrapers; mail chutes in office buildings and
hotels; automatic slot devices; paper drinking cups. These
are only a few of the hundreds of little conveniences and
mechanical devices which do not exist in Russia.

Other sharply etched differences between the two countries soon force themselves on one's attention. In Russia
one takes for granted the difficulty of obtaining an apartment,
or even a room, unless the seeker happens to be provided
with that most valuable possession in the Soviet Union —
some other currency than the Soviet ruble. So it seemed
strange to walk along the streets in New York where a
"Room to Rent" or "Apartment to Let" sign hung on almost
every house. Two extremes, neither of which could be
regarded as desirable. In the same way I could contrast my
breathless struggle for a ticket in Sverdlovsk with the Pull-
man car on a Western railroad line on which I was the sole
passenger.

The coddling of the consumer in America is another
never-ending source of wonder to the visitor from Moscow.

In Russia the consumer's tastes and conveniences are about the last thing to be considered. Chronically scanty and irregular supplies of foodstuffs and manufactured goods have schooled the Soviet consumer to patient acceptance of what he can get, regardless of how deficient it may be in quality. In America, on the contrary, the consumer seems to occupy the position of a sovereign. Sales are announced to tempt his pocketbook. Competitors in every field ask for his patronage. The dark side here, of course, is that so many consumers have seen their purchasing power largely or entirely wiped out that there is a more intensive scramble for the custom of those who remain.

Russian worries are utterly different from those of Americans. Unemployment? I have known Russians who suffered such cruel misfortunes as execution or banishment; but I have not known one who, during recent years, was unable to obtain work. Bank failures? Soviet state-controlled banks could not fail. Moreover, the ruble represents such a depreciated and uncertain unit of purchasing power that no one is much concerned about saving money anyway. Stock losses, difficulties with mortgage payments? Neither stocks nor mortgages exist in the Soviet Union. But some of the worries of a different kind which have been peculiar to the Soviet Union in recent years are crisply summed up by one of the characters in a popular Soviet play, *Fear:* "The Communist fears that he will be accused of heresy or disloyalty. The Soviet employee fears the *chistka*, or purge, that may blacklist him. The engineer fears an accusation of sabotage. The peasant woman fears that she may be called a kulak and have her property confiscated."

America and West European countries during the last

years have been passing through an acute phase of the periodic pains of individualism; the Soviet Union offers a varied exhibit in the growing pains of collectivism.   It is a matter of taste and opinion which one regards as more bearable and more curable.

VII

GOVERNMENT BY PROPAGANDA

PROPAGANDA and repression are the twin engines of the Soviet régime. It is only by the skillful, unremitting combination of these two potent instruments of government (and Soviet propaganda is unmatched in intensity, just as Soviet repression is unequaled in ruthlessness) that the Communist leaders have been able to keep themselves firmly in the saddle during a period when heavy sacrifices and deprivations were being imposed on the whole population and some classes were being literally crushed out of existence.

Propaganda alone would not be so effective if there were any means of voicing counter-propaganda. Repression alone would be ineffective in the long run if there were no effort to rally the people to the support of the government by constantly dinning into their ears its objectives and policies. But when both weapons are used simultaneously in dealing with a population of which more than half was illiterate before the Revolution, of which perhaps only 10 per cent, at a liberal estimate, had any fixed or definite political convictions before the Soviets came into power, the effect, as one might reasonably expect, is very great.

The success of the Soviet technique of government is attested by the imitation, conscious or unconscious, which it has excited in other countries. Germany under Hitler and

Italy under Mussolini are pursuing different social objectives from those of the Soviet Union; their régimes emerged, to some extent, from the struggle to suppress Communism. Yet the same formula of domination, propaganda plus repression, holds good for Italian Fascisti and German National Socialists as well as for Russian Communists; and some of the similarities in methods of governing which are a result of this circumstance are at once striking and almost amusing. These three dictatorships of the modern style are all sharply distinguished from old-fashioned military or monarchial absolutism because they have behind them the conscious support of large disciplined masses of followers, whom they are constantly strengthening in the faith by injecting new doses of propaganda. They are differentiated with equal sharpness from democratic governments because they are utterly intolerant of organized opposition and because they set up certain absolute ideas to which the individual citizen must profess allegiance, or remain discreetly silent.

Suppose that behind America's New Deal stood a tightly disciplined political party which possessed an iron grip on the whole machinery of administration and could not be peacefully voted out of power. Suppose that this party had control of every newspaper, every book-publishing company, every theatre, every radio broadcasting company — in brief, every agency of instruction and entertainment. Suppose that the penalty for the slightest opposition to the new measures were banishment at hard labor. Suppose that even the suspicion of not being actively in sympathy with them would expose an individual to loss of his post in the public service and to probable inability to find other employment. It is rather obvious that under such conditions the New Deal would have taken a very different course and that measures which have been withdrawn or modified in response to popular criticism would have been driven through with ruthless disregard of the objections which they might arouse.

The chief Soviet agency for preventing any "dangerous" thoughts from reaching the minds of the population is the Glavlit, a supreme board of censorship, without the permission of which nothing may be printed in the Soviet Union and no foreign books or newspapers may be brought into the country. Even theatre and concert programmes must bear the stamp of the Glavlit. How minute and sweeping this thought control may be is evident from the fact that a concert programme which included an orchestral composition, Brahms's Variations on a Haydn Theme, had to be abruptly changed at the last moment. The Variations were based on an old religious chorale; an erudite censor had discovered this circumstance and had decided that Soviet auditors should not hear it.

I once had the opportunity of discussing with a former head of the Glavlit, Mr. Lebedev-Polyansky, the principles which guided its work. "In general," he declared, "books which are published must correspond with the policies of the government." He explained that a main objective of the censorship was to prevent any ideas which were out of line with Party policies from reaching the masses. So it might be permissible for a scientific work, published in a very small edition, to touch on controversial ground, but such a work might not appear in a large number of copies.

Less than 1 per cent of the books which are submitted to the Glavlit are forbidden publication, according to Mr. Lebedev-Polyansky. This is a result not of the liberalism of the censorship, but, as the censor himself said, of the fact "that people who are hostile to the Soviet régime usually do not write books." Moreover, the directors of publishing houses, anxious to preserve their own reputation for orthodoxy, are seldom inclined to accept a manuscript which may be rejected by the Glavlit.

No religious literature may be printed in the Soviet Union, with the exception of two or three small church journals, extremely limited in circulation. The importation of religious books or publications from abroad is strictly prohibited. How careful the control over the receipt of unauthorized printed material from abroad is may be judged from an amusing incident which recently occurred in the office of a foreigner in Moscow. A charwoman, barely literate and certainly quite innocent of any knowledge of foreign languages, had asked for old newspapers for purely household uses. The secretary gave her a bundle, whereupon a Communist in the office building came in and warned the secretary against any such unlicensed distribution of foreign newspapers. While the foreigners are permitted to receive foreign newspapers for which they subscribe, there is almost no sale of foreign newspapers, except Communist ones, on news stands or in bookstores. The Soviet Union is far more thoroughly and hermetically sealed against the infiltration of questionable political, economic, and philosophical ideas from outside than any other large country in the world. Foreign technical books and journals are willingly imported, so far as currency restrictions permit; but every conceivable effort is made to prevent the poison of "bourgeois" ideas from reaching the Soviet population, especially the younger generation, which has been vigorously drilled in Communist ideas.

The huge Soviet propaganda machine works with every available resource to remould the mind of the nation. School and theatre, press and lecture platform, radio and poster, even moving-picture performance and circus, are all pressed into service on what is sometimes called "the ideological front." From the time when a child can toddle, a red flag is pushed into its hand; it learns the new Soviet songs and is taught in nursery and kindergarten to lisp Soviet slogans. The stream of propaganda, all directed to the purpose of making a new type of man and woman, entirely devoted to Soviet and Communist ideas, becomes intensified as the child grows older.

No one can visit a Soviet school without being impressed by the thorough manner in which the pupils are taught to hate "capitalism" and the "bourgeoisie" and to regard the Soviet system as the best in the world. I was once the witness of an amusing scene when a six-year-old American child was showing a picture book to a Russian playmate who was three or four years older. At first the Russian girl enjoyed the colored illustrations. Then an idea came to her; and, turning to her mother, she said: "Mother, this book is bourgeois. It can't be good, can it?"

Wherever he goes, the Soviet citizen cannot escape the pervasive flow of thought-moulding propaganda. If he walks the streets by day he sees red streamers calling on everyone to subscribe to the latest state loan, to join the Osaviakhim, a civilian military training organization, or to give some voluntary labor to the Moscow subway. The same appeals are blazoned forth in electrical signs at night.

If one turns on the radio in Moscow one is apt to hear, instead of the foolery of a (nonexistent) Russian "Amos an' Andy," a dissertation on the glories of collective farming or on the allegedly amazing strides of the nonferrous metal industry. The theatre repertory abounds in plays which, with slight variations, adhere to a common plot formula: a new industrial plant built at record speed and triumphantly completed ahead of scheduled time, despite the machinations of a villain in the shape of a sabotaging engineer or a kulak who has sneaked in as a worker and plays the part of a wolf in sheep's clothing.

Typical of film propaganda was an unconsciously amusing production which I saw where the heroine, a factory girl, contracts a union with an unworthy, careerist type of Young Communist, who persuades her to leave the factory bench and live with him in the ignoble comfort of domestic ease. The moral problem involved was not in the least that the girl had apparently not considered it necessary to register her union in the Zags, or Soviet marriage bureau; it was that she was a "deserter from the labor front." Bit by bit her proletarian conscience began to stir until she finally broke off with her unworthy lover and took her old place at the machine, whereupon the production plan of the factory, which had been lagging, was fulfilled by 106 per cent and the percentage of *brak*, or damaged goods, miraculously declined from 35 per cent to 4 per cent.

Even the circus has not been overlooked, and a special order once instructed the clowns to give a proletarian twist to their jokes and tumbling. While most of the items on the bill at a circus performance which I attended consisted of politically neutral exhibitions of acrobatics and animal-taming feats, there was a dutiful attempt to carry out this order by making jokes about bad-fitting clothing, ending up with an appeal to the workers to do better in this field in the future. And the Moscow circus is certainly the only establishment of

its kind in the world which would spread out for the benefit
of its spectators such a solemn streamer placard as: "We shall
meet the Seventeenth Party Congress with a general achievement of the 'technical minimum.'"   (The "technical minimum," it may be noted, is a test of mechanical skill which
is required in all factories.)

The poster is a means of propaganda which the Soviet
Government has liberally utilized since its establishment.
The artistic fancy of the Russian is usually considerably
more developed than his knack for mechanics; and it must be
said that posters depict the attractions of life in a collective
farm as considerably more alluring than one finds them in
life.   There are posters large and small, with single and
group themes, on every conceivable subject: bureaucracy, sanitation, industrial progress, military preparedness — all, of
course, pointing the way to the realization of Soviet policies.

Sometimes, no doubt, the preparation of posters diverts
attention from more practical activity.   A Soviet journalist,
Mikhail Koltzov, once described a case when Ukraina was
plagued with an especially large number of malignantly
biting flies in the summer.   The local Commissariat for
Health, instead of taking steps to provide fly paper and other
means of destroying the insects, confined its efforts to the
printing of eloquent poster appeals to destroy the flies "as
class enemies."   But the poster has its place with press and
radio, film and play, as a means of shaping ideas along new
lines.

Art has also been mobilized for the "class front" in recent
years.   (What has n't been on the "class front" during the
Iron Age?   Science, literature, music — even, alas, statistics.)   With the disappearance of the well-to-do private
patron of art, painters and sculptors have become dependent

on state, trade-union, and other public patronage; and many, especially of the younger artists, are attached to institutions, which pay them salaries and instruct them as to just what subjects they are to depict. In one year 347 artists were sent into industrial regions and to state and collective farms, and commissioned to paint scenes of new Soviet life. It is easy to imagine that there would have been short shrift for the artist who endeavored to represent weeds and hunger, rather than glowing prosperity, as features of life on a collective farm, or who preferred to paint an old church or monastery rather than a new factory or dam.

Employing the economic phraseology that is habitual in Russia in discussing literature, art, and drama, the newspaper *Soviet Art* complained that "the artists did not receive from their organizations definite production assignments," with the result that "we had unsatisfactory production." The Rabis, the artists' trade-union, thereupon decreed that "the sending of artists must be carried out in strict accordance with production plans, and every artist must receive a definite concrete assignment as regards production and theme, linked up with proposed exhibitions — as, for instance, 'For the Strengthening of the Defensive Capacity of the Soviet Union,' 'The Storm of the Second Five-Year Plan,' and so forth." Such a system fits the artist firmly into the propaganda machine and leaves little scope for the proverbial whimsies and caprices of the artistic temperament.

The press is naturally a very important cog in the well-oiled, high-powered machinery for the moulding of public opinion. No newspaper or magazine in the Soviet Union is or could be privately owned or published; the entire press is the obedient mouthpiece of the Party and the government. A press department attached to the Central Committee of the Party helps to supervise, guide, and coördinate editorial policy and can set every newspaper in the country, from Archangel to Tashkent and from Minsk to Vladivostok, roaring, exhorting, or denouncing, all on one theme and in very similar words, even though publications, in conformity with the Soviet nationality policy, are printed in many different languages.

A main point of contrast between the Tsarist and the Soviet régime is that the former, resting on tradition and authority, was inclined to look with a suspicious eye on educational effort in general, whereas the Soviet Government is eager to teach the people to read and write — so long as they read and write only the correct things, from the more or less mystical "class standpoint." So it is not surprising that there has been an enormous expansion of newspaper reading since the Revolution. Before the war there were 859 newspapers in Russia, with a total circulation of 2,700,000 copies. Now there are officially reported to be 9700 newspapers, with about 36,000,000 copies. It must, of course, be borne in mind that many present-day newspapers are extremely sketchy affairs — district organs which appear twice a week, and factory newspapers which are even more irregular.[1] But, whatever one may think of the quantity and of the quality of the news which is supplied to Soviet readers, it certainly reaches far more people than was the case in Tsarist days.

The rules which guide Soviet journalism are in many ways the precise reverse of those which govern the conduct of mass-circulation newspapers in other countries. Compe-

---

[1] Some 3000 of the publications officially classified as newspapers are small propaganda sheets issued by the political departments in the country districts.

tition is nonexistent, and Soviet editors do not vie with each others in "scoops" and "beats." Ordinary crime and scandal are rigidly barred from the columns of Russian newspapers. One would also look in vain for household hints, fashion and society articles, crossword puzzles, stock-exchange quotations, professional sport news, rotogravure supplements, and comic strips. On the other hand, there is very full reporting of important speeches and decrees. A fair proportion of foreign news, with a distinctly tendentious coloring, appears in the larger newspapers; provincial organs print the barest scraps of international news and satiate their readers with accounts of the fulfillment or nonfulfillment of production programmes in factories and collective farms. The Soviet press suffers from a constant shortage of paper; even such leading newspapers as *Izvestia* and *Pravda*, organs respectively of the Soviet Government and of the Communist Party, are restricted to four large pages; provincial publications are even more meagre in size.

Just as the Soviet press omits or restricts to a minimum many things which are supposed to appeal to readers in other countries, it treats at great length subjects which would only be described in business or trade supplements in foreign newspapers. Every large new factory that is opened is described in detail as a new victory on the "industrial front"; every sowing and harvesting "campaign" commands many columns of description, of praise for districts which are doing well and reproof for those which are lagging.

The numerous bridles, blinders, and curbs which are placed on the Soviet press, the necessity for repeating faithfully every Party shibboleth, the fear of transgressing, however slightly, that indefinable but imperative rule of thought and expression known as the Party line, the strict prohibition of publishing any news or comment which has not been passed for approval by the official department which may be affected — all this imposes on the Soviet press a tone of monotonous and colorless uniformity, which is only occasionally broken by a witty *feuilleton* or a sarcastic article on foreign affairs.

Not that criticism is excluded from its columns.   But the criticism is sharply restricted to minor details of execution, and stops abruptly if larger issues of policy are concerned. A Soviet journalist, for instance, could describe quite frankly the poor working of a collective farm.   He could not, however, even hint that collective farming is an undesirable system.   Such things as the famine, the wholesale arrests carried out by the Gay-Pay-Oo, the sufferings of forcibly deported peasants, are barred subjects for Soviet newspapers, which repeat, like parrots, such demonstrable untruths as that there is no forced labor, no persecution of religion, no poverty in the Soviet Union, until the editors and perhaps some of the readers may come to believe them.[2]

Soviet newspapers have a number of stock methods of suggestive reporting.   Whenever the annual state loan is issued (subscriptions of three weeks' or a month's salary to such loans are actually if not nominally compulsory for workers, employees, and members of collective farms) it is always "in response to the overwhelming demand of the workers" of Leningrad, Tula, Magnitogorsk, or some other

---

[2] *Pravda*, which in Russian means "Truth," on July 28, 1933, asserted, "The Soviet Union is the only country which does n't know poverty" — this about a country which in the preceding six months had witnessed an enormous dying off of people for sheer lack of anything to eat.   In the same month a writer in Moscow's English-language newspaper, the *Moscow Daily News*, made the cheerful but unfortunately highly inaccurate claim that Russia had "no more dying villages, no more hungry centres."

industrial centre. What makes this annual comedy more diverting is that the issuing of subscription blanks and other preparatory work in connection with the loans inevitably require more time than is permitted to elapse between the "initiative" of the workers and the government's acceptance of it.[8] When an ardent shock-brigade worker, trying to speed up the other workers, is beaten or killed, a kulak genealogy is almost automatically attributed to his assailant. Any international dispute in which the Soviet Government is involved, any trial of persons accused of treason or sabotage, is always the signal for a vast outpouring of very similarly worded resolutions from factories, institutions, and organizations, all expressing their support of the government, their detestation of the persons on trial, and the resolution of the signers to work harder as a response to the incident in question. One of the engines that rather painfully and creakingly hauled along the train in which I was traveling to the opening of the Turksib Railroad was labeled "Our Reply to the Pope," His Holiness being an object of especially violent denunciation at that time because of his protests against the persecution of religion in Russia.

The Communist Party is the cementing force which coördinates all the various agencies of propaganda. It has a familiar and easily recognizable method of hammering new policies into the minds of the masses. First Stalin makes a speech, or the Central Committee of the Party publishes a resolution, covering the noteworthy current problems of the day. Then Stalin's chief lieutenants — Kaganovitch in Moscow, Kirov in Leningrad, Kossior in

---

[8] In 1934 the precise amount of the loan was set down in the state budget months before the Magnitogorsk workers "proposed" that it be raised.

THE VOICES OF AUTHORITY IN THE COMMUNIST PARTY

(1) Stalin; (2) Voroshilov; (3) Kalinin; (4) Kaganovitch; (5) Ordzhonikidze; (6) Budenny; (7) Molotov; (8) Kuibishev; (9) Rudziatak; (10) Litvinov; (11) Jaroslavsky; Gorky (un-numbered) is in the centre

Ukraina, and others — repeat the speech or the resolution with minor variations of addition and comment at gatherings of the higher Party officials of their regions.   These officials pass the word on to the provincial and district Party leaders, who then in turn communicate it to the subalterns of the Communist army, the secretaries of the local Party branches.   Then every Party member is supposed to become an agitator and a propagandist for the new measures among his fellows in factory, shop, or office.   It is a case of an organized minority continually working over an unorganized mass, endeavoring to overcome its inertia and its resistance to polices which may be strange and unpopular.

Soviet propaganda, while it is an unmistakably powerful weapon, is not an invincible one.   When the economic shoe is pinching too sharply, the official statements lose their effect.   A Ukrainian peasant who knows that his brother and some of his friends perished during the famine will not be impressed, except unfavorably, by a newspaper assurance that poverty has ceased to exist in the Soviet Union; and few workers are stupid enough to believe that the annual forced loans are really voluntary.

But among those classes which feel themselves a part of the existing régime the effects of the gigantic Soviet propaganda effort are potent and significant.   One never hears among the Soviet youth the fatalistic, self-deprecatory statement which was so familiar during the first years of my stay in Russia: "We are a dark people."   The propaganda of common ideas and aims has welded together Young Communists from Moscow and from the Caucasus, from the Tartar Republic on the Volga and from the old lands of Central Asia which are gradually becoming modernized. The unremitting political agitation has averted any serious outbreaks in the Red Army during a period when news from home must have often been disquieting to the peasant soldiers. Again and again I have found Young Communists in student dormitories, in workers' barracks, in communes, living under conditions which seemed to an outsider extremely difficult, who were entirely convinced that their system was the best in the world, and that its physical hardships would be quickly overcome. The political stability of the Soviet régime during a period when sacrifices almost unprecedented in any country in peace time were being required of the population must be attributed not only to a machinery of repression which in many ways exceeds that of the Tsars in ruthlessness, but also to the fact that it has won a host of loyal supporters who are on fire with zeal for Communism as a new faith. And while some phases of the Communist propaganda campaign are crude and overdone and miss the mark, it represents an essential agency in the remoulding of the mind of the country which is a prerequisite of the ultimate success of the Communist cause. The effect of the propaganda on different classes is naturally varied. It is least effective with older and middle-aged peasants and with members of the pre-war educated classes. It is accepted most unquestionably by the masses of the Soviet youth who know pre-war conditions only from what they are told in Soviet schools, and life in foreign lands only from what they read in Soviet newspapers.

Soviet propaganda has its external as well as its internal side. Its chief attentions are reserved for well-known politicians, business men, and publicists who come to the country as individuals or in groups; but almost every visitor to Moscow comes into contact with it to some extent.

During recent years there has been a growing stream of

tourists, especially Americans, to the Soviet Union. This movement will doubtless grow as a result of the establishment of Soviet-American diplomatic relations. Increased familiarity with the physical appearance of modern Russia, with Soviet political and economic ideas and constructive achievements, with Russian literature and art, music and drama, is certainly most desirable. But some visitors who spend a short time in the Soviet Union do not fully grasp the immense difference between the handling of a foreign tourist in the Soviet Union and in England, or, for that matter, in any West European country.

In England the foreign visitor goes where he pleases, meets whom he chooses, — from the Fascist leader, Sir Oswald Mosley, to the Secretary of the British Communist Party, — forms his impressions without official aid or interference. The political or economic or social observer in Russia, however, whether he realizes the fact or not, is faced with an utterly different situation. Between him and an impartial, all-round view of the country and its living conditions are barriers which in England do not exist at all: barriers of language (extremely few foreign tourists possess any knowledge of Russian); of fear and repression, which make many Soviet citizens positively afraid to talk with a foreigner; finally, of a very centralized and highly organized state propaganda system.

Most visitors to the Soviet Union come under the auspices of Intourist, the Soviet State Tourist Organization. Indeed, under present conditions of shortage of food and hotel accommodations and lack of railroad travel facilities, it is decidedly difficult for the foreigner to get about in any other way. Intourist undertakes far more than similar agencies in other countries. It acts as a showman not only for places of scenic, historical, and artistic interest, but also for the whole Soviet system. Its programme includes visits to model factories, model *crèches*, model children's homes, model prisons, model collective farms. The tourists are conducted by guide-interpreters who have been put through a special training course in propaganda and who know that failure to create a favorable impression, if it leaks out through the indiscretion of a foreigner, may have decidedly unpleasant consequences for themselves. In their training course they have not only been drilled in general Soviet ideas, but have also been taught how to explain most satisfactorily such sights as the demolition of a church or the queue outside a food shop.

There is a significant difference between what is and what is not shown to the foreign visitor. He is readily taken to the Sokolniki Prison, where conditions for the inmates, measured by Russian living standards, are almost luxurious. (Prince Kropotkin tells us in his memoirs that the Tsarist Government had a habit of building a few admirably equipped prisons for the purpose of making an impression on foreign visitors.) Our present-day tourist is not, however, given an inside view of the Inner Prison of the Gay-Pay-Oo, or of the grim Butirky, which has an unsavory reputation for chronic overcrowding, bad physical conditions, and frequent actual and attempted suicides among its inmates. He is conducted to the pleasantly located colony for reclaimed waifs which the Gay-Pay-Oo maintains in Bolshevo, near Moscow — an excellent institution of its kind. He is not shown one of the numerous forced-labor concentration camps, where conditions are very different from those in Bolshevo. If he wants to get a view of Soviet agriculture, a model commune in Tambov Province — highly unrepresentative if only because it was founded, not by native peasants, but by returned emigrants who brought a good deal of their own machinery — is at his disposal. Ukrainian and North Caucasian villages where 10 per cent or more of the population perished of famine and related causes during the winter and spring of 1932–1933 are not on the Intourist schedule.

The Russians are natural actors and stage managers, and the contemporary art of Soviet showmanship has ancient and distinguished antecedents. When the Empress Catherine II traveled by boat on the Dnieper through newly annexed Ukraina, her favorite, Prince Potyemkin, hastily erected stage villages in the sparsely populated country through which the Empress would pass. What is surprising in Russia at the present time is not the persistence of the "Potyemkin villages" traditions, but the readiness with which some foreign visitors, not infrequently men and women with a reputation for scholarship and critical acumen in their respective fields at home, accept the Soviet conducted tour at full face value without apparently realizing that they are seeing only the bright sides of a picture which has some distinctly dark sides.

I have sometimes wondered whether there is some undetected magical quality in the air or the climate of the Soviet Union that makes some of its sociologically-minded visitors cast away all sense of proportion and all capacity for criticism. Why is it that the people who raised such vigorous protests when Sacco and Vanzetti were sentenced to death after an unjust trial are so silent when forty-eight Russians are shot in a batch without any trial at all? Why does a more or less well-known British lawyer make himself eternally ridiculous by stating in print that the right to arrest is

more limited in Russia than in England?[4]   Why does Mr.
Bernard Shaw, who has said so many consciously funny
things, make himself responsible for an extremely good
unconscious joke by asserting in all seriousness that the
British engineers who were arrested on charges of sabotage
would have a fairer trial in Moscow than anywhere else in
the world?   Why does a newspaper magnate, after spending a few days in Moscow, during which his talks have been
restricted to foreigners and to Soviet officials, undertake to
enlighten the world as to just what percentage of the
160,000,000 inhabitants of the Soviet Union supports the
existing régime, what percentage opposes it, and what percentage is neutral?

In some cases, no doubt, a glowingly overfavorable view
of Russia is a possibly unconscious psychological reflection
of an unfavorable view of the existing social and economic
order in other countries.   But it would seem that people who
want to build utopias ought to place them in the sky, instead
of twisting the features of an existing order out of all imag-
inable recognition in response to an apparent urge to believe
that just because the Soviet Union is assumed to be new it is
therefore beyond criticism.

Foreign journalists with fairly long terms of residence in
Russia are naturally less susceptible to feats of social and
economic showmanship than are visitors who come to Russia
for short visits, especially if the latter have no background
of previous Russian experience.   The Soviet authorities have
worked out a number of regulations, to say nothing of
methods of indirect pressure, for the purpose of keeping the

---

[4] The absurdity of this statement is evident from the fact that on one of
Russia's numerous forced-labor construction jobs, the Baltic–White Sea
Canal, more people were employed than one would find in all the prisons
of England.

less pleasing aspects of Soviet life out of the columns of the foreign press. First of all, there is the preliminary censorship of all press telegrams, a system which does not exist as a permanent institution in any other European country. Mailed articles are free from censorship; but news developments of first-hand importance, which cannot wait for the slower mails, can be legally dispatched only in the phrasing which meets the censor's approval.

This censorship has almost automatically become intensified in severity since I described the system in my earlier book, *Soviet Russia*. A new correspondent is sometimes unctuously assured that the sole purpose of the Soviet censorship is "to prevent inaccuracies." This is a regrettably inaccurate definition. The sole concern of the Soviet press censor — as of any press censor, for that matter — is expediency. He is interested, not in the factual truth of the message which is submitted to him, but in the effect which its publication will produce in the country to which it is being sent.

Now during recent years the number of things which the Soviet authorities quite understandably desired to conceal from the attention of the outside world very considerably increased. Since 1929, executions, admitted and secret, have greatly increased in number; an entirely new system of widespread forced labor has grown up; the persecution of religion has been greatly intensified; the country experienced a major famine. In the light of these facts the censorship could not but become stricter. Although the officials of the Commissariat for Foreign Affairs who administer the censorship are above the Soviet bureaucratic average in tact and intelligence, they are themselves closely limited in their decisions and must often refer border-line and debatable messages to mysterious individuals and organizations "higher up." Their task is far from an enviable one; their careers may be ruined if a message which they have passed should impress a high Soviet or Communist official as unduly outspoken.

The Soviet brand of censorship, like all others, not infrequently makes itself ridiculous, as when it solemnly lays an interdict on the mention of some incident of diplomatic negotiations which is already well known abroad, or forbids a correspondent to send the startling information that the Turksib express was stalled in the desert for a few hours, or refuses to permit the news of the departure of Foreign Commissar Litvinov for America (Litvinov's departure was veiled in the most ludicrous atmosphere of college-fraternity mystery) to be sent from Moscow, or forbids the sending of the news of a fire in the tall Gay-Pay-Oo building, which is directly across the street from the Commissariat for Foreign Affairs.[5] More serious, from the standpoint of giving the outside world a genuine view of Russian conditions, are such things as the well-nigh complete suppression of news of the famine, the concealment of a very large number of characteristic incidents of Gay-Pay-Oo terror, and the inevitable bowdlerization of style of a correspondent who knows from experience what will and what will not get past the censor's blue pencil. As I have said, the scope of Soviet control over foreign press messages was considerably extended in the spring of 1933, when a new rule was established forbidding any foreign corre-

---

[5] This last bit of censorship brought its own appropriate punishment. Some two weeks after the fire had occurred (it affected two upper stories in the Gay-Pay-Oo headquarters and apparently caused no loss of life) a garbled and greatly exaggerated story to the effect that the whole Gay-Pay-Oo prison had burned down, with numerous casualties among its inmates, appeared in a foreign newspaper.

spondent to leave Moscow without submitting a precise itinerary of his route and obtaining the permission of the authorities. The obvious intention of this innovation was to prevent any first-hand description of the famine. The prohibition went into effect in early spring; the first permits to travel in the country districts were issued in September, when the new harvest was largely gathered in and the raw visible traces of famine had been removed. One official explanation of the prohibition of travel was that the presence of foreign correspondents would obstruct the gathering of the harvest. What was even more amusing than this suggestion that a few itinerant correspondents might seriously affect the fate of harvesting operations over almost one sixth of the surface of the globe was that some foreigners were naïve enough to take it seriously.

Permits to reside in the Soviet Union are granted to foreigners for a maximum period of six months at a time; and the foreigner who leaves the country even for a short time must reapply for an entrance visa. This is a convenient Sword of Damocles to suspend over the head of an unruly correspondent; a delay in granting the return visa is a recognized way of warning the journalist that his writing is not regarded as satisfactory, or "objective," to use a word of which the Soviet authorities are fond. Mr. Paul Scheffer, distinguished correspondent of the *Berliner Tageblatt*, against whom no charge of factual inaccuracy was brought, was kept out of the Soviet Union, when his views and judgments had become distasteful, by the simple device of refusing him a return visa.[6] A well-known journalist is rarely directly expelled; this involves too much publicity and

[6] This same threat of finding reëntry to the Soviet Union barred in the event of too specific or too emphatic references to the "forbidden" aspects of the Soviet régime applies to writers, lecturers, and students, as well as to journalists.

scandal.   On the other hand, surreptitious private efforts of Soviet agents abroad to undermine the position of unpopular correspondents with their home offices are quite frequent. Some of these efforts have been successful; in cases when the home office has vigorously supported its correspondent it has usually succeeded in keeping him in Moscow.

That this unusual régime of controlling press messages and restricting the freedom of movement of journalists within the country clouds foreign understanding of the Soviet Union and makes the task of the correspondent in Moscow more difficult and more delicate than it is in many other capitals is obvious.   Despite the occasional unmistakable successes of the censorship in misleading foreign opinion, I am personally inclined to doubt whether, in the long run, it serves the best interests of the Soviet Government.   Its existence is known, at least to intelligent readers, and casts a natural shadow of inhibition over messages from Moscow. Censorship furnishes the sole reason and excuse for the occasional outburst of untrue or grossly exaggerated alarmist rumors about Russia from places outside the Soviet frontiers.   Moreover, there are leaks even in the tightest system of news repression.   When a sensational message gets out in some way, despite the censorship, it carries more weight than it would if it emanated from a capital where there was no restraint, simply because it is assumed that it must have been officially passed.

Censorship implies that some things must be concealed. Its abolition would afford the most persuasive evidence of improvement in Soviet conditions.   Despite these considerations, which have all been repeatedly laid before the authorities by correspondents resident in Moscow, the impulse to secrecy and concealment is so strong in Russian and especially in Soviet official nature, there are still so many bleak and raw spots in Soviet reality, that it would be most surprising (as well as most gratifying) if the system were completely abandoned in any near future. The new ruling which forbids travel outside of Moscow without special permission might conceivably be dropped, especially if there are no more famines to conceal. But it seems probable that the battle of wits between journalist and censor, the bartering of a vivid adjective for a qualifying phrase, of a mild verb for a strong noun, will go on. And readers who wish to obtain a full picture of the Russian situation from Moscow messages will be well advised to remember that while, of course, no self-respecting correspondent ever consciously sends untruth from the Soviet capital, it is often impossible, under the present system, for the most conscientious journalist to send the whole truth.

VIII

GOVERNMENT BY TERROR

WHEN Lady Astor, in company with Bernard Shaw and Lord Lothian, met Stalin in the summer of 1931, she blurted out the unconventional question: "How long are you going to continue killing people?" And Stalin, possibly taken a little off his guard, shot back the retort: "As long as it is necessary."

Here one has in a nutshell the philosophy of the terrorism which has always been an integral part of the Communist dictatorship. The right of the rulers to decide how long it may be necessary to go on killing people is absolute and unquestioned. The right of the individual to live does not weigh in the balance. And the absence of *habeas corpus* in Soviet jurisprudence has often led to the application of a sterner substitute: *habeas cadaver*.

The degree of Soviet terrorism has always varied with time and circumstances. One of its fiercest outbursts was in the late summer and early autumn of 1918, when the military situation was critical and an attempt had been made on the life of Lenin. According to official reports, which certainly did not err in overexaggeration, the numbers of people who were rounded up and shot at this time ran into thousands. Another major example of "Red Terror" occurred in the Crimea in the winter of 1920–1921, after the defeat of the last White leader, Baron Wrangel. The former President of the Hungarian Soviet Republic, Bela Kun, and a fanatical veteran woman Communist, Zemlyachka, were sent to the Crimea with sweeping powers to root out counter-revolution; and under their orders there was a wholesale slaughter of former White officers and individuals of all classes who were suspected of having been in any way connected with Wrangel's régime.

As against these high points of terror, there were times when the Soviet régime during the civil war was relatively mild, when spokesmen for opposition parties were given a very limited freedom of speech and press, something which was not permitted after the end of the civil war. At one moment, in the winter of 1919–1920, when the victory over the chief anti-Bolshevik leaders, Kolchak and Denikin, was virtually complete, the Soviet Government even made the striking gesture of abolishing the death penalty (a step which proved extremely short-lived, if, indeed, it ever went into practical effect). In the same way there has been a considerable variation in the intensity of terrorism in more recent years. From 1922 until 1928, when life was, on the whole, becoming easier and more comfortable, there was a substantial relaxation in the pressure which the Gay-Pay-Oo, as the grim Cheka of the civil-war period had been renamed, exercised on the population. Judged by any Western standards, the processes of law and justice even in those years were decidedly abnormal; exile without open trial was frequent; and executions by administrative order occurred from time to time.

But during the Iron Age, from 1929 until 1934, the scope of terrorism immensely expanded. Some of its hardest blows were struck at the peasantry, much the largest class in the population, which had been comparatively free from the attentions of the Gay-Pay-Oo during earlier years. During the autumn and winter of 1929, when the initial drive for collectivization was at its height, two foreigners who made separate and independent studies of the Soviet provincial press reached the conclusion that daily executions over a period of some months averaged from twenty to thirty. Most of the victims were recalcitrant peasants who were accused of resisting grain requisitions, and there was a fair sprinkling of priests among those who were shot.

In the autumn of 1930 even the jaded nerves of Russians were somewhat shocked by the announcement that forty-eight persons, including some distinguished professors and specialists, had been shot by summary order of the Gay-Pay-Oo for alleged sabotage in the food industry. Alleged confessions of the victims, who were obviously in no position to challenge and repudiate, were published after the shooting had taken place. In the spring of 1933 there was another wholesale slaughter; thirty-five officials of the Commissariat for Agriculture were put to death, again without public trial. The posthumous bill of indictment against them contained such strange items as "causing the growth of weeds and burning and destroying tractors and other agricultural machines." Inspired rumors were spread about that one of the persons executed, Konar-Polishchuk, had been head of an espionage organization which was working on behalf of Poland. Whatever may have been the degree of truth in this, some of the men who were executed, such as the former Vice Commissar for Agriculture, Wolf, had been engaged for many years in responsible posts in the Soviet agricultural service; and their motives for lapsing into crude and clumsy forms of sabotage, which were certain to be detected and to bring condign punishment, like the motives of the unfortunate professors and experts of the food industry, remain, to put it mildly, difficult to comprehend.

Before 1930 the forced labor of prisoners and exiles was of slight importance in Soviet economic life. After the first huge wave of kulak liquidation the timber industry and many large construction projects have depended very largely for their labor supply on the victims of the government's ruthless measures of repression. Most of these conscript laborers are peasants who opposed collectivization; but the terror has also taken a heavy toll of the city intelligentsia. Engineers, agronomes, historians, bacteriologists, statisticians, art experts, men of the most varied intellectual pursuits, have been arrested, usually on the vague and formidable charge of sabotage. Some have been executed; others have been sent to chop wood in the forced-labor camps; still others have been forced to work at their professions, but in the technical status of prisoners, in new construction enterprises where unfavorable food and housing conditions would have made it difficult to attract professional men voluntarily.

The secrecy with which Soviet terrorism is cloaked, the fact that many executions and the great majority of sentences of imprisonment and exile are carried out without any publicity, make it impossible to give precise data as to its scope. The very size of the country also makes it easier to conceal acts of repression than it would be in a smaller land with better communications. A resident in Moscow, Russian or foreigner, would in many cases only learn by accident, if indeed he learned at all, of such episodes of "class war" as the death from hunger of many exiled peasant children in remote Luza, in Northern Russia, in the summer of 1931; or the wide-spread scurvy among the forced laborers in the Karaganda coal mines, in Kazakstan, as a result of inadequate diet; or the perishing of cold of kulak families which were driven out of their homes in winter near Akmolinsk, in Kazakstan; or the development of diseases of the female organs among the women exiles in bleak Khibinogorsk, beyond the Arctic Circle, as a result of the complete absence of sanitary provision in the severe winter.

It is only very infrequently that an official statement indirectly casts some light on the scope of the Soviet terror. In August 1933, it was announced in the Soviet press that over 12,000 prisoners employed in the construction of the canal which links the Baltic Sea with the White Sea (an extensive chain of lakes and rivers has been utilized in this connection) had received a complete amnesty and that over 59,000 more had received reductions of sentence, in celebration of the speedy completion of the canal. If one considers that there were probably tens of thousands more prisoners on this enterprise who did not benefit by the amnesty and the reduction of the sentences, it would seem that the number of prisoners on this single enterprise would easily exceed the total number of political prisoners in all the countries of Europe, and this at a time when many countries are under dictatorships which employ ruthless methods with political opponents.

The Baltic–White Sea Canal accounts for only a small fraction of the political prisoners and exiles of the Soviet Union. I could testify from personal observation that tens of thousands of such prisoners, mostly exiled peasants who had been guilty of no criminal offense, were employed at compulsory labor in such places as Magnitogorsk, Chelia-

BARRACKS FOR THE PRISONERS WORKING ON THE
BALTIC–WHITE SEA CANAL

THE PRISONERS AT WORK

binsk, and Berezniki.[1]   I was reliably informed on one occasion from a source that must remain anonymous that there were about three hundred thousand prisoners in concentration camps in Siberia alone.   The number of persons in prison and exile fluctuates from time to time as some people finish their terms and others are sent out; but the total number of Soviet citizens who, during the Iron Age, have been deprived of liberty without anything that could plausibly be called "due process of law" can scarcely be less than two million.

What marks out the Soviet terror in an age that has been full of examples of governmental ruthlessness in many countries is not so much individual acts of revolting cruelty — although these have certainly not been lacking — as the enormous number of persons affected (compared with the puny efforts at terrorism instituted in European countries, there is something majestically Asiatic about the Soviet system, with its millions of victims) and the vile conditions of food and housing which almost invariably prevail in places of imprisonment and exile.   The latter are the result not so much of deliberate cruelty as of the generally strained food situation of the country and of the inhospitable and remote places to which exiles are sent.   When free workers

[1] A little incident which occurred during my visit to the Cheliabinsk tractor plant, then in the last stages of construction, in the summer of 1932, throws some light on the value of the Soviet conducted tour. My wife, who speaks Russian much more fluently and idiomatically than I do, began to talk with some of the prisoners who were at forced labor. A Communist foreman, feeling that this was no proper subject of inquiry for a foreigner, stepped up and asked her, with significant emphasis, whether she was a Soviet citizen.   When he learned that she was not, he retired; but the incident indicates how much an actual Soviet citizen, acting as interpreter, would feel free to communicate to a foreigner about forced labor, famine, persecution of religion, and other forbidden subjects.

and peasants have often been hungry and undernourished it was hardly to be expected that "class enemies," as political exiles are considered, would be better fed; and letters and stories of prisoners which I have read and heard generally agree in complaining of terrific overwork (the Soviet labor laws do not apply in practice to forced labor), of extreme and insanitary overcrowding in fetid and verminous barracks, of the well-nigh complete lack of meat and fats, fruit and vegetables.

In the centre of Moscow, on the former Lubyanka Square (now called Dzerzhinsky Square, in honor of the fanatically idealistic and devoted Polish Bolshevik who founded the Cheka), is a tall gray building.   If one looks closely enough one can distinguish near the top a bit of sculpture depicting the Parcæ, the Greek Fates, cutting short the threads of human life.   There is grim and profound symbolism in this pre-war decoration, for the building houses the headquarters of the Gay-Pay-Oo, to use the familiar Russian abbreviation for its full official title, United State Political Administration.   No single organization in the world, it is safe to say, bears the responsibility for cutting short so many human lives as the Gay-Pay-Oo, which is simply the old Cheka, dreaded instrument of Red Terror during the civil war, under another name.

The Gay-Pay-Oo annually celebrates the birthday of its organization in December 1917.   On such occasions it is habitually referred to in laudatory speeches as "the unsheathed sword of the proletarian dictatorship."   It certainly is the incarnation of the terroristic side of Soviet administration.   For the Gay-Pay-Oo, during the Iron Age, has been quite above the restraints, scanty though these are, which Soviet law places on the operations of the ordinary courts.

Every Soviet citizen, except a few highly placed Communists, has been at its mercy. It has repeatedly made use of its extraordinary power of shooting whom it might choose after a "trial" *in camera,* where it performed the triple function of accuser, judge, and executioner. The Gay-Pay-Oo may arrest anyone and hold him for an indefinite period of time without bringing any accusation. It can subject anyone, without the sentence of an open court, to several degrees of administrative banishment, ranging from the relatively mild "minus six," which forbids one to live in Moscow, Leningrad, and four other important cities, to imprisonment at hard labor for a period up to ten years in a concentration camp in the Arctic wilds.

The Gay-Pay-Oo at times has almost shown signs of becoming a state within a state, although the present tendency is to clip its wings slightly. It has its own army in the shape of a number of crack regiments, which correspond to the Guards Regiments of the Tsar in their supposed special reliability and in the care and attention which they receive. It has under its command more serfs than the richest mediæval Russian boyar, in the persons of the involuntary laborers who are herded in its concentration camps. Its officials ride around in the shiniest and newest automobiles and generally live in a style which betokens their power. Whoever else may go cold or hungry in the Soviet Union, the Gay-Pay-Oo official and his family are always well provided for. A post in the Gay-Pay-Oo is the ambition of every Soviet young man who wishes to make a successful career and is not encumbered by "bourgeois" humanitarian scruples.

The saying, "All hope abandon, ye who enter here," must have occurred to many who have been rounded up in the familiar nocturnal raids of the Gay-Pay-Oo, for this organization has much more than power of life and death over its victims. Under the peculiar Soviet juridical practices it is also in a position to bring the strongest kind of pressure on its victims by threats directed not only against their persons, but also against members of their families.[2]

On this point we have the interesting testimony of the wife of Professor Tchernavin, a distinguished scientist who was arrested on the familiar charge of sabotage and was fortunate enough to escape from the Soviet Union, with his wife and son, in 1931.[3] "I learned afterwards," she writes, in describing her own arrest, "that the examining officer had confronted him with the dilemma of either signing the statement that he was a 'wrecker' or of being the cause of my arrest. . . . After my arrest my husband was presented with another alternative: either he must confess his 'guilt' or he would be shot, I would get ten years penal servitude and our son be sent to a colony for homeless children."

[2] The holding of wives and other relatives as hostages for the return of Soviet citizens who go abroad is a very familiar practice. At the time of the visit to Russia of Bernard Shaw, Lady Astor, and Lord Lothian, a Russian professor named Krynin who was living in America asked the intercession of Shaw and Lady Astor for his wife, who was forbidden to leave Moscow and go abroad, apparently as a reprisal for Krynin's failure to return. After the excitement which had been aroused over this incident had subsided, the Gay-Pay-Oo exiled Madame Krynin to some unknown place.

[3] Many of the books which profess to "expose" the Gay-Pay-Oo are so grossly exaggerated and uninformed that they are worse than worthless from the factual standpoint. A distinguished exception is Madame Tchernavin's *Escape from the Soviets*, a narrative of her own and her husband's experience and of their final escape. Anyone who wishes to read an account of the state of ghastly terrorism in which the old intelligentsia were living, especially in 1930 and 1931, written with transparent honesty and on a basis of definite personal experience, cannot do better than turn to Madame Tchernavin's book.

This is a useful bit of first-hand testimony to remember in considering the psychological background for the curious sabotage trials which were such a characteristic feature of the Iron Age.

Professor Tchernavin's experience closely coincides with an instance of Gay-Pay-Oo methods with which I happen to be personally acquainted. For obvious reasons names must be withheld. A man who was fairly well known in some circles abroad had made himself obnoxious to the Gay-Pay-Oo by his intercession with other Soviet authorities on behalf of political prisoners. It was considered inexpedient to arrest him on account of his age and because his arrest would have attracted attention abroad. So it was intimated to him that if he did not abandon his practice of interceding his son would be banished.

It is difficult to estimate how many people have been secretly put to death during recent years. I may cite two typical cases within a limited circle of personal acquaintances. Julius Rozinsky was formerly an employee in the service of the Commissariat for Foreign Affairs. In the autumn of 1929 his father-in-law, an elderly man who had been refused permission to join his family in Riga, made an unsuccessful attempt to cross the frontier illegally and was caught. Shortly after this, Rozinsky himself was arrested; and in the spring of 1930 the old man whose crime was his desire to join his family, and Rozinsky, who may have been suspected of knowing of the plan without reporting it to the authorities, were both shot without publicity and without any kind of open trial.

It is noteworthy that Rozinsky was a man of distinctly Communist sympathies, the best proof of which was that he had frequently been assigned as an interpreter to sympathetic radical visitors. If he encountered such summary treatment it is easy to imagine what kind of "justice" an omnipotent Gay-Pay-Oo tribunal would mete out to anyone who, by very class origin, was guilty in advance — a priest or a well-to-do peasant, a professor or engineer of the old school, for instance.

The other victim of secret execution was a certain Sergei Treivas, who, as secretary of Voks, the Society for Cultural Relations with Foreign Countries, was in the habit of showing off the achievements of Soviet culture to admiring visitors. His fate was perhaps a realistic commentary on his glowing expositions.

When one distinguished scientist after another disappeared into the clutches of the Gay-Pay-Oo, the familiar official explanation was that they had been guilty of that extremely elastic crime known as sabotage. Toward the end of 1930, eight professors and engineers were brought to a public trial on a formidable bill of indictment, charging them with deliberately misplanning and mismanaging industrial enterprises which were under their charge, with maintaining connections with French and British military authorities with a view to promoting intervention and the armed overthrow of the Soviet Government, and with organizing a so-called Industrial Party to set up a military dictatorship after the Soviet Government was overthrown. The defendants all obediently confessed practically everything that was laid to their charge, professed edifying repentance, and got off with their lives. So they were luckier than their predecessors, the alleged *saboteurs* of the food industry, who were shot without benefit of public trial.

This spectacular trial was brilliantly staged to make a proletarian holiday — the courtroom filled with loud-speakers and flashlights, the papers full of resolutions from all sorts of bodies, from the members of the Moscow bar [4] to Young Pioneer school children, all demanding the shooting of the prisoners, even the Young Communist son of one of the defendants duly demanded the death of his father. But the reality of the scene was impaired when the head of the alleged Industrial Party, Professor Ramzin, included in his confession some items which were obviously and even absurdly untrue. Indeed, if there had been one free opposition newspaper in Russia, the trial would probably have broken down amid gales of general laughter on the day when Ramzin's "confession" was published. For the man who was mentioned as the destined Premier of the counter-revolutionary government which the self-confessed plotters were proposing to set up was one P. P. Ryabushinsky, a well-known pre-war Russian industrialist. And P. P. Ryabushinsky — very thoughtlessly, from the standpoint of the organizers of the trial — had died in Paris several years before the trial was held. A "conspiracy" of which the prospective chief was a dead man would seem to be a more suitable subject for a comic paper than for a serious trial, especially as another of the "proposed Ministers," Vishnegradsky, was also no longer among the living. There were other amusing discrepancies in the testimony, as when Ramzin told of a "meeting" in London with Colonel Lawrence at a time when it was conclusively evident that

---

[4] The sanguinary resolution of the Moscow lawyers was withdrawn, as an afterthought, on the ground that it might embarrass the conduct of the defense, since the lawyers who were appointed for this purpose might feel bound by the resolution. Any "defense" of persons accused of a political offense under Soviet conditions is bound to be farcical, because a lawyer who would say anything displeasing to the court would soon feel the strong hand of the Gay-Pay-Oo.

Lawrence had been stationed, as an aviator, on the northwest frontier of India, or when he spoke of meeting a certain "Sir Philip," whose last name he did not know — because, he said, in England lords are always called by the first name with the prefix "Sir."

An intelligent Communist acquaintance admitted to me in private conversation that "perhaps 50 per cent of the Ramzin case was imaginary"; had he raised his estimate to 90 per cent, I could have agreed with him.   In the other outstanding "sabotage" case which was heard shortly after the Ramzin trial, when a number of alleged Mensheviki who had occupied positions in the Soviet economic and statistical service were brought to trial, there was also a careless slip: the prosecution insisted that the Menshevik leader Abramowitsch had been in Russia on a secret visit during a period when he was able to prove a complete "alibi."

Other sweeping arrests, which were not followed by open trials, occurred among historians, bacteriologists, and other classes of scientists.   Among the large number of historical scholars who were arrested were men of international reputation, including four members of the Academy of Science — Professors Platonov, Tarle, Likhachev, and Lubavsky. Most of the historians were middle-aged and elderly men; Platonov and one of the others implicated in this affair died in exile; two suffered mental breakdowns as a result of the rigors of confinement, interrogation, and exile.   In the absence of any official explanation of this wholesale arrest of Russia's historical scholars, which affected scores of people, one can only repeat the rumor that Platonov, while abroad, had met his former pupil, the Grand Duke Andrew.   If this really occurred, it was a highly indiscreet action on the part of Platonov, although it is not altogether clear how a talk between a venerable professor and a forgotten scion of the Romanov family could have greatly endangered the stability of the Soviet state. But the penalty for Platonov's supposed action fell not only on him, but on many of his friends, associates, and pupils, who had no responsibility for the meeting and knew nothing about it.

It would require an entire book to give an adequately detailed picture of Soviet repression during the Iron Age. The cases that have been cited, however, convey some idea of the state of absolute terror which was created for considerable classes of the population: the old intelligentsia, any peasants who could be suspected of being well-to-do, and, of course, the pariah caste of the *lishentsi*, or disfranchised, ex-aristocrats, former merchants and traders, pre-war officers and Tsarist officials, and so forth.

Every historical period of terrorism has, of course, its definite causes. Not all the victims of the Gay-Pay-Oo can be regarded as innocent, although the utter defenselessness of the individual against the omnipotent state does make it conceivable, and in some cases even probable, that a man who was innocent, or guilty of some trivial offense, might accuse himself falsely, if this were the price of life for himself and of security for his family.

There is foreign espionage in Russia, just as there is Soviet espionage in other countries; and here and there the Gay-Pay-Oo has doubtless caught real spies along with imaginary ones. Cases of corruption and slackness in industrial administration also undoubtedly occurred. Some Soviet citizens, on the rare occasions when they could travel abroad, probably yielded to the temptation — humanly understandable, although quite inexcusable considering the risk to which this exposed them, their families, and their friends — to indulge in surreptitious meetings with old friends among the émigrés. In view of the far-flung network of Gay-Pay-Oo espionage abroad as well as in the Soviet Union,[5] such meetings were almost certain to be discovered, with the most disastrous consequences for the Soviet citizens concerned.

In very infrequent cases an engineer or technical expert might have been so desperately embittered against the Soviet régime that he indulged in deliberate sabotage in the enterprise where he was employed. But, with the knowledge that the penalty for sabotage was death or a long term of exile at hard labor, it taxes one's credulity to believe that many of the proverbially soft Russian middle-class intelligentsia possessed either sufficient fanaticism or sufficient nerve to resort to it.

Of course, if skepticism regarding the advisability of Soviet industrial and agricultural policies and discontent with material hardship could be regarded as sabotage, a very large part of the pre-war educated class was undoubtedly guilty of this offense. But this was something very different from the actual damaging or wrecking of plants and machinery.[6]

[5] A former Gay-Pay-Oo agent, George Agabekov, who fled from the Soviet service, has published a description — plausible, in the main — of Soviet espionage methods in Persia, where he worked personally, showing how agents and informers were recruited from the most unlikely classes, so that former Tsarist officers and prelates of the Armenian Church in some cases were making regular reports to the foreign representatives of the Gay-Pay-Oo.

[6] An incident reported in *Izvestia* late in 1930 showed on what curious material a charge of sabotage could be based. A certain Professor Tushnov, in an institute in Kazan, was accused of saying that every scientific student abroad had his own microscope and other equipment, a situation which does not exist in the Soviet Union, and of adding that "some who come to study in the Soviet Union cannot even handle an oil stove." The Kazan proletarian students promptly accused the Professor of "ideological sabotage," and *Izvestia* solemnly characterized Tushnov's statement as being "direct solidarity with those who, in the name of saving capitalism and its 'culture,' strive to destroy the sole proletarian state in the world."

One can only understand the sweeping arrests for sabotage, often on what seem fantastically improbable charges, if one bears in mind the white heat of fanaticism which the Communist leaders whipped up among the masses, and to some extent also among themselves, in connection with the fulfillment of the five-year plan. When plans went awry, when deprivations, instead of disappearing, became more severe, when promised improvements in food supply did not materialize, the subconscious temptation to seek scapegoats became almost irresistible. And who were more natural scapegoats than intellectuals of the old school who were out of sympathy with the new order anyway?   Nero, one feels, could have understood the reality behind many Soviet sabotage trials and arrests.   His effort to cast the blame for the burning of Rome on the Christians is one of the first "sabotage trials" recorded in history; and the Christians, it must be said, had imprudently furnished circumstantial evidence to Nero's Gay-Pay-Oo by indulging in dark prophecies about the approaching end of the world.

The effect of the huge Gay-Pay-Oo system, with its army of spies and provocators, on Russian daily life is formidable and prodigious. Anecdotes abound on the theme that, where three Russians meet, one is certain to be an agent of the Gay-Pay-Oo.   No doubt the omniscience of this organization is exaggerated; but the terror which it strikes is real and ever-present and is by no means confined, as its apologists would like to suggest, to incorrigible enemies and critics of the Soviet régime.   I have seen a plain-clothes agent take a man off a train for talking too freely, and the flow of critical conversation in queues is substantially checked by the general belief that the eyes and ears of the Gay-Pay-Oo are everywhere.

My chief personal grievance against the Gay-Pay-Oo is the number of friendships with educated Russians which its system has cut short or made impossible. Many Russians would as readily spend an evening with a man in an advanced stage of typhus as with a foreigner; and one certainly cannot blame them if one bears in mind the all-pervading espionage and the amazing imagination of Gay-Pay-Oo examiners in making up accusations of bribery, spying, and what not on the basis of the most harmless social contacts between Russians and foreigners. I know of one case where a Russian was arrested and held in prison for months because a servant (in the households of foreigners, servants are very apt to be willing or unwilling spies) had overheard and misunderstood some fragments of conversation in which he had been advising a foreigner about walking trips on the famous Caucasian Military Roads. The Russian was suspected of betraying secrets about military roads.

On one occasion I had invited to my house two Communist Party members, whom I shall call A and B. The latter arrived late, and asked whether there were any other guests. When he heard that A was there he turned pale, mumbled an unconvincing excuse, and bolted away with a speed that would have been amusing if it were not pathetic. I cannot say whether there was any foundation for B's apprehensions about being seen by A in the home of a foreigner; that the apprehensions existed was unmistakable.

It is noteworthy that high Soviet diplomats and public officials who should, one would suppose, be exempt from the functioning of the repressive system unbend visibly and behave much more like normal human beings as they get farther away from Moscow. When I was in China, in 1927, I found that a Soviet official was apt to be much more communicative in Shanghai than in Harbin, where the clammy restraining influence of Moscow was already felt.

An amusing official confirmation of the close surveillance under which foreign residents of the Soviet Union are kept was supplied to a foreign correspondent in the course of an argument with an official in the Commissariat for Foreign Affairs. The official was reproaching the correspondent for alleged remarks in private conversation which the correspondent denied having made. Finally, losing patience and discretion at the same moment, the official pointed to a thick *dossier* which lay on a shelf and triumphantly exclaimed: "Everything is reported. *Everything* is reported." This is the ideal of the Gay-Pay-Oo for foreigners and Russians alike. Unfortunately, as is bound to be the case under such a universal espionage system, while much is reported, much more is certainly misreported.

There is a sharp line of administrative demarcation between what the Gay-Pay-Oo is permitted to do to foreigners and what it habitually does to Russians; it is one of the many amusing inconsistencies of Russian life that while the Soviet Government, in principle, is strongly opposed to any form of extraterritorial privileges, it actually concedes, in fact if not in name, an extraterritorial status to foreigners resident in the country. A foreigner in Moscow may say and do many things which would place a Russian in a concentration camp, and go unscathed. Occasionally the line is overstepped, as when the Soviet Government in 1924 caused the arrest, trial, and conviction — on highly improbable charges, including participation in a plot to murder Stalin and Trotzky — of three German students, Kindermann, Wolscht, and Von Ditmar. The students were released when a Soviet revolutionary agent named Skobelevsky, who had been sentenced to death for organizing a terrorist group among German Communists, was released by the German authorities. A German engineer and two mechanics were brought to trial in the Shachti sabotage case; and, although they were acquitted, the circumstances of their arrest and investigation created a considerable temporary coolness between the Soviet Union and Germany. More recently, in the spring of 1933, the Gay-Pay-Oo endeavored to cast six British engineers in the employ of the Metro-Vickers Company for the familiar rôle of villains in a sabotage trial; and still more recently there were a number of mysterious arrests among foreigners in the service of the International Control Company, an organization which had been functioning in the Soviet Union for a number of years, certifying the quality of grain and other cargoes which were dispatched from Soviet ports. Citizens of Belgium, Denmark, Germany, and Austria were arrested in this case, held for many weeks, and finally let go and expelled from the country without being brought to trial.

Such cases of arresting foreigners on political and economic grounds are rare, however; they involve too many disagreeable diplomatic consequences. Normally the Gay-Pay-Oo, where foreigners are concerned, confines itself to such harmless activities as opening and reading their letters, and keeping voluminous records of their associates, personal habits, and political views. Spies and provocators are reserved for those who are regarded as more important. When a new journalist or man of affairs applies for an entrance visa, the Gay-Pay-Oo scans his record closely, apparently oblivious of the fact that people's original views, favorable or unfavorable, often change very much after a period of residence in the Soviet Union. There have been so many disillusioned liberals and radicals that I have sometimes wondered whether the Soviet Government, if it must control admission to the country so strictly, would not be better advised to grant entrance visas only to hardened conservatives, who would come without great expectations and presumably leave without pained disillusionment.

The Gay-Pay-Oo makes the lives of foreign diplomats in Moscow rather dull by restraining all Russians, outside a narrow licensed official circle, from paying calls at embassies; the suspicion of espionage is only too easily aroused.[7] Some of its clumsier efforts at espionage and telephone wire-tapping furnish permanent topics of dinner-table conversation.

Early in 1934 there were persistent rumors that the Gay-Pay-Oo would be reorganized as a Commissariat for Internal Affairs and stripped of some of its more sweeping powers, such as that of executing persons without open trial.[8] At the moment of writing, these rumors have not been officially confirmed; but several circumstances make some sort of reorganization of "the unsheathed sword of the proletarian dictatorship" not improbable. First of all, the internal situation, definitely eased as a result of the favorable harvest of 1933, has convinced the Soviet leaders that the

[7] There was unconscious humor in a newspaper dispatch which appeared early in 1934 to the effect that members of the staff of the American Embassy in Moscow would be expected to mix with the Russian people, as well as with officials. It takes two to "mix"; and Americans, like other diplomats, have probably learned by this time that the average Russian does not regard a foreign diplomat as a suitable acquaintance, from the standpoint of his personal safety.

[8] By a curious coincidence these rumors arose shortly before the sudden death, from heart failure, of Vyacheslav Menzhinsky who had headed the Gay-Pay-Oo since the death of its founder, Felix Dzerzhinsky, in 1926. Like his predecessor, Menzhinsky was a Pole, a man of good education and of fanatical idealism — in other words, a model Grand Inquisitor.

worst of the agrarian crisis is over. The improvement
in the Soviet international situation, reflected in America's
recognition and in the more cordial relations with France,
also furnishes a motive for improving the international
reputation of the Soviet régime by curbing its terrorist arm
of administration. As far back as 1931, Stalin publicly
stated that it was time to cease regarding every old engineer
as an uncaught criminal; and privately the Soviet leaders
can scarcely fail to recognize that the virtually uncontrolled
hand which the Gay-Pay-Oo has enjoyed in arresting and
banishing alleged *saboteurs* has had a demoralizing effect
upon the class of old technical experts on whom the success of Soviet industrial projects still depends to a very
considerable degree. Finally, too great independent authority for the Gay-Pay-Oo is not consistent with the
position of absolute domination which Stalin has built
up for himself in the Soviet and Party machine of government.

As I pointed out at the beginning of the chapter, Soviet
terrorism has gone through successive phases of relaxation
and intensification in the past; and a milder period may be
in store for the immediate future. It would be a grave
mistake, however, to associate the ruthlessness of the Soviet
régime exclusively with the Gay-Pay-Oo, or to assume that
a renaming and reorganization of the latter will mean an
end of ruthlessness, although it doubtless will herald a
period of somewhat greater formal legality and administrative mildness. Some of the fiercest measures of recent
years — the law authorizing the liquidation of the kulaks
as a class, the law of August 7, 1933, which permits the
application of the death penalty for *any* theft of state property
(a definition which, under Soviet conditions, covers almost

all property), the mass deportations from Kuban villages in the winter of 1932–1933, the decision to let the famine take its course in the winter and spring of 1932–1933 — were acts of the general Party leadership, for which the Gay-Pay-Oo bears no special responsibility.

A final and complete abandonment of terrorism as an instrument of government will only come when the grimly pragmatic philosophy which assumes that the individual has no rights which the state is bound to respect is discarded. So long as that philosophy prevails, one may expect a continuance of executions for crimes which would not be regarded as capital offenses in Western countries — hoarding silver coins, for instance, or stealing grain from a collective farm field, or negligence leading to wrecks and accidents. The Soviet Government is proud, with some reason, of the modern humanitarian methods which it has introduced in dealing with common criminals and in reclaiming street waifs and prostitutes.[9] But it clings to an idea which even the least progressive penologists in other countries have discarded for many generations: that the application of the death

[9] As a general rule there is an effort in Soviet prisons and prison labor camps to avoid affixing a stigma of inferiority on the criminal through the requirement of wearing a special uniform. Sentences are indefinite and are made progressively shorter in the event of good behavior, and efforts are made to teach trades to the prisoners. Although the maximum prison sentence is ten years, criminals of a very hardened type are sometimes shot as "socially dangerous." Common criminals who have been convicted of more serious offenses are often sent to the rougher and more unpleasant places of exile, such as the Solovetzky Islands, in the White Sea, or the Narim region, in Siberia, where they are employed at hard labor along with kulaks and other "class enemies" of various brands. It is the general testimony of people who have been in concentration camps that common criminals get better treatment than those whose offenses are of a political or economic type. The Gay-Pay-Oo overseers apparently believe that a murderer or a bandit is easier to reclaim than a priest, a kulak, or an anti-Soviet intellectual.

penalty for a most varied list of offenses has a permanently wholesome reformatory effect.

A new proof that terrorism remains an essential element in Soviet administration was furnished by a law prescribing penalties for treason which was promulgated on June 8, 1934, and which, in several of its provisions, is a worthy companion piece of legislation to the notorious law of August 7, 1932, with its establishment of the death penalty for theft of state property. This law makes the death penalty mandatory in the case of soldiers who are guilty of espionage, betrayal of military or state secrets, or flight abroad. Civilians may also be put to death for any of these offenses or may be given the milder punishment of ten years' imprisonment with confiscation of all their property.

Members of the family of a soldier who knew of his intention to flee from the country without informing the authorities are to be punished with imprisonment from five to ten years and confiscation of all their property. The law contains one further clause which certainly could not be duplicated in the legislation of any civilized country. It prescribes that other adult members of the "traitor's" family, living with him and dependent on him, even though they may have had no knowledge of his act and no responsibility for it, are to be deprived of electoral rights (which means also deprivation of food cards) and face "exile to remote regions of Siberia for five years." (The entire text of the law is published in *Izvestia* for June 9, 1934.) It is a matter of common knowledge that the Gay-Pay-Oo extorts confessions from its prisoners by threats against the safety of members of their families. But this is the first time that the Soviet Government has itself supplied public documentary proof of its policy of treating relatives of its offending citizens as hostages who may be punished for no crime of their own. The purpose of this extraordinary law is apparently to check desertions from the Red Army and, still more, flight from the huge forced-labor camps of Eastern Siberia.

Until the individual's right to live and to enjoy liberty is regarded as superior to the state's right to put him to death or to exile him to forced labor, the Soviet Union, in its treatment of political offenders of various kinds, seems destined to remain where Tsarist Russia stood: somewhat more ruthless than the dictatorial European régimes, somewhat less ruthless than the more backward Asiatic countries.

The Gay-Pay-Oo was replaced as an institution by the Commissariat for Internal Affairs, according to a Soviet decree of July 10, 1934. Inasmuch as the new Commissar for Internal Affairs is Yagoda, former acting head of the Gay-Pay-Oo, and his two assistants were prominent figures in the Gay-Pay-Oo, it seems reasonable to assume that the Commissariat for Internal Affairs, in methods and personnel, will be very similar to the Gay-Pay-Oo, just as the latter organization, when it was created in 1922, took over to a large extent the working apparatus of its predecessor, the Cheka, or Extraordinary Commission for Combating Counter-Revolution.

The most important change indicated in the new decree is that the Commissariat for Internal Affairs, unlike the Gay-Pay-Oo, will not be able to pass summary death sentences. This right is reserved for the ordinary and special courts. It may be recalled that a similar change was announced when the Cheka was renamed as the Gay-Pay-Oo; but the abstention from inflicting summary death sentences was very brief. It remains to be seen whether the Commissariat for Internal Affairs, unlike the Gay-Pay-Oo, will remain within the limitation which the decree imposes upon it. The Commissariat for Internal Affairs retains the right to inflict the penalty of exile at hard labor up to a term of five years without trial before a public court. It also retains the management of the numerous large forced-labor camps which have grown up in Russia during the last few years.

IX

THE AUTOCRAT OF ALL THE
SOVIET REPUBLICS

FORMALLY the Soviet Union is a federation of Soviet Republics. Formally Stalin is not a member of the Council of People's Commissars, the Soviet Cabinet, and therefore bears no responsibility for its decisions. Actually this son of an obscure Georgian cobbler rules Russia with more absolute power than any of the self-avowed Romanov autocrats who preceded him, with all their pomp and trappings of traditional imperial splendor.

It is no exaggeration to say that Stalin concentrates in his hands more power than any other man in the world at the present time. In many respects, of course, his position is analogous to that of Mussolini in Italy and of Hitler in Germany. He is the unquestioned leader of a governing party which permits no other parties or political groups to exist legally. But because the Soviet state, with its immense assumption of economic functions, with its unrivaled apparatus for persuading its citizens by means of propaganda and for coercing them by means of terror, is by far the strongest in the world, its leader may rightly be considered the world's most powerful sovereign.

Stalin's authority is supreme in the most varied fields. His word is final on any important decision of foreign or internal policy. His decision on a disputed point of economic policy, on the pace at which industrialization is to be pushed, on the methods which are to be used in promoting collective farming, can exert the most profound influence upon the lives and fortunes of tens of millions of people. Let him detect heresy in an article in a historical magazine and write a letter to the magazine sternly denouncing "contraband Trotzkyism and rotten liberalism toward it," and scores of young "Red professors," as eager for his approval as courtiers about the throne of a Tsar, will leap into action, repeating and emphasizing all the points in Stalin's message. History in Russia can be and has been rewritten at his will, mainly with a view to minimizing and discrediting the part which his great fallen rival, Leon Trotzky, played in the Revolution and in the civil war.

Stalin's power extends far beyond the frontiers of the Soviet Union. The Communist International, that world union of Communist parties, is held on the tightest disciplinary leash from Moscow. It rests, in the last analysis, with Stalin to decide what instructions are to be given to underground Communist agents in Germany and Poland, to the Red partisan forces which are fighting in various parts of China, what slogans and tactics are to be recommended to American and British Communists.[1]

The time has long passed when Stalin was acquiring the realities of domination while affecting to deprecate any tributes to his personal authority. Now he basks in a

---

[1] Interesting testimony in this connection is furnished by D. Manuilsky, an outstanding Russian leader in the Communist International, who writes: "Not one important document of big international significance was issued by the Communist International without the most active participation of Comrade Stalin in its composition." (*Cf. Stalin*, a collection of reminiscences and laudatory tributes, published by the State Publishing Company, p. 93.)

flood light of varied adulation which might have appealed to a Byzantine Emperor. Not one speech can be made at a Party Congress or on any other important public occasion by any Communist, of high or low degree, without some sweeping tribute to his genius. Typical of the style of such tributes is one which recently emanated from one of his most faithful henchmen, Kirov, the head of the Leningrad Party organization: —

It is difficult for one to imagine the figure of such a giant as Stalin. During the last years, during the time when we have worked without Lenin, we do not know of one change in our work, of one big slogan, enterprise, or direction of our policy which was not initiated by Stalin. All basic work proceeds according to the instructions and initiative and under the leadership of Comrade Stalin. . . . The powerful will and colossal organizing talent of this man assure the Party the timely carrying out of great historical changes, connected with the victorious building up of socialism. Everything that we achieved during the first five-year plan was achieved on the basis of his instructions.[2]

All the signs of respect and homage that are usually paid to the head of a state or to the wielder of dictatorial power are Stalin's. His name, along with that of Premier Molotov, is affixed to every important government decree. Portraits of this tall, strongly built, black-haired and black-moustached man, with the typically Caucasian olive skin, hang in every Soviet office. His pictures far outnumber those of all other Communist leaders, dead and living, at anniversary celebrations.

Stalin is always the first to dispatch a congratulatory message on some extremely distinguished feat of physical

[2] *Cf. Izvestia* for January 24, 1934.

daring, scientific research, or industrial achievement. It is
to him that delegations of workers and collective-farm
members address their greetings and representations. And
it would be difficult to count the number of factories, state
and collective farms, schools, public enterprises of all kinds
that bear his name. Four cities in various parts of the
Soviet Union pay him a similar honor: these are Stalingrad,
an industrial town on the lower Volga; Stalinsk, a new factory
and mining centre in Central Siberia; Stalinabad, capital of
remote Tadjikistan, in Central Asia, not far from the frontier
of India; and Stalinogorsk, site of a large new chemical plant.

Like the tragic hero of Moussorgsky's great opera, the
mediæval Tsar Boris Godunov, whose cool, calculating
character suggests some points of similarity to that of the
present Soviet dictator, Stalin might say: "I have achieved
supreme power." Whether this has brought him the
happiness that was denied to Boris is a question which no
outsider can answer. He is not only the most powerful,
but also the most secretive and reserved of modern dictators.
One feels that he will never publish an autobiography,
like Hitler, or communicate his views on international subjects to the world press, like Mussolini.

The main traits of his character were forged during
the long period before the Revolution when he was a
podpolschik, or underground revolutionary, arrested again
and again by the Tsarist police and sent to places of distant
exile, from which he escaped five times to resume the work
of secret organization of conspirative groups and the surreptitious spreading of revolutionary pamphlets among the
workers of Baku, the large oil centre of his native Caucasus,
and other industrial towns. Stalin's activity included still
more daring and risky phases; he was the guiding spirit be-

hind the raids on banks and state funds which were carried out by the Armenian Bolshevik Ter-Petrosian, better known under his pseudonym of Kamo.   One of these raids involved the throwing of a bomb in the crowded streets of Tiflis and the killing and wounding of a considerable number of people.

Stalin's official biographical sketches are silent on this aspect of his career.   These "expropriations," as revolutionary raids on state funds for the purpose of replenishing the Party treasuries were called, were a debatable and much-discussed point of revolutionary tactics.   The line between "expropriation" for revolutionary purposes and ordinary robbery was one which, for weaker and less reliable characters, might easily become obscure; and Lenin, who at first welcomed the proceeds of the raids, ultimately decided that the disadvantages of this method of raising funds outweighed its benefits.   Whatever may have been the case with some other participants in "expropriations," no shadow of suspicion ever rested on the personal integrity of Stalin himself, or of Kamo, who was a very Caucasian type of Bolshevik, a Robin Hood of the pre-war underground movement, who made himself famous by the number of his flights from prisons and by several almost miraculous escapes from death sentences which were passed on him.

Secrecy and distrust of his fellow men became almost second nature to the underground revolutionary in Tsarist times.   Not only were the numerous police themselves always on the watch for subversive activities, but every revolutionary group was infested with provocators—that is, police agents who pretended to be revolutionary sympathizers in order to ferret out the secrets of the movement and to arrest its participants.   One can readily understand how Stalin developed the extreme reserve which has always been one of his chief characteristics, and how the saying, "Lenin trusts Stalin, Stalin trusts no one," which was very much in vogue at the time when I arrived in Moscow in 1922, came into being.

Pre-war Bolshevik leaders fall into two main groups. There were émigrés who lived in Geneva and Paris and London, edited little newspapers and magazines, fought fiercely among themselves over points of dogma and practical tactics, kept up communication with Russia by various surreptitious channels, and maintained a precarious living as best they could. These were, in the main, the intellectual leaders of the Party. Others remained regularly in Russia, leaving the country only on rare occasions to attend Party Congresses, which were always held abroad because of the risk of detection and wholesale arrests in Russia. They performed the task, very hard and thankless in the period of reaction which followed the collapse of the 1905 Revolution, of keeping alive the Party organization, circulating semilegal and illegal literature, struggling with the rival Social Democratic organization, the Mensheviki, for control of such workers' organizations as were permitted to exist. Stalin was in this second category; and it is quite probable that he conceived a feeling of aversion, compounded of contempt and envy, for the men who remained abroad, who escaped the painful spade work in Russia, and who were so glib with their pens and their ideas. It is certainly not without significance that not one of the men who enjoy the highest mark of Stalin's confidence, a seat in the Political Bureau of the Party, has ever spent much time outside of Russia, speaks any foreign language, or can be reckoned as an intellectual in background and training.

Stalin was always a figure of considerable weight in the Communist Party councils, although at the time of the Revolution he was little known outside the Party ranks.   His rise to supreme power was based on a shrewd appraisal of the enormous strategic value of mastering what is often called in the Soviet Union the "Party apparatus" — that is, the group of professional Party workers who are at the head of the important city, provincial, and local organizations.   In his capacity of General Secretary of the Party he gradually filled these offices with men who were personally and politically devoted to him; his opponents were gradually displaced, demoted, sent on missions abroad.   His astuteness in building up a personal "machine" in the Party officialdom is indeed one of the few things in his life which would command at once the understanding and the admiration of the late Mr. Charles F. Murphy, or any other American political "boss."

To say that Stalin is an extremely cunning politician is not for a moment to deny that he is a man of strong views and definite policies, sincerely devoted to the Communist cause as he understands it.   History is full of examples of fanatics who in pushing forward their ideas displayed qualities of practical shrewdness that would put to shame the most cynical opportunist.

Stalin's first concern after the death of Lenin was to rid himself of Trotzky, who was obviously his most brilliant and most dangerous competitor for Party leadership.   Once this had been achieved (the destruction of Trotzky's almost legendary civil-war reputation through a nation-wide campaign of belittlement was one of the first noteworthy achievements of the Communist propaganda machine), it was an easy matter for Stalin to turn on his original allies, Gregory

Zinoviev and Leo Kamenev, who were men of very different mettle from Trotzky, and to eliminate them from positions of Party leadership. And when the remaining three members of the Political Bureau which had existed at the time of Lenin's death — Premier Aleksei Rykov; the head of the trade-unions, Mikhail Tomsky; and the editor of the Communist Party newspaper, Nikolai Bukharin — raised voices of protest against the speed of industrialization, the methods which were being employed in promoting collectivization, and the hardships which were being imposed on the population, Stalin was so firmly in the saddle that he was able to brush them aside with little difficulty.

As a ruler Stalin is adept in the employment of methods which would have commended themselves to Niccolo Machiavelli. One of these is never to admit that he was mistaken or that the Party "general line," or policy, was wrong. When a crisis arises that calls for a striking and definite change of policy and there are no old professors or engineers who can plausibly be offered up as scapegoats, it is the Soviet and Party minor officials who are sacrificed. The blame for the difficulties is cast on them; there are a few exemplary trials; Soviet public opinion is satisfied. This method was used in the spring of 1930, when the excesses of forcible collectivization were clearly threatening a complete breakdown of agricultural production; it was employed again in the spring of 1932, when there were belated official acknowledgments that too much grain had been squeezed out of the Ukrainian peasants. It has the advantage of appealing to a very old Russian tradition of attributing oppression and misfortune, not to the distant Tsar, but to the unpopular local official.

Stalin's name will always be associated with the great

changes which were wrought during Russia's Iron Age: the sweep toward industrialization, and the reorganization of agriculture along the lines of what might fairly be called state landlordism. More than one striking parallel may be drawn between Stalin and the most forceful and purposeful of Russia's Tsars, Peter the Great. For both the Bolshevik who was born in a cobbler's hut and the Tsar who was born to the purple have been obsessed with one overmastering idea: that their country was backward and must be pushed ahead at all costs.

If Stalin ever stops in the press of work to dream of a utopia, it probably assumes the shape of the Soviet Union transformed into a "socialist America" — that is, a land where American high-speed technical achievement is mated with a socialist form of economic organization. His speeches abound in references to the importance of mastering technique, of overcoming Russia's traditional technical backwardness. As Peter's eyes were turned toward Europe, Stalin's eyes are turned toward America. And the technical experts, skilled artisans, and shipbuilders whom Peter recruited in Germany and England and the Netherlands have their modern successors in the American engineers who made their contribution to erecting Russia's network of new big factories and electrical power plants.

It is noteworthy that both Peter and Stalin took a one-sidedly materialistic view of what constitutes Western culture and civilization and saw no fundamental contradiction between the ideal of "progress" which they proclaimed and the methods of barbarous cruelty with which they endeavored to bring about this progress. In a revealing outburst of self-confidence Stalin exclaimed on one occasion: "When we put the Soviet Union on an automobile and the muzhik on a tractor, let the worthy capitalists, who boast so loudly of their 'civilization,' try to overtake us."

So Stalin is inclined to interpret civilization in terms of automobiles and tractors. He does not admit that there might conceivably be other standards of measurement — the number of executions without trial, for instance, or the numbers of persons imprisoned in concentration camps. It was the tragedy of Peter the Great that he endeavored, in the eloquent phrase of the great historian Kluchevsky, "to square the circle" by attempting to superimpose Western material progress on Russia while withholding those elements of individual initiative and political liberty, limited and slight though they were, which existed in Western Europe and contributed toward its material progress. Perhaps a future historian, if history can ever be freely written in Russia again, will pass a similar judgment on Stalin.

Like many men of slight formal education, Stalin has a genuine respect for classical literature; and he has occasionally intervened to moderate the grosser excesses of the bureaucratized literature and drama which have grown up as an inevitable fruit of regimentation and censorship. On one occasion a group of young "proletarian" writers [3] paid a visit to Stalin and presented him with copies of their latest works. Stalin picked up one of the books and asked the author how long it had taken him to write it. Expecting to be praised for his "Bolshevik tempo," the author replied that it had been a matter of a few weeks. "Then I won't read it," Stalin declared, tossing it back to the discomfited writer, "because I am sure it cannot be good. Take much

[3] A proletarian author in the Soviet Union is not necessarily, or usually, a worker by origin, but rather a man who accepts completely and without reservation the Communist theoretical outlook on life and art.

longer time for preparation; read Shakespeare and other classics, as I do; and then you will be able to create something that will endure."

If Stalin has a weakness it is his desire to be regarded as a leading Marxist theoretician. The original trinity of the theoretical founders of Bolshevism, "Marx-Engels-Lenin," has now been amended to read "Marx-Lenin-Stalin." As a matter of fact, Stalin's mind is at its best in approaching a practical problem. Here he is clear-cut, logical, incisive. On the other hand, he does not make the impression of being on congenial ground when he attempts to discuss abstruse philosophical and economic questions.

He is a prodigious worker, as any man in his position would have to be; and his attention to detail is remarkable. I know of two quite minor grievances which were brought to his personal attention when all other means had been exhausted, and were speedily redressed. In one case a foreign scholar was confronted with bureaucratic red tape when he tried to take some historical material out of the country; in another instance the family of a Soviet employee had been threatened with unjustified eviction from their apartment.

The Communist leader is to be seen very rarely at the opera or the ballet; on such occasions he sits inconspicuously far back in one of the side boxes. In summer he takes a holiday on the beautiful "Caucasian Riviera," in the neighborhood of Sochi or Gagri. He has a mansion in the country some distance to the west of Moscow, and habitually drives in to work every morning in a high-powered automobile, closely followed by another automobile manned by reliable Gay-Pay-Oo guards. Elaborate precautions are taken to protect his life; and on the day in the autumn of

1932 when he marched in the funeral procession of his wife there was an impressive mobilization of Gay-Pay-Oo troops and mounted police, and casual spectators were kept at a respectful distance.

Stalin has three children, an adult son by his first wife, who died during the civil war, and a younger boy and a girl by his second wife, Nadyezhda Alleluyeva, who died suddenly in November 1932. The latter was the daughter of a veteran Petrograd Bolshevik worker, in whose house Lenin had once hidden. Her death, the cause of which was not stated officially, unloosed a flood of speculation and rumors of suicide. It was as mysterious as the death of a mediæval Tsarina, and some day in a far-distant future it may be a theme for an investigating historian. Stalin has now contracted a union with the sister of his chief aide, Kaganovitch.

A strenuous campaign to make Stalin a popular figure among the Russian masses is under way. He receives delegations of collective-farm peasants and the interview is described at length. He exchanges messages with the women in the collective farms of a remote district in the North Caucasus. It is a question, however, whether he will ever rank among the intimately beloved leaders of history. Apart from the ruthlessness of his régime, his rise to power was accomplished by means of subtle moves on the chessboard of Party politics, and was quite over the heads of the great majority of the people. His character is calculated to inspire respect and fear rather than affection; and it is significant that Communists in private conversation usually refer to him as the *khozayen*, or "boss."

Immortality is a gift which is not vouchsafed to the most potent dictator; and a question of succession to the unwrit-

KAGANOVITCH

STALIN

VOROSHILOV

ten but all-powerful post of Party leader (experience would seem to show that the Soviet mechanism of power requires a single directing hand at the helm) would arise in the event of Stalin's death. The two men who would seem to stand the best chance of inheriting his mantle are K. E. Voroshilov, the War Commissar, and Lazarus Kaganovitch, his right-hand man in matters of Party and Soviet organization. Although Voroshilov is a Russian and Kaganovitch is a Jew, the two men have strikingly similar backgrounds. Both are of genuine working-class origin, Voroshilov being the son of a casual laborer and a former metal worker himself, while Kaganovitch followed his father's trade as a leather worker in the town of Gomel. Both are self-educated men, having enjoyed only the scantiest elementary schooling.

Voroshilov is Kaganovitch's senior by more than ten years (the latter has barely passed forty) and naturally played a more distinguished part in the civil war, where he was a fighting commissar, attached to Budenny's rough-riding cavalry army for the purpose of ensuring its military discipline and its loyalty to the Soviet régime. Voroshilov was on bad terms with the imperious Trotzky during the civil war, and was therefore a natural candidate for the post of War Commissar when Trotzky's immediate successor as War Commissar, Mikhail Frunze, succumbed to the consequences of an unsuccessful operation. Although Voroshilov had no formal military training in his youth, he is a good horseman and a crack rifle shot; to be able to shoot like Voroshilov is the ambition of every Young Communist. A warm-hearted, quick-tempered, impulsive man, something of his buoyant temperament brims over in the orders which he signs and in the speeches which he delivers to the troops on the big revolutionary holidays, May the first and November the seventh.

Kaganovitch has risen to power by methods which are more similar to those of Stalin himself, although up to the present time he has carefully avoided arousing the jealousy of his chief. He has acquired the reputation of a capable, hard-working, indispensable administrator and organizer. A number of important measures in agriculture, notably the establishment of the political departments in the machine-tractor stations, are attributed to his initiative; and he has played a leading rôle in the reconstruction of Moscow. Stalin left him a free hand in framing the recent important measures for the reorganization of the Party and of the Soviet apparatus of administration, with the main objective of simultaneously giving greater authority and greater responsibility to the men at the head of the Party organizations and of big industrial enterprises. In the event of Stalin's disappearance from the scene, Kaganovitch would seem to be more strategically situated to take hold of the Party organization; he has already established his right to be publicly characterized as "Stalin's best collaborator." Around Voroshilov, on the other hand, is the aureole of a military hero with indisputably Communist and proletarian antecedents. The racial question, which still has some significance in Russia, despite the constant educational campaign against "racial chauvinism," would also operate in favor of Voroshilov.

It is still perhaps premature to discuss hypothetical successors to Stalin, for the latter, whose fifty-fifth birthday is in December 1934, is in full health and vigor and might conceivably outlive Voroshilov or Kaganovitch, or both of them. There are periodic rumors that Stalin will add formal to factual power by assuming the post of Premier. Such a change could be accomplished at a moment's notice; the pale and colorless Molotov, who owes his Premiership entirely to Stalin's patronage, would, of course, step aside immediately to make way for "the boss." The most valid objection to it is that it might be diplomatically difficult, in these days of general establishment of regular relations with other countries, to reconcile the formal obligations of the head of a state with those of the leader of world Communism.

Whatever office he may choose to hold, there is every probability that Stalin will remain master of the Soviet state as long as he lives. He has carved out for himself no inconsiderable place in Russian history as a modern Peter the Great, the symbol and incarnation of the Soviet Iron Age.

X

THE SHADOW OF WAR

BORN in revolution, the Soviet Union has always lived under a real or imaginary shadow of war menace. Every Communist believes that in some more or less distant future the issue between socialism and capitalism will be fought out in a gigantic Armageddon. Lenin and Stalin have always emphasized the view that, while rivalries and antagonisms among other states may delay the formation of a united front against the Soviet Union, the likelihood of an onslaught on the latter, as the standard bearer of world revolution, must always be borne in mind.

The apprehensions of the masses are regularly kept alive by suggestive reports of impending aggression from without. On one occasion I made a collection of newspaper headlines on this subject, and within a short time had collected the following typical samples (at that time the supposed threat was believed to be in the West, rather than in the East): —

Programme of the Rumanian King: Enslavement of the Country and War with the Soviet Union.

Stages of Military Preparations against the Soviet Union.

Rehearsal of the Attack on the Soviet Union.

Conspiracy against the Soviet Union under the Flag of Union of Europe.

The Imperialists Are Anxious to Seize the Soviet Oil; They

Prepare a Blow at the Oil Wells of Baku; Suspicious Journeys of British Agents.

To Turn the Armed Attack on the Soviet Union into Revolutionary Struggle for the Soviet Union.

The effect of the newspaper articles which are heralded by such headlines is, of course, intensified by the absolute uniformity of political opinion which is imposed on the Soviet press. No suggestion that the war menace is exaggerated, to say nothing of any pacifist propaganda, would be printed.

Another device for whipping up the martial spirit of the population was a play which has been running for several seasons at the Meierhold Theatre under the title, *The Last Decisive*, which is suggested by the line in the "Internationale" about "the last decisive struggle." The author is Vsevolod Vishnevsky, who has served in the Soviet Army and Navy. The most striking feature of this drama is the last act, where twenty-seven Soviet sailors and border troops are shown defending themselves against hopeless odds. The scene is made very realistic: a machine gun barks; rifles crack; the boom of the enemy's cannon is heard; the theatre is filled with the smell of powder. In the end the gallant twenty-seven are wiped out by the superior forces of their opponents. Various artificial means are used to arouse the excitement of the audience; women who have been placed in various parts of the theatre begin to weep hysterically. Then the last survivor among the twenty-seven lurches over to a blackboard, where he works out the comforting calculation: "162,000,000 − 27 leaves 161,999,973." (The 162,000,000 refers to the supposed population of the Soviet Union.)

After this a stentorian-voiced figure stalks out on the

stage and shouts: "Why do you weep? Tears make it difficult to shoot straight. Who in the audience is in the army?" A number of men in uniforms rise. "Who is in the reserve?" A larger number of people in civilian clothes stand up. "Who will defend the Soviet Union?" Everyone leaps from his seat, and the loud-voiced figure on the stage thunders: "The performance is finished. The continuation — on the front."

Up to 1931, Soviet apprehensions of armed attack were primarily directed to the West, with France and England alternately playing the rôle of hypothetical aggressor. At no time does there seem to have been any serious foundation for these continually expressed suspicions. The strongly marked and growing antagonisms among the European powers were the best possible guaranty that no power would assume the risk of precipitating hostilities with the Soviet Union, even if any adequate *casus belli* had existed. The continual beating of the war drum by the Soviet leaders may be attributed to three causes: dogmatic belief in the ultimate inevitability of a clash with the "capitalist" powers, desire to stiffen the morale of the population in the face of increasing material hardships by representing the danger of foreign attack as imminent, and a somewhat juvenile overestimate both of the significance of the country's industrial achievements and of the envy and fear which these achievements were causing abroad.

Since the autumn of 1931 the war threat has become more concrete and more realistic. The Japanese seizure of Mukden and the inauguration of a forward policy in Manchuria tore down the buffer which semi-independent Manchuria had formerly constituted between Russia and Japan. The Soviet zone of political influence in North Manchuria disappeared when Japanese troops marched into Harbin and occupied the stations along the line of the Chinese Eastern Railroad. Confronted with this new situation, the Soviet Government adopted two main guiding lines for its policy: not to risk a conflict over Russia's interests in Manchuria, and to prepare energetically for the defense of the country's Far Eastern frontiers. And, while a Japanese surprise attack in 1931 or in 1932 might have encountered little effective resistance, the Soviet Union by 1934 was in a position to put up a strong fight for its vast although sparsely populated Far Eastern territories.

By this time the double-tracking of the Trans-Siberian Railroad had been almost completed. A picked, well-equipped Far Eastern Army, with a numerical strength estimated at about 150,000, was stationed along the Manchurian and Korean frontiers. Steel and concrete fortifications had been erected at strategic points. Japanese command of the sea could not be disputed, as there is no considerable Soviet naval force in Far Eastern waters; but the harbor of Vladivostok, the main Soviet window on the Pacific, had been carefully strewed with mines, and coast-defense batteries had been erected along the shores in the vicinity. A few submarines were transported to the Far East by train.

The commander in chief of the Far Eastern Army is General Bluecher, who emerged into prominence during the Russian civil war, and subsequently, under the pseudonym of Galen, acquired valuable Oriental experience as military advisor to the Chinese nationalists at the time when they were working in close coöperation with Moscow and with the Chinese Communists. His army is supplied with such modern mechanical weapons as armored trains and tanks, and three or four hundred Soviet airplanes have been concentrated in the Far East. There is widespread belief in Moscow that this air fleet could lay Japan's chief cities in ruins within a few days after the outbreak of hostilities. Several cavalry divisions were also sent to the Far East; it was believed that they would prove effective in the Siberian and Manchurian plains.

During the winter of 1933–1934 the most prominent Soviet leaders used extremely strong and unqualified language in accusing Japan of offensive designs against the Soviet Far East. Premier Molotov and Foreign Commissar Litvinov both stated in public addresses that Japan was preparing for aggressive war against the Soviet Union. Stalin's chief lieutenant, Kaganovitch, made the following uncompromising declaration in the course of a speech in Moscow in January 1934: "The situation in the Far East is strained. We must expect an attack at any moment. Every imperialist is hypocritical and cunning, and the Japanese imperialists especially remind us of this. . . . We shall not yield in the Far East to the Asiatic ideologists of imperialism, but shall create there the biggest industrial base of the Soviet Union and will fight for every foot of the Far East." And in the following month General Bluecher, addressing the Communist Party Congress, stated that Japan was feverishly preparing for war, cited as evidence for this statement the building of roads and railroads of strategic significance in Northern Manchuria, the alleged concentration of Japanese troops, and the building of over fifty airdromes and air bases in Manchuria. He boasted: "If war breaks out in the Far East our army will reply with a blow from which the foundations of capitalism will shake and, in some cases, crumble."

Now it not infrequently happens that in the Soviet Union, which is the country of secret diplomacy *par excellence*, there is more than meets the eye in militant official statements, or in the absence of them. The Soviet press and Soviet public men have sometimes been most silent just when the apprehension of attack was greatest; and the converse of this statement may apply to the unusual flow of grave warnings of imminent war during the winter of 1933–1934. The fact that America had just established diplomatic relations with the Soviet Union must also be taken into account. There was apparently a feeling in Soviet official circles, correct or incorrect, that strong anti-Japanese declarations would not be displeasing in Washington.

While the Far Eastern war cloud may eventually roll away, like the much more imaginary clouds which Soviet leaders at one time persisted in seeing on the horizon of Western Europe, there are serious causes of difference between the Soviet Union and Japan which will have to be settled before the tense atmosphere along Russia's far-flung frontier in the Far East can be altogether removed. These causes, in the order of their relative importance, may be stated as follows: —

1. Vladivostok, in the opinion of Japanese who think exclusively in terms of military security, is too close to Tokyo and Yokohama. In extremist Japanese military circles the opinion is held, and has sometimes found public expression, that the menace of devastating Soviet air raids should be banished by the rounding out of the Japanese Empire through the severance from the Soviet Union of Northern Sakhalin and Eastern Siberia, where a puppet state on the Manchukuo model, under White Russian domination, might be created. That the Soviet Union would

fight rather than permit the realization of such plans may be taken for granted. It remains to be seen whether some kind of mutual agreement for air disarmament on both sides of the frontier, which might satisfy both Russian and Japanese aspirations for security, can be worked out.

2. The Chinese Eastern Railroad — in the operation of which the Soviet Government, according to its agreement with China in 1924, has an equal share — has become a prolific source of disputes and "incidents" since the Japanese military authorities have virtually taken over Northern Manchuria. Arrests of Soviet citizens employed on the railroad on various charges have been frequent and have led to acrimonious protests. The Soviet Government in the spring of 1933 plainly intimated its willingness to withdraw from Manchuria by proposing to sell its interest in the railroad to Manchukuo. But this solution of the problem has been delayed by differences regarding the price which should be paid, the Soviet Government having reduced an original price of 250,000,000 gold rubles to 200,000,000 gold rubles, while the Manchukuo negotiators have refused to increase their original offer of 50,000,000 paper yen, which is little more than a tenth of the Soviet demand.

3. The westward trend of Japanese expansion has raised the question of the status of Outer Mongolia, which has been in fact, if not in name, a Soviet protectorate for more than a decade. Russian military instructors have trained the Mongolian Army, and Russian civilian "advisors" have shaped the political and economic features of the Mongolian state very much along Soviet lines. It is unlikely that the Soviet Government would go to war for the sake of the Mongolian People's Republic, which has been set up under its tutelage. Yet a westward push that would bring the Japanese advance into Mongolian territory would encounter

more or less serious opposition from Soviet-trained Mongols and might lead to Soviet-Japanese complications.

4. Disputes repeatedly crop up about the terms under which the Japanese may fish in Soviet territorial waters and operate coal, oil, and timber concessions in Northern Sakhalin and on the mainland of Siberia. These disagreements, while they are sometimes sharp and protracted, are not of major consequence and would scarcely lead to an outbreak of hostilities.

The outlook for the Soviet Union in the event of war with Japan obviously depends not only on the special preparations which have been made in the Far East, but also on the general state of the country's armed forces and on the morale of the population as a whole. With all its shortcomings and failures in other fields, the first five-year plan unmistakably and considerably increased the military preparedness of the Soviet Union.

Russia in 1934 is vastly stronger in the air, in tanks and heavy artillery, in capacity for manufacturing shells and high explosives and poison gas, than it was in 1929. This fact alone, to Communists who think exclusively in terms of force, is a sufficient justification for the enormous sacrifices which were demanded of the population. (It is a question whether a country's real fitness for war can be measured merely in terms of weapons and munitions. At any time during the last few years the acute food shortage, the disorganization of railroad transport, — most important of all, the depressed morale of the peasantry who would have to furnish the largest proportion of recruits for a large-scale war, — would have been serious negative factors to weigh in the balance against the larger quantities of airplanes, shells, and poison gas.)

The Soviet Union has three lines of defense. First is

the standing army and the navy, the numbers of which are officially given as 562,000 officers and men. It has never been made quite clear whether this figure includes the special regiments and the border guards under the authority of the Gay-Pay-Oo, the numbers of these units being generally estimated at about 100,000. Service in the regular Red Army is for two years, with longer periods in special branches. Almost all the aviation, armored-car, and gas units are attached to the regular army.

The second line of defense consists of the territorial force. This is a militia, the members of which receive annual training, for periods ranging from one to three months over a total of five years, in camps near their homes. The territorial troops are provided with a permanent staff of commissioned and noncommissioned officers.

The third line of defense consists of what might be called the armed citizenry: civilians who have not served in either the regular or the territorial forces, but who have received instruction in elementary marching and drilling, rifle practice, use of gas masks, and so forth. There has been a very sweeping growth of this civilian military training during the last few years; and Osaviakhim (the Society for Promoting Aviation and Chemical Defense), which has been officially described as "the military reserve of the Red Army," now numbers over thirteen million members.

Not everyone who belongs to Osaviakhim can be regarded as a full-fledged military recruit. Some of its members merely pay small annual dues and listen to an occasional lecture on what to do in the event of an air raid or a gas attack. But an ever-increasing proportion of the Osaviakhim members (of whom over three million are women) are receiving more or less thorough elementary military training. Significant of its progress in this respect is the fact that 215,000 of its members passed the difficult test which permits them to wear the badge of the "Voroshilov Sharpshooter" in 1933, as against 10,000 in 1932. The un-uniformed Osaviakhim units, consisting largely of students and factory workers, have become increasingly numerous in the big military parades on the first of May and the seventh of November. All students in the middle and higher schools and all members of the Union of Communist Youth are required to take military training, even if they are not called to the colors with the regular and territorial troops. Groups for rifle practice are organized in every large factory and public institution.

Soviet military progress in recent years has been especially marked in aviation and in mechanized war implements, such as tanks and armored cars. The Soviet Union now possesses over two thousand fighting airplanes (the number is steadily and rapidly increasing) and has recently concentrated its efforts on the production of heavy bombing planes. The tanks, which may be seen at large parades, are of all types, shapes, and sizes, from diminutive whippets to huge, lumbering castles on wheels. A peculiar weapon which was invented during the Russian civil war by Makhno, the resourceful Ukrainian partisan chieftain, has been taken over by the Red Army and may receive its test should the Soviet Union become involved in a war of quick movement. This is a machine gun mounted on a *tachanka*, or peasant cart.

In line with this policy of militarizing the entire population (or at least those classes which are regarded as loyal to the Soviet régime) was a speech which President Kalinin delivered in April 1934, calling for more active work in this direction by village Soviets and by collective farms. He recommended that the rural Soviets train women and children in agricultural tasks, so that work would not be upset in the event of a mobilization of large numbers of able-bodied men, and that "military sections" be organized in the country districts with a view to training the peasants in a knowledge of local geography and the best means of beating off attacks on their villages and resisting air raids. The machine-tractor stations are becoming in many cases centres of military training, especially in the use of mechanical weapons, as well as of state economic domination of the peasantry.

The Red Army is unquestionably one of the most noteworthy achievements of the Soviet régime. The best proof of this is the fact that there were no cases of serious disaffection in the army at a time when the peasant villages were seething with discontent over the measures which were being employed to push ahead collectivization.

There were several reasons for this. First of all, there is a very careful selection of the soldiers and of the officers of the Red Army, according to the presumption of loyalty. In 1933 over 70 per cent of the officers (or, as they are called in Russia, commanders) of the Red Army were Communist Party members and candidates or Young Communists. Almost half of the whole army, officers and men being counted together, fell into these categories. There can be little opportunity for loud grumbling, to say nothing of mutiny, when every other soldier and three officers out of four have Party tickets and are bound by Party discipline.

There has also been an important change in the class composition of the Red Army. In 1927, 63.4 per cent of its members were peasants and 23.8 per cent workers. On January 1, 1934, the proportion of peasants had fallen to 42.5 per cent,[1] the proportion of workers had risen to 45.8 per cent. So the workers outnumber the peasants in the army, although in the country there are about six peasants to every one worker. Moreover, the percentage of Communists is especially high in just those branches of the service which are strategically most important, where mutiny might have especially unfortunate results — in the tank corps, in the armored-car divisions, in the air force. Children of the disfranchised classes are rigorously excluded from active military service.

Apart from this careful selection of the recruits from those classes and political groups where loyalty can most safely be taken for granted, the conditions of service in the Red Army are genuinely attractive and are calculated to win over the peasant recruit who may come from his village hostile and distrustful. The soldiers get much better food than the majority of them eat in their own homes, and discipline, while strict, is humane and intelligent. Beating of soldiers, which was quite common in the Tsarist Army, is now strictly forbidden. A big educational work is carried out among the men, and one is often struck by the number of officers and soldiers who may be seen at operas, concerts, and theatres. Not only has the Red Army resisted successfully the waves of disaffection which would have seeped into a less carefully selected and trained armed force from the discontented villages, but it has prepared a considerable number of future directors of collective farms from among its recruits.

[1] *Cf*. the report of War Commissar Voroshilov at the Seventeenth Communist Party Congress, published in *Pravda* for February 4, 1934.

So experience has shown that the peace-time Red Army, well treated and intensively drilled in propaganda as well as in rifle and bayonet practice, is a reliable bulwark of the existing régime. In the event of a big war it would be impossible to pick and choose so carefully among the vast numbers of recruits that would be needed at the front; and then the mood of the most discontented elements might make itself felt. This is only one of several reasons why the Soviet Government is, I believe, altogether sincere in its expressed desire to avoid a clash with Japan at the present moment.

Time works on the Soviet side in several ways. It makes possible a building up of transportation facilities capable to some extent of reducing the enormous handicap that would inevitably confront the Soviet régime if it became involved in hostilities in the Far Eastern theatre of war, which is thousands of miles away from Russia's main centres of population and industry, while it is conveniently close to Japan. The completion of actual and potential munition centres in Siberia, the development of the extensive Biro-Bidjan territory set aside for Jewish colonization on the Amur River, the state-encouraged settlement of sparsely populated Eastern Siberia, where sweeping tax exemptions and reductions have recently been announced as part of an effort to attract new settlers and to prevent old ones from leaving — all this requires time.

If the new revolutionary fanaticism of the Soviet Union should some day clash with the traditional patriotic fanaticism of Japan, the stakes of the conflict would be tremendous. Crushing military defeat is the one conceivable factor that might bring the whole Soviet edifice, so imposingly based on the foundations of propaganda and repression, tottering to its fall. More than once lost wars have brought to Russia far-reaching, even revolutionary consequences. The liberation of the serfs and the reforms of Alexander II were the direct sequel of the Crimean War; the Russo-Japanese War of 1904–1905 brought on the first, ultimately unsuccessful revolution; the World War was the most direct cause and prerequisite of the Bolshevik Revolution. These lessons of history are probably not lost on Stalin and his associates.

A decisive Soviet victory would have equally portentous consequences for Asia and for the world. It might mean revolution in Japan; it would almost certainly give a tremendous stimulus to Bolshevism in China, where the Communist Party claims 400,000 members. Large areas in south-central China are under more or less permanent Soviet control.

It is a grave question whether a Soviet-Japanese war would not tend to become world-wide in its scope. How would other powers with large Far Eastern interests react to a Japanese victory which would certainly tend to make Japan the absolute master of Eastern Asia, or to a Soviet victory which would confront colonial and trading nations with the formidable spectre of the greatest land mass in the world under the red flag, with 400,000,000 Chinese added to the 160,000,000 inhabitants of the Soviet Union, with Bolshevism knocking at the doors of Shanghai and Hongkong, of French Indo-China and the Dutch East Indies, of Singapore and Calcutta?

Just because the stakes are so great, just because the risks of defeat for either side are so grave, the much-predicted and much-threatened Soviet-Japanese war may never take place. But the Far East is the most clouded part of the international horizon, from the Soviet standpoint, at the present time; and recent Soviet international policy has been shaped in all its more essential features by the desire to improve the country's defensive position on its far-flung Siberian frontier.

The Far Eastern war cloud may or may not lose its importance with the passing of time. Larger and more permanent is the broad question whether the Bolshevik Revolution, in the long run, will bring the outside world peace or a sword. The desire for peace of the Soviet Union at the present time, despite the occasional militant speeches of its leaders, is convincingly genuine. The big transformation inaugurated by the five-year plan is still far from complete; the situation as regards food and transportation is decidedly unfavorable, from the standpoint of war.

Suppose, however, that all goes for the best in the Soviet Union, that the peasants become broken in to the yoke of collectivization, that transportation is pulled up to a normal level, that food difficulties are gradually overcome. Suppose, in addition, that intensive arming in Russia proceeds at the present pace; that by 1940, for instance, the country has ten thousand combatant airplanes instead of its present two or three thousand. Is it certain that the Soviet will-to-peace will prove permanent and unchangeable under such circumstances?

One cannot answer this question with a simple Yes or No. There are considerations that speak powerfully on both sides. The international revolutionary fanaticism which is still nourished in Russia, the possibility that an energetic, self-confident Young Communist generation, brought up to regard their system as infinitely superior to that of "dying capitalism," might some day feel the impulse to help along revolutions in other countries by military action, the ease with which the Soviet propaganda machine could represent any kind of war as defensive — all these are factors which must be seriously considered. The threat persists because the inability of Russia to measure up to West European countries in mechanical instruments of warfare is rapidly disappearing.

On the other hand, the Soviet Union is free from any biological or economic stimulus to aggression. It does not feel the strain of being cooped up within narrow frontiers or of lacking essential natural resources. It has no population pressure for expansion at the expense of weaker neighbors. Like America after the Civil War, it may conceivably devote generations of peaceful effort to the many projects of internal development which suggest themselves to anyone who looks at an economic map of the Soviet Union.

The future trend of Soviet policy toward war or toward peace does not depend exclusively on Moscow. It depends on the course of events in those countries with which the Soviet Union comes into closest physical and political contact. A policy of genuine appeasement and armament limitation, initiated by Russia's neighbors, would strengthen those forces inside the Soviet Union which work for peace, just as any acts which are calculated to revive the chronic nervous Soviet apprehension of "imperialist aggression" will have a contrary effect. And whether the Soviet régime at some future time might embark on a campaign of nationalist militant expansion that might easily assume the guise of "wars of proletarian liberation" depends very largely on whether the countries which might be the objects of such expansion, the Baltic States, Poland, Rumania, and China, for instance, look ripe for the revolutionary plucking.

XI

THE SOVIET UNION AND
THE OUTSIDE WORLD

THE triumph, in a country of Russia's size and natural resources, of a revolution which set up a new social and economic order and which vigorously proclaimed, especially in the first years of its existence, a militantly international character was bound to excite strong repercussions outside the Soviet frontiers and to raise a number of interesting questions. How would the Soviet régime adjust its diplomatic dealings with the governments of "capitalist" states? What kind of commercial relations would develop between a country where the state monopolized foreign trade, along with other branches of economic life, and lands which adhered to the competitive system? How could the activities of the Communist International be reconciled with normally friendly relations between the Soviet Government and the governments which the International was endeavoring to destroy? How infectious would the new ideas released by the Bolshevik Revolution prove in other parts of the world?

Not all these questions have been fully answered at the present time, when the Soviet Union is well advanced in the second decade of its existence. But some main trends of Soviet contact with the outside world are already pretty clearly determined.

The year 1933 will be remembered in history as a year of

major importance in Soviet diplomatic annals. With the aid of a diplomacy that has been, in the main, skillful and adroit, unsentimental and realistic, the Soviet Union for some time had been conquering for itself the recognition accorded to a major power. The year 1933 witnessed the completion of this process by the establishment of diplomatic relations with the United States, the sole great power which had hitherto persisted in a diplomatic boycott of the Soviet Union, and by the bridging over of the deep gulf which had previously separated the Soviet Union from France and France's chief East European ally, Poland.

The formal establishment of Soviet-American diplomatic relations on November 16, 1933, was hailed in Moscow as an event of first-rate international importance; and Soviet satisfaction was enhanced by the appointment of an outspoken and friendly American Ambassador in the person of Mr. William C. Bullitt. A few days after his arrival in Moscow, Mr. Bullitt was given an opportunity to talk personally with Stalin — a privilege which has very seldom been extended to any foreign diplomatic representative.

A few years ago — more specifically, before the Japanese seizure of Mukden in the autumn of 1931 — American recognition would have been regarded as primarily economic in its significance. Now, although commercial possibilities are not ignored, Soviet emphasis is rather on the political aspects of Mr. Roosevelt's decision. Russian public opinion is inclined to be very optimistic about the American attitude in the event of a Soviet clash with Japan. Much of the strong talk in Moscow last winter about readiness to smash any Japanese attack was delivered with one eye turned toward Washington. Every piece of news, however unimportant, that seems to point to strained relations between the United States and Japan is prominently displayed in the Soviet press. It is widely believed in Moscow that one of the purposes of American recognition was to ward off the threat of a Japanese attack on Siberia; and even non-Communist Russians are apt to take it for granted that American support, at least in the form of munitions and supplies, will be forthcoming if the threatened Russo-Japanese conflict breaks out.

In the matter of Soviet-American trade it is reasonable to expect that a sequel of recognition will be some degree of recovery from the state of virtual stagnation which prevailed in this field from 1931 until the end of 1933. The establishment in America of a special bank, under government auspices, for the financing of exports to and imports from the Soviet Union was the first concrete step looking toward a revival of Soviet-American trade. Cold facts and figures, however, lend little support to the optimists who profess to believe that the establishment of diplomatic relations with the Soviet Union will open up a market of inexhaustible wealth to the American business man. The Soviet share in the enormously depleted world trade of 1933 was in the neighborhood of 2 per cent. The value of Soviet exports (the basic measure of the country's capacity for paying for its imports) has been declining steadily during recent years, as may be seen from the following figures (in gold rubles).[1]

	1930	1931	1932	1933
Exports	1,036,371,000	811,210,000	563,844,000	495,600,000
Imports	1,058,825,000	1,105,034,000	698,693,000	348,200,000

So exports have been declining, until in 1933 they were less than half of the figure for 1930 and less than one third

[1] The gold ruble is worth a little over 51 gold American cents.

of Russia's exports (calculated in gold rubles) of 1913. There is little sign of a "Red trade menace" here (one of the emptiest of the unfounded scares which have been put into circulation about the Soviet régime). But there is also little "Red trade promise" in import figures which have shrunk to less than a third of the 1930 figure, which, in its turn, was less than the 1913 figure.

The enthusiastic Congressman who declared on one occasion that the United States, by not recognizing the Soviet Union, was losing $500,000,000 worth of trade annually [2] was apparently oblivious of the fact that the total receipts of the Soviet Government from exports (the main source of paying for imports) have been far short of $500,000,000 ever since 1930. Moreover, in these days of intense economic nationalism and trade restriction, it would be impossible for the Soviet Government to divert more than a very modest share of its export receipts to purchases in America. The time when the Soviet Union could acquire a large favorable trade balance in Great Britain and use the proceeds to redress an unfavorable trade balance in the United States has irrevocably passed. The new Soviet-British trade agreement, concluded early in 1934, provides that the Soviet Union must spend an increasingly large proportion of the receipts from its sales to Great Britain for purchases in Great Britain, until by 1937 a balance of 1.1

[2] Political non-recognition was a very minor factor in the sharp decline in Soviet purchases in America which began in 1931. The basic reason for this decline was that the Soviet Union, feeling the pinch of the world crisis, was obliged to cut down all its purchases abroad. The total Soviet purchases in America from the beginning of October, 1933, until the end of February, 1934, amounted to only about $6,000,000, and it will be surprising if the total of Soviet purchases in 1934 or in 1935 reaches the total of $110,000,000, which was achieved, without recognition, in 1930.

for Soviet sales as against 1 for Soviet purchases is reached.

Litvinov's statement at the London Economic Conference that the Soviet Union was prepared to place orders to the value of one billion dollars, over and above its planned purchases abroad, provided that credits were forthcoming, may be set down as a piece of window dressing, which owed whatever success it may have achieved to the ignorance of Soviet economic realities which is very widespread in foreign countries. Assuming that the Soviet Government desires to preserve its credit, it is hard to see how it could afford to accept credits to the amount of a billion dollars, even if any country were willing to grant them, unless it could be assured of a corresponding expansion in the value of its exports. And countries with far greater competitive exporting power than the Soviet Union would find it very difficult, in these days of high tariffs, quota restrictions, and other barriers to trade, to discover markets for the extra sale of a billion dollars' worth of their products abroad.

America's experiences with overlending to South America and to Central Europe during the years which preceded the depression would seem to dictate a more sober and discreet credit policy in regard to the Soviet Union. Russia unquestionably needs large quantities of many American goods: railroad and factory equipment, machine tools, excavating and dredging machinery, copper, cattle, and cotton, to mention only a few of the more obvious. America, on its side, can absorb a certain amount of Soviet timber, manganese, platinum, furs, bristles, matches, and miscellaneous articles.

A wise and discriminating credit policy, coupled with a liberal attitude toward imports from Russia, will doubtless bring about, over a term of years, a substantial although not a phenomenal advance in Soviet-American trade from its present extremely low level. A bold and reckless policy of sweeping credits for Soviet purchases in America, unaccompanied by any effort to ensure that there should be a corresponding growth in Soviet sales to America, would merely pave the way for a repetition of the South American and Central European financial disillusionments. When one makes every allowance for the desire of the Soviet Government to honor its own foreign commitments, and for the improvement in its credit standing which has come with the discharge of a substantial part of its obligations to Germany,[3] it is quite obvious that heavily one-sided trade between two countries, under present world conditions, carries with it, in the long run, a definite risk, indeed almost a certainty, that the side with the unfavorable balance of trade will be unable to discharge its obligations.

American failure to recognize the Soviet régime before the Roosevelt Administration came into office was mainly attributable to three causes: the repudiation by the Soviet Government of debts to the American Government and to American citizens contracted by the Tsarist and by the Kerensky régime; the failure of the Soviet Government to compensate American citizens for confiscated and national-

[3] According to Stalin, the Soviet commercial debt abroad by the end of 1933 had been reduced to a little over 450,000,000 gold rubles, and there has been a notable fall in the abnormally high charges which were formerly made for discounting Soviet bills of exchange. In considering Soviet possibilities of payment for foreign imports, one must also reckon with domestic gold production, which is officially stated to have reached a figure of about 100,000,000 gold rubles a year by the end of 1933, and with receipts from the Torgsin stores. But the latter seems likely to be a diminishing source of income (the country's hoarded stocks of gold and foreign currency have been pretty well drained); and along with these "invisible assets" the Soviet Union has "invisible liabilities" in the shape of shipping charges, upkeep of missions and trade agencies abroad, etc.

ized property; and the organized propaganda for revolution in America sponsored by the Communist International. The debts fall under two main headings: loans totaling about $86,000,000 advanced to the Tsarist Government by American banking syndicates, and a capital sum of $187,000,000 advanced by America to the Kerensky Government in 1917. It is safe to predict that any payments which the Soviet Government will make on these debts will be of a distinctly "token" character, so far as the amount is concerned. American intervention in Russia during the civil war, which had extremely little effect on the course of hostilities in the decisive campaigns, is retrospectively convenient, inasmuch as it gives the Soviet Government material on which to base elastic counter-claims.[4] If America adheres to the principles of the Johnson Act and refuses to sanction any credits to the Soviet Union until the Kerensky debt is paid in full, even the modest measure of Soviet-American trade which would seem economically feasible will not take place. Private compensation claims may be settled on a basis of individual agreements with the more influential claimants, accompanied, perhaps, by some minor "token" payment to the lesser creditors, or they may be allowed to languish in neglect indefinitely, as has been the case with the much larger British and French claims.

In the matter of Communist propaganda, Foreign Com-

---

[4] Litvinov in Washington renounced Soviet claims connected with the presence of American troops in Eastern Siberia from 1918 until 1920, a gesture which was not unconnected with the existing Far Eastern situation. Actually the very limited American intervention in Siberia was beneficial rather than otherwise to Soviet interests, because it exercised a restraining influence on the Japanese troops, who entered Siberia in much larger numbers. The Soviet Government, however, reserves its claims for damage in connection with the American military activity in the Archangel Region of Northern Russia.

missar Litvinov gave President Roosevelt one sweeping assurance which cannot be paralleled in Soviet discussions of this delicate subject with other governments. Under this assurance the Soviet Government undertakes "not to permit the formation or residence on its territory of any organization or group — and to prevent the activity on its territory of any organization or group, or of representatives or officials of any organization or group — which has as an aim the overthrow or the preparation for the overthrow of, or bringing about by force of a change in, the political or social order of the whole or any part of the United States, its territories or possessions."

The phrasing of this pledge is legalistic and clumsy. But if words have any meaning this undertaking would seem to obligate the Soviet Government to suppress or to expel from its territory the Communist International, which, if one may trust the evidence of its numerous long-winded published resolutions, is certainly working for the overthrow of the United States Government, as of every other "capitalist" government. But the Soviet Government obviously has no intention of doing any such thing; it was announced early in 1934 that a Congress of the International would be held in Moscow later in the year. So this sweeping "anti-propaganda" pledge must obviously be interpreted in a Pickwickian sense — that is, it is not being, and will not be, carried into effect. To sticklers for fidelity in the execution of governmental pledges this may seem regrettable. But practically the Communist menace to the stability of the American Government is certainly so negligible as to be scarcely worth considering.

For reasons of revolutionary prestige the Soviet Government could not sacrifice the Communist International on the altar of American recognition, desirable as the latter certainly was. But in smaller details the Soviet authorities have shown a disposition to spare American susceptibilities. In 1932 a number of American Negroes of Communist and radical views were brought to Russia to act in a moving-picture production which was to depict the exploitation and oppression of the black race in America according to the best canons of "class art." Before the film reached the stage of completion, however, an influential American business man strongly remonstrated with the Soviet authorities, declaring that the showing of the film would have disastrous effects on prospects of recognition. The practical advice of the business man outweighed the claims of international revolutionary propaganda; the preparation of the film was suddenly stopped, and the bewildered and disillusioned Negroes were abruptly sent about their business.

Whether the establishment of Soviet-American diplomatic relations will go much beyond the obvious convenience of creating diplomatic representation and consular services would seem to depend largely on the course of events in the Far East. The act of formal diplomatic recognition can do little to change the realities of the economic situation, which are that America does not seem able or willing to absorb any very large quantity of Soviet exports and cannot with any safety sell to Russia very much more than it buys from Russia. There would seem to be no reason why the diplomatic relations which were perhaps established rather tardily should not be permanent, unless there should be an unforeseen and improbable relapse of the Soviet Government into extremist propaganda methods.

The year 1933 was marked not only by an establishment of diplomatic relations with America, which Soviet diplomacy will certainly endeavor to turn into a thoroughgoing rapprochement between the two countries, but also by a fundamental and sweeping reorientation of Soviet foreign policy in Europe. One after another the familiar features of Soviet diplomacy in the European field were discarded or reversed. Litvinov, at the beginning of his career as Commissar for Foreign Affairs, had issued a statement emphasizing the special sympathy of the Soviet Government for the countries which were defeated in the World War. Now Karl Radek, the leading Soviet publicist, defends the Versailles Peace settlement, on the ground that it could only be changed by war, which would be a catastrophe in itself and would end in a still more undesirable redrawing of the map of Europe. Up to the latter part of 1933 one would search in vain for a friendly reference to the League of Nations in the speech of a Soviet leader. Abuse and contempt were heaped on the Geneva institution, which was usually represented as a centre for preparing interventionist war against the Soviet Union. Now the value of the League as an instrument, if not a very effective one, for the preservation of peace has been suddenly recognized by Stalin, Molotov, and Litvinov. Soviet membership in the League, which would have seemed grotesquely impossible as recently as 1932, is now a quite probable development. The political and economic ties which bound together the Soviet Union and Germany for more than a decade after the signature of the Rapallo Treaty in 1922 [5] have been completely loosened; and new bonds, the stability of which will be

[5] Germany was the first large country to extend *de jure* recognition to the Soviet Union and to make a provisional renunciation of the property of its citizens which had been nationalized and confiscated under Soviet decrees and administrative measures.

tested by the future, have been forged with France and with Poland.

The cooling off in Soviet-German relations set in when Franz von Papen became Chancellor of Germany in the spring of 1932. Von Papen was regarded in Moscow as the advocate of a conservative entente between France and Germany, the spearhead of which was to be directed against the Soviet Union. This process of cooling off has gone much farther since National Socialism became dominant in Germany early in 1933.

Hitler's merciless drive against German Communism was by no means the decisive factor in the change. Cold-bloodedness is a quality on which Soviet diplomacy prides itself. The fact that a number of the few Turkish Communists on one occasion were sewed up in sacks and thrown into the Black Sea has not prevented the Soviet Union from cultivating the most friendly relations with the nationalist régime of Mustapha Kemal. Mussolini is also reckoned among the international friends of the Soviet Union, despite his vigorous repressive measures against Italian Communists.

A combination of factors has created the sense of estrangement between the Soviet Union and Hitlerite Germany. There was the tendency of National Socialist leaders — before, and in some cases after, they came into power — to invest their movement with an international anti-Bolshevik mission and significance. There was the Hugenberg Memorandum at the World Economic Conference in London in the summer of 1933, which demanded for Germany opportunities for colonial expansion in Eastern Europe. Alleged conversations of Alfred Rosenberg, prominent National Socialist theoretician, with Ukrainian separatist émigrés, and the repressive measures which were in some cases taken against Soviet citizens during the first months of the National Socialist régime, also helped to create strained relations between the two countries and to promote the conviction on the Soviet side that in the future Germany might be as threatening in the West as Japan is considered to be in the East.

Still another factor in the change of Soviet international front was a shrewd appraisal and exploitation of the reaction in France and in Poland to the rise of militant German nationalism. Neither of those countries could be indifferent to the political and strategic advantages of destroying the former close contact between Moscow and Berlin. They were willing to meet Soviet overtures for friendship halfway.

So one of the paradoxical immediate results of the coming into power of the German National Socialists, who had dreamed of a crusade against Bolshevism on an international scale, was that it created a new, much friendlier atmosphere between the Soviet Union and France, the strongest European military nation, and thereby considerably strengthened the Soviet position in the concert of European powers.

Among the signs of the new trend of Soviet foreign policy one may note the signature of non-aggression pacts with France and with Poland; the acceptance by Poland and by the Little Entente and Baltic States in the summer of 1933 of the Soviet formula defining aggression; the visits to Moscow of M. Herriot, leader of the French Radical Socialist Party, and of M. Pierre Cot, French Minister of Aviation, in the autumn of 1933. Military attachés have been exchanged between Paris and Moscow for the first time since the Revolution. Exchanges of friendly visits of artists and of groups of journalists have been arranged with Poland and with the Baltic States, and early in 1934 Colonel Beck arrived in Moscow for the first visit ever paid to the Soviet capital by a Polish Foreign Minister. Even the thorniest question on the Soviet western frontier — the Rumanian occupation of Bessarabia, which the Soviet Government has never recognized as legal or valid — has lost a good deal of its sharpness since the Soviet Government, under its own formula defining aggression, would not have the right to intervene in Bessarabia if a revolution should break out there.

While it would not be accurate to say that the pre-war Franco-Russian alliance has been fully restored (the Soviet Union would scarcely be in a position to undertake aggressive commitments in Europe until it felt more secure in the Far East, and a resumption of large-scale lending by France to Russia seems, to put it mildly, improbable), the coöperation between Paris and Moscow which was so evident at the session of the Disarmament Conference in late May and early June is a most important factor in contemporary European politics. Both its direct and its indirect consequences may well be far-reaching. For one thing, it marks the definite emergence of the Soviet Union from its former attitude of self-righteous revolutionary isolation from the combinations of other powers. The Soviet press now ardently takes sides with France and attacks Germany and England, forgetful of the old tradition of attacking impartially the "imperialists" and "capitalists" of all countries. A new balance of power may be in the making. One speedy result of the Soviet-French rapprochement was the establishment of diplomatic relations between the Soviet

Union, on one side, and Czechoslovakia and Rumania, on the other, on June 9, 1934.

It would be premature to reckon Poland as a fast and unchanging friend of the Soviet Union; Polish policy at the present time seems to aim at a delicate balancing between Moscow and Berlin, accompanied by a desire to extract the maximum benefit from friendly relations with both Germany and the Soviet Union. But Soviet-Polish relations have improved almost beyond recognition by comparison with the feeling which prevailed between the two countries a few years ago. Soviet diplomacy has also been active in the Baltic States, where existing pacts of non-aggression, at the Soviet initiative, have been prolonged for a period of ten years. The Soviet Government also proposed to guarantee the independence and territorial integrity of the Baltic States by means of a common declaration, which was to be signed by Poland and Germany; Germany rejected the suggestion on the ground that it was superfluous and unnecessary.

This new Soviet foreign policy is dictated not only by apprehension of future German ambitions, but also by the desire to secure the rear of the Soviet Union in the West, through understandings with France and Poland, in the event that all the country's military resources should be required in the Far East. This same defensive motive is visible in the special Soviet effort to cultivate cordial relations with Turkey, which holds the key to the Black Sea. Not only have there been exchanges of ceremonial visits between representatives of the two countries, but the Soviet Union has given Turkey a helping hand in its first efforts at industrialization by granting to the Turkish Government a long-term loan in kind, in the form of machinery and equipment, which has made possible the building of a large new textile plant in Cæsarea, in Anatolia.

A further implication of American recognition and of the probable admission of the Soviet Union to the League of Nations is a disappearance of the Ishmaelite status which was attached to the Soviet Government, in the international field, for many years after the Revolution.   There are now only a few secondary European powers which do not maintain regular diplomatic relations with the Soviet Government; and the number of these is likely to be diminished in the near future.

In the economic field the Soviet Union has justified neither the fears of those observers who raised the cry of the "Red trade menace" nor the hopes of those who saw in Russia a fertile field for foreign investment and development.   The idea that Russia would constitute a grave competitive threat to other countries in the field of international trade was based on several misconceptions in regard to the results of the first five-year plan and the character of Soviet economy.   The greatest of these misconceptions was that the big new plants so actively under construction would soon turn out a surplus of goods which would be unsalable on the home market and would, therefore, be dumped abroad at ruinously low prices.

Some forcing of export there certainly has been.   In order to obtain foreign currency with which to pay for imported machinery and equipment, the Soviet Government has shipped abroad and sold at low prices food products which were badly needed at home.   But the fact that Soviet exports in 1933 were less than a third of pre-war Russia's exports in 1913, measured in gold rubles, is a sufficient commentary on the idea that the Soviet Union, after the completion of the five-year plan, would have enormous surplus stocks of goods, with which it might flood the markets of the world. The new steel, copper, chemical, and other plants are as yet quite unable to supply the needs of the country's programme of industrial development; and the date when the production needs of the country and the consumption needs of its inhabitants will be satiated certainly seems to lie in a very distant future. Nature has made the Soviet Union one of the most potentially self-sufficient countries in the world. Its economic difficulties, acute as they are, are difficulties of poor organization, ill-advised reckless experiments, inadequate technical knowledge, not of poverty in natural wealth.

On the other hand, the experience of the last few years certainly does not mark the Soviet Union out as a promising field for the investment of foreign capital. The Iron Age witnessed the termination of almost all the scores of concessions (mostly of small size) which had been granted to foreign firms for the operation of factories, mines, farms, and timber tracts. In some cases the concessions were brought to an amicable close; in others there were sharp protests on the part of the concessionaires against chicanery and duplicity on the part of the Soviet concession authorities, who were accused of either directly breaking contracts or interpreting them arbitrarily and unfairly. The Soviet authorities were apt to accuse the holders of concessions of putting too little money into Russia and of taking too much money out in the form of profits. Without attempting to pass judgment on the varied merits of each case, it may be said that two fundamental difficulties almost invariably cropped up whenever a foreign *entrepreneur* endeavored to operate an enterprise in Russia.

First, the foreigner was obliged to deal with a monopolistic state, which was prejudiced against him anyway as a "bourgeois" and which could, whenever it desired, cut off his transportation facilities, boycott his products, and impose on him the observance of labor conditions which were much better than those which prevailed in the state industries. There was no impartial tribunal to which a foreign concessionaire could appeal. One contract which was concluded with the Lena Goldfields Company did provide for the creation of such an arbitration tribunal, to consist of representatives of the company and of the Soviet Government, with an impartial chairman in the person of a foreign technical mining expert. But this arrangement was repudiated by the Soviet Government as soon as it was invoked by the company.

Secondly, the foreigner, as soon as he began to earn profits in Soviet rubles, often found himself confronted with great difficulties in obtaining permission to exchange these rubles for foreign currency. The rubles were quite valueless outside the Soviet frontiers; they could only be used for operating expenses inside the country. While in some disputes over concession terms the Soviet Government seems to have been at fault, and in others the concessionaires were probably guilty of sharp practice, the almost unbroken record of failure of foreign concessions to function on a mutually satisfactory basis would suggest that the concession system is simply not suited to Soviet conditions, and that foreign business firms will in the future be well advised not to invest capital in the Soviet Union in this way.

Apart from diplomacy and trade, the Soviet Union has another means of contact — hostile contact, in this case — with the outside world, in the Communist International. It might have been expected that during a period of widespread unemployment and profound economic crisis the revolutionary gospel of the International would have gained in popular appeal. Actually, under the test of the last few years, the International has proved pitifully weak and ineffective. In the light of recent experience one might even venture the prediction that any socialist revolutions which may take place in the future will come about in spite of the self-styled "general staff of the world revolution" and not on account of its singularly unsuccessful efforts.

The collapse of the German Communist Party, supposedly the strongest branch of the International outside of Russia, before the onrush of Hitlerism without the firing of a shot, without even a strike of protest, plainly revealed the clay feet of an organization whose significance has been grossly overrated both by Communists and by extreme conservatives. In this connection I recall a conversation which I had in Berlin with a well-informed and experienced foreign observer of German conditions in the latter part of 1932, a few months before the clamping down of the National Socialist dictatorship. My acquaintance had what might be described as a left-wing Social Democratic outlook — that is, he regarded the official Social Democratic policy as too cautious and compromising, without, however, sharing the views of the Communists.

"If I were a capitalist, I would subsidize the Communist International," he exclaimed in an outburst of indignation. "It is the surest guaranty that there will never be a revolution in Germany, except of the Fascist kind. It has hopelessly split the labor front, and its made-in-Moscow slogans and tactics can never win the confidence and support of the German masses."

Of course it is a matter of opinion whether the break-up of the pre-war unity of the European labor movement is more attributable to the doctrinaire extremism of the Communists or to the excessive moderation of some of the Social Democratic parties. But that this break-up was perhaps the biggest of several factors which opened the doors wide for the victorious upsurge of Fascism is unmistakable. It is significant that in Austria, where the majority of the workers had remained united under Social Democratic leadership and where the Communist Party was very weak, there was heavy fighting in the working-class districts of Vienna before the new dictatorial régime could establish itself. In Italy and in Germany, where the Communists had driven a much deeper wedge into the working-class movement, Mussolini and Hitler came into power without any resistance that called for the use of military force.

The Russian Orthodox Church was gravely weakened by its close pre-war association with the Tsarist state. And the Communist International, far from benefiting, is rather injured by the fact that it is completely dominated from Moscow and is not infrequently utilized as a cat's-paw of Soviet foreign policy. The strict subordination to Moscow, the Russian stamp that is placed on all the propaganda of the International, the frequent deposition, on summary orders from Moscow, of trusted and popular leaders of the national Communist parties — all these things tend to cripple Communist agitation outside of Russia,[6] to alienate many of the more sincere and intelligent revolutionaries,

[6] Communist slogans were often almost incredibly inept and unreal. In 1932, when one might have expected that all the energy of the German Communists would have been concentrated on the struggle with the rising tide of National Socialism, the posters at large Communist meetings displayed such empty appeals as "Defend the Soviet Union" and "Defend China," although it is rather unclear what German workers could have done either to "defend China" or to protect the Soviet Union against an attack that never took place.

and to make of the "general staff of the world revolution" a lifeless bureaucratized institution, formidable only on paper.

Stalin is as much of an autocrat in the International as he is in the All-Union Communist Party. And his régime tends to eliminate vigorous personalities and original thinkers [7] and to bring to positions of leadership in Communist parties throughout the world colorless bureaucratic mediocrities, who are trained not to think until they have received instructions from Moscow. Now the faithful Party bureaucrat who always does what he is told may have useful functions to perform in a going concern like the Soviet Union. But this is emphatically not the type of man who can lead a successful revolution, a task for which independence, daring, and initiative are required. Lenin was fortunate in that no Communist International existed in 1917 to tell him when and how he was to launch the Bolshevik Revolution.

It is sometimes suggested that the Soviet leaders have given up all hope of revolutions on the Russian model in other countries. This is, I think, an overstatement. While there can certainly be little immediate optimism about the progress of Communism outside the Soviet Union, — except, perhaps, in China (and there what passes for Communism seems to possess many traits of traditional peasant insurgence, with a veneer of Moscow-trained leadership), — the picture might change in the event of another world war. And if the Soviet Union should itself become involved in hostilities Communist propaganda would be used to the uttermost as a military weapon against the enemy. The foreign Com-

[7] Ruth Fischer, Brandler, and Thalheimer in Germany; Doriot and Frossard in France; Lovestone, Lore, and Nearing in America, to mention only a few of those who have been excommunicated by the International.

munists would be useful, in such an eventuality, for espionage and diversion work in the rear of the anti-Soviet forces.

As time goes on, it seems increasingly probable that the main historical significance of the Russian Revolution outside the frontiers of the Soviet Union will be not economic, but political. No country at the present time seems likely to imitate the economic and social features of the Bolshevik Revolution. But two large European countries, Italy and Germany, have taken over with conspicuous success the Bolshevik formula for successful government: unlimited propaganda plus unlimited repression.[8]

And there is a deeper reason than the incompetence and blundering of the Communist International for the sweep of various brands of Fascism in countries where parliamentary democracy has broken down. What can Communism, to judge from the Russian experience, offer to the numerous middle class, to the still more numerous landowning peasants and farmers of Western Europe and America? Nothing but social and economic extermination — "liquidation," if one prefers the Soviet term. But the middle class and the peasantry are vastly more powerful in almost any European country than they were in pre-Bolshevik Russia, with its notoriously thin middle class and its huge mass of desperately poor, shiftless, and land-hungry peasants. They

---

[8] In this connection I recall the interesting remarks of a Russian Communist who had spent some years in Italy. Needless to say, they were made in the course of an extremely private conversation. The Communist observed that such political discontent as existed in Italy was almost entirely confined to the older and middle-aged workers, who could still remember that there had once been a Social Democratic movement in Italy. The youth, with few exceptions, had been brought up in the Fascist spirit and was full of enthusiasm for Mussolini. "It is really very much in Italy as it is here," he concluded, "except that in Italy the people have enough to eat."

will not permit themselves to be "liquidated" voluntarily. And when the strain of economic crisis becomes too acute they are almost historically predestined to turn to Fascism of some kind as an alternative to and a defense against Bolshevism.

The Bolshevik Revolution imagined itself the herald of an international working-class revolution. It has actually been the predecessor of the nationalist middle-class revolutions headed by Mussolini and Hitler.[9] It is not the first time that great historical expectations have been sharply and ironically deceived.

[9] In more than one way Bolshevism (unconsciously and unwillingly, of course) has paved the way for Fascism. It has provided the whole Fascist technique of government: a single party, headed by a leader of unquestioned authority, bound by severe discipline, monopolizing all governmental power; a deluge of propaganda and emotional appeals for the masses; concentration camps and, in extreme cases, firing squads for the few obstinate spirits who resist. Moreover, Fascism is definitely a reaction to a real or imaginary threat of Communism. It is certainly no accident that in those countries where Communism has never taken serious root (America, England, France, the Scandinavian countries, Belgium, the Netherlands, Switzerland, for instance) there is also no Fascist movement of any consequence.

XII

NEW RUSSIA

Nowhere in the world is there such a sharp line of demarcation, as regards tastes, habits, outlook on life, between the older and the younger generation as there is in the Soviet Union. Whether a Russian takes a hopeful or a gloomy view of his own living conditions and his country's prospects often depends upon whether he is under or over thirty. Of course it would be an absurd oversimplification to set down all the Russians over thirty as pessimists and all those under thirty as optimists; there would be plenty of exceptions in both camps.

But there is something very distinctive in the outlook of most of the young people who have grown up entirely under the Soviet régime, singing Soviet songs, studying in Soviet schools, getting their training in the extensive Soviet youth organizations. For every adult Communist there are several young people who are receiving intensive Communist training. In addition to the four and a half million Young Communists and the six million Young Pioneers, there are two million Octobrists,[1] children of kindergarten age who are being moulded along Communist lines.

[1] According to the old Russian calendar the Bolshevik Revolution occurred on October 25, and is hence often referred to as the October Revolution.

I brought away a vivid first-hand idea of how this moulding is carried out from a visit to a kindergarten which bears
the name "Communist International" and is attached to a
Moscow clothing factory. In many ways this kindergarten,
which is one of the best in Moscow, was quite like similar
institutions in other countries. The children were divided
into groups according to age and had regular periods for
study, play, and rest. They cut out and pasted pictures,
built with blocks, and took care of plants.

Three distinctive features of the kindergarten were the
cult of Leninism, the intensive antireligious propaganda,
and the concentration upon military toys and games.
Prominently displayed in one of the rooms was a placard,
made by the children themselves, with the inscription:
"How We Fulfilled the Commandments of Lenin." Various children had carried out these commandments in different ways. Some had collected money for Mopr, an organization which helps Communist prisoners in other countries, and for the construction of an airplane. Others had
sent toys to a collective farm. One proud youngster claimed
credit for having removed ikons from his home. A crude
drawing showed the removal of the ikons, and beneath was
an inscription: "There is no God; we don't want Christmas;
we shall make our parents also godless."

I asked a boy of seven, who stood near by, to explain the
meaning of this scene. His face became tense and serious.
"There is no God," he declared with firm conviction.
"That is why we remove the ikons. Only the priests and
capitalists say there is a God, because they are enemies of
the workers and want to enslave them."

Two other boys came up. "Of course there is no God,"
they chimed in. "And abroad workers' children are not

allowed to go to school, because they don't want them to learn that there is no God."

"Do any children abroad go to school?" I inquired. The question created some confusion. "Some go and some don't," was one reply. "The children of the rich go," was another.

The ideas of the children were very directly turned toward military things. The walls were covered with pictures of War Commissar Voroshilov, General Budenny, and Red soldiers and sailors. In the more advanced group, for children of six and seven, practically all the toys suggested war. A table was full of miniature tanks, cannon, rifles, machine guns, and armored trains, and on the floor was a large toy wooden cannon, which the children had made themselves. Several boys ran around the room with toy rifles, firing imaginary shots at each other. I asked one of the teachers why there was so much emphasis on war and she replied: —

"We are not pacifists. Our children are taught to love and admire the Red Army, and they all want to become soldiers when they grow up. We take the children on excursions to the Red Army schools and barracks, and the soldiers visit us. We know that we shall be attacked by the capitalists, and we prepare for it and live up to the commandments of Lenin," she concluded, pointing to the placard on the wall.

Almost all the children in this kindergarten, as soon as they are old enough, will join the Young Pioneers, the organization for children between the ages of eight and sixteen, who have been steadily increasing in numbers and are more and more in evidence in Russian public life. Distinguished by their red scarfs, bands of Young Pioneers

Soyuzphoto

A Factory School in the Donetz District

are often to be seen in the summer marching out to camps, where they are given courses in physical training, woodcraft, and so forth, not unlike those which are found in Boy Scout camps in other countries.

At Christmas time it is the duty of the Young Pioneers to convince the unconverted children of non-Communist families that it is wrong and improper to have Christmas trees. To help them in this and to strengthen them in the antireligious faith, they are supplied with little primers which contain a curious smattering of Marxism, comparative religion, mythology, and information about the five-year plan, which is supposed to be inimical to Christmas trees.

No Soviet election is complete unless a troop of Young Pioneers marches in and, through its leader, gravely announces its *nakaz*, or instructions, to the Soviet delegates. These instructions usually contain a point about closing more churches and turning them into schools or Pioneer clubs. When a *chistka*, or purge, of a Soviet institution is in progress, it is not uncommon for a ten-year-old Pioneer, properly coached, to get up and solemnly accuse some victim of the purge of bureaucracy or sabotage.

A feature of the training of the Young Pioneers is the extraordinary precocity which it seems designed to inspire. If one picks up a copy of the *Pioneer Pravda*, the newspaper of the organization, it suggests very much the senior *Pravda*, rewritten in simpler language. Through this newspaper the Young Pioneers, of whom 70 per cent are under thirteen years of age, are told about the latest measure of agrarian policy, about the "legends" which are circulated in "capitalist" countries about Soviet forced labor, about the revolutionary movement in China.

This forcing of the social activity and mental development of young children has been carried so far that it often leads to harmful psychological results in the form of excessive nervousness, heart trouble, and the like, and the present tendency is to put some curb on it. An educational investigator made the interesting discovery that what many children most desired in summer camps was simply to be let alone, to rest, not to be called out for the endless group activities. And early in 1934 the Soviet authorities issued specific instructions against cramming the brains of elementary school children with too much *politgramota* (Communist economics and political theory) and against posing questions to them based on the last decisions of the Party Congress.

There has also been a reaction against the complete outlawry of fairy tales and imaginative animal stories which at one time went into effect. At this time there had also been a crusade against conventional dolls and other toys; and one zealot, Mr. D. Popov, in all seriousness made the suggestion that Soviet children should be entertained and edified in the following way: "Show the children malignant caricatures of Tsars, capitalists, gendarmes, priests, and Fascisti. Show them the faces of saboteurs, bureaucrats, kulaks, and Nepmen [private traders]. Show proletarians of Europe, Asia, America, and Africa."

But, while there is now a more general realization of the fact that propaganda, like other things, may be overdone to such an extent that it defeats its own purpose, there is an unremitting effort to bring up the Young Pioneers as loyal and enthusiastic Soviet citizens, to train them to guard the crops in the country districts and to perform other public tasks in the towns.

When the Young Pioneer puts on his red kerchief, when

the Young Communist puts on the khaki uniform and Sam Browne belt which is a frequent although not an invariable sign of membership in that organization, he is taught to regard obedience to the orders which come from the Party as the first and supreme duty, a duty which must take precedence over family ties and relationships. Cases when children denounce their own parents are common and are always mentioned with approbation in the Soviet press. Thus in the spring of 1934 a Tartar schoolgirl named Olya Balikina informed the local authorities that her father and some other peasants were taking for their own use grain which belonged to the collective farm. This offense, under the notorious Law of August 7, exposed those who were guilty of it to the death penalty. Olya was held up as an example of young Soviet virtue and, as a reward, was transferred at state expense from her village school to a model school in the city of Kazan.

The Union of Communist Youth, with its four and a half million youths of both sexes, plays a very important rôle in Soviet life to-day. It is at once a social and recreational body, an agency for imparting a firm grasp of the ideas of Marx and Lenin to the rising generation, a nucleus which is supposed to make for harder and more efficient work in every factory and institution, and a labor corps of shock troops. Whenever there is an odd job for which there are not enough hands, or whenever the speed and effectiveness of work show a tendency to sag, Young Communists are mobilized by their organization and sent to the place in question. Every effort is made to surround this extra labor with a glamour of heroic achievement; the groups of Young Communists who are dispatched to timber camps and freight-car sidings, to steel mills and coal mines, are sent off with bands and songs and congratulatory speeches, in which Stalin's phrase that "labor in the Soviet Union is a thing of honor and glory, of courage and heroism," is often quoted.

Moscow is now in the very visible throes of building a subway. Ten thousand Young Communists have been mobilized for this work. As a means of celebrating the fifteenth anniversary of the establishment of the Union of Communist Youth, it was decided to hold a *subbotnik*, or day of voluntary work on a holiday, the extra pay of which would be contributed to the country's "iron fund of defense." No doubt the organizers and leaders of the Young Communists are unconsciously adept in the psychological appeal which Mark Twain's Tom Sawyer skillfully employed when he persuaded all the boys in the village that it was a privilege to be permitted to help whitewash his back fence.

Stalin and other Soviet leaders are keenly appreciative of the contribution which this closely welded, strongly disciplined, enthusiastic body of youth is making to the building up of the Soviet Union; and on the occasion of its fifteenth anniversary, in 1933, warm congratulatory messages poured in from the most prominent Party and Soviet leaders. The Young Communists responded with a vow, addressed to Stalin and couched in the romantic language that appeals to youth in every country. They vowed to fight for the abolition of classes and exploitation, for the dictatorship of the proletariat, for mastering industrial technique. They also pledged themselves to become model soldiers, fearless aviators, brave sailors, capable tank drivers.

One of the most interesting considerations, to anyone interested in Russia's future, is the type of human being that is emerging from the Young Communist school, through which so many of Russia's younger people, especially in the towns, are passing. Of course no general answer can be absolutely correct, because a mass organization of four and a half million members obviously takes in different types of individuals. At the same time the theoretical training, the discipline, and the obligations which are imposed upon every Komsomol (the Russian abbreviation for Young Communist) do tend to emphasize certain qualities and repress others and to create something of a standardized type.

The typical Komsomol has a narrower range of thought, a more limited general culture, and a much more cocksure, dogmatic attitude on almost any debatable question than the average young man of education in pre-war Russia. There are several reasons for this. A very large part of the Young Communists are recruited from classes which had little or no education before the Revolution; their incessant preoccupation with the extra tasks which are assigned to them outside of working hours restricts their possibilities for wide reading and general thought.[2] Finally, it is drilled into the Komsomol from the moment he joins the organization that obedience to its orders is his first duty, and that any criticism of these orders is a sin of the gravest kind. All this, taken together, makes for a certain hardness and narrowness that one often senses in Soviet young people of both sexes.

[2] In this connection I recall the remark of a West Indian Negro who had somehow drifted to Russia and was employed on the Turksib Railroad. He declared that the capacity of the young engineers left something to be desired and suggested in explanation, "They usually don't come from educated families, and they have too much sociable work to do." (By "sociable work" he meant the obligations in the way of public activity which fall on the Young Communist: speeches at workers' meetings, courses for teaching literacy, etc.)

However, if one takes another standard of comparison, the young peasant or worker of pre-revolutionary days, the Young Communist is a definitely more advanced type. He reads more books, goes to more concerts and theatres, leads a more alert and intelligent existence. The best type of Young Communist is distinguished by physical fitness and athletic tastes; and it is significant that the most striking feats of graduates of the Young Communist organization, such as the stratosphere flight of Prokofiev and the record parachute jump of the aviator Evseev, have been in the realm of practical achievement and physical daring. The Young Communists at the present time are placing great emphasis upon technical education and training, and no doubt many future "captains of industry" are being trained in the Soviet ranks.

I remember very well a meeting with a rank-and-file Komsomol at the end of an exhausting day during which I had been endeavoring to get some information about the automobile plant at Gorky (formerly Nizhni Novgorod). The general impression of the day had been depressing; food was bad, and housing and sanitation were worse; there seemed to be an atmosphere of chaotic irresponsibility in the management of the plant; and, so far as I could judge from talks with foreign experts and from scanning back numbers of the local factory newspaper, the automobile works had apparently suffered from an acute attack of all the "growing pains" that are apt to afflict new Soviet industrial enterprises. By contrast this ardent Young Communist was a ray of optimism. He admitted the defects, but was sure they would be overcome in time.

Along with thousands of other Young Communists he had been mobilized for "shock work" in the building of the plant. The conditions which had confronted these youthful soldiers of labor had been far from easy. Meals were irregular; hours of labor were unlimited ("Often," as the Young Communist told me, "when we had just lain down to sleep after an exhausting job of carrying bricks we would be called out to mend something that had broken down in another part of the plant"); for a time the bare ground had been the only sleeping place.

"There were some mama's boys," said my acquaintance with great scorn, "who said it was too hard and ran away. We don't want sneaks like that in our organization. A real Komsomol would no more think of running away from a hard job than he would think of running away in battle."

He fairly bubbled over with enthusiasm in describing the new factories which were going up all about the city. This Young Communist had come from the log cabin of a poor peasant household in North Russia. What might have seemed to a foreigner a dreary spectacle of hardship and desolation was to him a field of opportunity. This element of opportunity, incidentally, must never be overlooked in judging the psychology of Russia's younger generation. With all the hardships which it has brought to the whole population, with all its ruthless inhumanity toward classes and individuals which are regarded as hostile, the Iron Age has bequeathed to young men and young women who feel themselves a part of the existing system many openings in industry and agriculture and study. Up to the present time, at least, the Soviet Union has not experienced the problem of an excess of trained people; indeed, its main difficulties are attributable in no small degree to a precisely opposite cause: that too many responsible posts are in the hands of bungling amateurs.

It would be a mistake to regard the entire Soviet youth as a massed block of enthusiasts for the existing régime. Contrary to the enthusiastic Komsomol of Gorky I have an equally distinct recollection of a young man whom I met in the course of a walking trip and whom I will call Kolya. He was little over twenty, and, therefore, a product of the Soviet schools and the Soviet régime, and was in his last year of training as an engineer. Kolya was making the trip with a group of young men and women, mostly advanced students or recent graduates.

Whenever he could get away from his companions and walk alone with me he would begin to express doubts and criticisms which somehow suggested a country boy who had come to college and was beginning to lose faith in Fundamentalist theology. Were things really so bad in foreign countries as the Soviet newspapers described? He had his doubts. And, sinking his voice and looking about for possible eavesdroppers, he went on: "And isn't it terrible to think of forty-eight people, two whole truckloads, being shot without trial for so-called sabotage? I'm not the only one who thinks that way, but of course we know better than to talk out loud about such things. And please don't say anything to my companions about what I have been telling you. For we have a saying in Russia that every man wants to eat, to live, and not to sit."[3]

Under a régime of cast-iron dictatorship it is difficult to estimate how numerous are the doubting Kolyas. But the heretics and dissenters are unorganized and inarticulate; it is the Komsomol who sets the tone for the present-day Soviet youth.

The eternal conflict of point of view and psychology

[3] "To sit" is a familiar Russian colloquialism for "to be in prison."

between the older and younger generation in Russia, which found its highest artistic reflection in Turgeniev's *Fathers and Sons,* is now more evident than ever. The spiritual clash is more natural and inevitable now, because a middle-aged, pre-revolutionary generation and a young Soviet generation stand face to face, with loyalties, tastes, and ideas that are often in sharp contrast. The Young Communist son or daughter cannot understand why the father and mother, even though they may have been revolutionists in their younger days, do not share his boundless enthusiasm over Magnitogorsk or Dnieprostroi. The father or mother cannot understand why the children accept so calmly and even approvingly such things as the liquidation of the kulaks, the banishments without trial, the complete suppression of criticism of Communist ideas.

It is not uncommon to see in a provincial newspaper a list of announcements to the effect that such and such young people have broken off all connections with their parents. There is often a distinct element of economic self-interest in such declarations, because children of disfranchised persons can only hope to escape from this pariah status if they publicly renounce their parents. But there are many cases when children of parents who are not suffering from such social disabilities strike out for themselves at an early age, simply because the home atmosphere has become distasteful.

I stumbled across a homely illustration of the clash of opinion between old and young when I visited the textile town of Ivanovo early in 1934. I had stopped for a chat in one of the little cabins where many of the less skilled workers live. The owner of the cabin, a middle-aged textile worker, worn and gnarled with years of service in the mills, was distinctly pessimistic in his outlook and complained especially about the food shortage. So did his wife, who insisted that things were better before the Revolution. A middle-aged friend, another worker, talked in the same strain. But a red-haired girl of sixteen or seventeen, the daughter in the family, argued vigorously on the other side. Had n't the Soviet régime given her a chance to attend a training course for teachers, an opportunity which a worker's child might not have had under Tsarism? And she knew and repeated the familiar official explanations for the food shortage: the resistance of the malevolent kulaks, the necessity for making sacrifices to build up industry, and so forth.

The difference of outlook between Soviet "fathers and sons" found more intellectual expression at a meeting of parents and teachers which took place in a Moscow high school. A modest middle-aged man took the floor and brought in an indictment against the younger generation in the following terms: —

"The Revolution was sixteen years old this year. My son is also sixteen years old and is a member of the highest class in this school. I think the school has ruined him and other young people of his age. . . .

"These young people are dry, egotistical, self-assured. They have n't read anything, but they are ready to discuss everything. They think they have real ideas. But are they ideas? We, of our generation, reached our convictions with blood and tears. Now the young man is given ready-made beliefs in school. . . . They are dry, crude rationalists. They talk excitedly about the mating of rabbits, but they cannot dream. They are insolent cynics, new business men, Soviet Americans. I can perhaps admire some traits in them, but I cannot love them."

This naturally evoked a storm of protest among the

students; and the critical parent was roundly denounced as a "petty bourgeois" (a term of vague but profound abuse in the Soviet Union) who was envious of the health and enthusiasm of the young builders of socialism. "You say we don't dream," cried an indignant girl. "Here is Pavel Ivanov, who is absorbed in organic chemistry and can quote fifty complicated formulas from memory. He pronounces them with the inspiration of a great poet. He dreams of making artificial protein. Another of our students wants to be a city planner and to lay out the socialist cities of our future. And one of our hydrotechnicians has thought of a scheme by which he will steal all the warm sea currents from the capitalist countries and envelop Siberia with them. Our epoch is so full and varied; there is so much to dream about."

Similar disputes between old and young in Russia have been argued out, against differing political and social backgrounds, more than once in the past. Sixty or seventy years ago the famous émigré publicist, Alexander Herzen, despite his own radicalism, which compelled him to live in permanent exile, conceived a keen dislike for the morals and manners of a younger generation of revolutionaries, whose creed he stated for them in the following caustic phrases: —

"You are hypocrites; we will be cynics. You were moral in words; we will be scoundrels in deeds. You were courteous to superiors and rude to inferiors; we will be rude to everyone. You bowed without esteeming; we will push without apologizing."

The Bolshevik Revolution has tended to create not only a new type of youth, but also a new type of woman, and it has very largely demolished old-fashioned family relations.

The Soviet theory has always been that woman's place is anywhere but in the home; and the positive shortage of labor which has been experienced during recent years has strengthened the drive to push women into factory and office work. So one now finds women in the Soviet Union working at almost every conceivable trade or profession, as engineers and aviators, hodcarriers and motormen. The barelegged bronzed girl tractor driver, with the red kerchief that may denote her membership in the Union of Communist Youth, is not an unfamiliar sight on the countryside; and one can find women acting as presidents of village soviets, managers of factories and collective farms.

The "lady," like the "gentleman," of leisure would be an absurd anomaly in the Soviet Union. It is not regarded as good form for the wives of even the highest Soviet and Party officials to be without occupation, and they are usually engaged in some branch of work or course of study. So Stalin's late wife was studying the process of making artificial silk along with her friend, the wife of Premier Molotov; Madame Litvinov gives English lessons and occasionally contributes to Moscow's English-language newspaper; President Kalinin's wife undertook the management of a state farm; Madame Bubnova, whose husband is Commissar for Education, for a time took charge of the ikon department of the Torgsin stores.

This varied activity of women has a double edge. It is naturally appreciated by the girls of independent temperament who want to make their own careers. I saw the other side of the picture when I talked with a woman, the wife of a worker at the Berezniki chemical works, who was a fellow passenger on a boat trip down the Kama River. She was going from Berezniki all the way to Stalingrad, because in Berezniki the food cards of unemployed wives of workers had been taken away, in an effort to force them to take employment in the factory. "I have enough to do with my three children without going into the factory," the woman said, "and I am going to Stalingrad to see whether a worker's wife can't draw her bread ration there, if she is n't employed herself."

One of Russia's outstanding social experiments has been the inauguration of a system under which divorce may be had for the asking, and without delay, by either partner in a marriage. I obtained an idea of how the Soviet marriage and divorce mechanism functions in practice by visiting the Zags, or marriage and divorce registration bureau, of my neighborhood in Moscow. The applicants for marriage and divorce waited their turns in the inevitable queues in an anteroom, where a loud-speaker entertained them with denunciations of the heresies of the "right deviationists" in the Communist Party. The inner room, where the registration took place, was simply furnished with two or three plain tables and chairs, while portraits of Lenin reading *Pravda* and of Kalinin absorbed in *Izvestia* hung on the walls.

A young woman of perhaps twenty sat behind one of the tables and hurried through the proceedings with a maximum of speed. People who came to get married could always be distinguished from those who desired divorce, because the former arrived in pairs and the latter singly. When a couple entered, the officiating young woman briskly invited them to sit down and followed this up with the stereotyped phrases, "You are to be married? Yes. Please show your documents and pay two rubles." This was the fee for marriage or divorce collected from workers and employees.

Members of the professional and disfranchised classes had to pay ten rubles.

Of the eight couples that were married during my visit to the Zags only one paid ten rubles, and this was because the bridegroom had forgotten to bring a certificate from his place of employment and was willing to pay the higher fee for immediate marriage. The only other questions asked of the future husband and wife were their nationality and whether they had been married before. After the marriage has been registered, both partners sign their names several times in large books for purposes of record. This is why the Soviet marriage usually goes by the prosaic term of "signing up" (*raspiska*).

The partners in a Soviet marriage may either keep their original names or take a common name, which may be that of either husband or wife. In the eight marriages which I witnessed six brides selected their husband's name, one couple decided to go by individual names, while one man expressed a desire to assume his wife's name. He was a peasant, and the registration clerk confided to me her suspicion that he was of a kulak family and wished to hide his ignominious, not to say dangerous, origin as completely as possible.

I asked the clerk about the causes of divorce. "Causes?" she replied, with a bored air. "We don't ask for them. Any married person may come here, apply for a divorce, and get it after paying two rubles. We then inform the other party to the marriage by post that he or she is divorced. If there are no children, the whole matter is quite simple. The mutual obligations of husband and wife cease when the marriage has been dissolved, except in cases where one of the two is diseased or disabled. He or she can then claim support from the healthy person for a few months. If there are children, they are usually left with the mother, while the father must pay a quarter or a third of his earnings for their support.   If the divorced couple cannot reach an agreement on this point here, we refer the case to a court."

To judge from talks with several people who were applying for divorce, the causes of matrimonial difficulty in the Soviet Union are not very different from what they are in other countries, with the exception that disputes over property are infrequent.   Women usually complained of drink, abuse, and desertion; men of slovenly housekeeping or lack of congeniality.   The most harassed-looking of the claimants for divorce was a Moscow policeman, who may have been a lion in battling with the city's criminal classes, but had apparently come out second best in arguments with a redoubtable mother-in-law whom he accused of ruining his domestic happiness.   The policeman's troubles were not necessarily ended when his divorce form was filled out; for every divorce case the clerk announces that neither partner in a dissolved marriage has the right to eject the other from a room which has formerly been in their joint possession.   Owing to the acute housing shortage in Moscow, it frequently happens that divorced people continue to live in the same room — separated, if possible, by a curtain or a piece of furniture.   Often the husband brings his new wife to his part of the room, or *vice versa.*

The Zags which I had visited registered in one year 3862 marriages and 2906 divorces.   Unfortunately, general statistics for marriage and divorce throughout the Soviet Union are not published.   In the textile town of Ivanovo, in 1932, there were 1731 marriages and 502 divorces; 1933 revealed almost the some proportion: 1700 marriages and 491 divorces. If one considers that no stigma attaches to unregistered unions, that the term "illegitimate child" has no meaning in Russia, and that changes are probably still more frequent in the case of unregistered unions, it seems safe to say that the extreme easiness of divorce in the Soviet Union makes for somewhat greater instability of marital relations than one finds in other countries. On the other hand, organized prostitution has very greatly diminished by comparison with pre-war time.

Divorce for the asking is not the only factor which has changed beyond recognition conventional family and home life in the Soviet Union. The whole tendency of Soviet education is to place loyalty to the Communist Party, to the supposed interests of the working class, above the older mutual loyalties of husband and wife, parents and children. The Soviet stage and Soviet literature abound in plays and books in which the wife denounces a counter-revolutionary husband to the authorities, or a son in the Red Army does not spare his own father if he finds him fighting on the side of the Whites. Such cases have been and are not infrequent in real life. Moreover, the economic dependence of wife on husband and of children on parents is greatly diminished under the Soviet system. The wife who does not work outside the home in the towns is an exception; on the collective farm the women work in field or dairy and get their share of earnings quite separately from their husbands. Students in the Soviet higher schools look, not to their parents, but to the state for support.

There has been a further upheaval in domestic relations because of the very great socialization of daily life. The extremist theories of the Communist Sabsovitch, who wished to make all future apartment houses communal in character and to educate children completely apart from their parents, have, indeed, been rejected, partly because they would have proved too expensive in practice, partly because they aroused too much popular protest. The principle of the individual family apartment is kept in new dwellings.

But life itself has tended to drive people out of their homes during recent years. The woman who works in a factory or office finds it convenient to turn over her young children to a *crèche* or kindergarten. Home cooking has lost its savor as a result of meagre and unappetizing rations; the most substantial meal is often to be had only in some kind of public dining room. Under prevalent conditions of overcrowding, the average Russian's living quarters are not very attractive; and this stimulates a tendency to spend leisure away from it, in the numerous workers' and employees' clubs in winter and in the public parks and on the boulevards in summer.

New Russia, this younger generation that has now grown up entirely under Soviet influence, is developing very largely without three of the oldest and most deep-rooted human institutions: religion, the family, and private property. In regard to the family and to private property, some compromise tendencies are already visible. The extreme sexual promiscuity which was both fashionable and general among the Young Communists and the "emancipated" Soviet younger generation a decade ago is now officially frowned on. Excessive loose living, like excessive drinking, is a recognized ground for expulsion from the Communist Party or from the Union of Communist Youth. There was a time when the typical Young Communist, rather amusingly and paradoxically, considered Western dancing immoral, while he looked on any kind of stable marriage with a good deal of contempt. Now the attitude is changing on both these subjects: Young Communist leaders extol the advantage of permanent marital relations, — provided, of course, that they are based on mutual love and comradely mutuality of interests, — and the fox trot and similar jazz dances are beginning to emerge from their former underground and surreptitious state as dance halls are being opened.[4]

While large fields of activity are barred forever to private ownership under the Soviet system, there is a marked and increasing tendency to insist on the principle of unequal pay for unequal work.   The importance of giving the individual more material stimulus by awarding higher pay and bonuses for more capable work is becoming more and more firmly embedded in Soviet psychology, as will be shown in detail in a later chapter.

Only in the case of religion does Soviet antipathy to this "opium for the people" remain uncompromising and unabated.   Here the great riddle of the future is whether Communism itself will assume the functions of a popular religion or whether the tendency to seek for some non-materialistic interpretation of life will ultimately, in some form, reassert itself.

When one makes every allowance for the unseen and unheard dissenters who exist under every dictatorship, there would seem to be no reason to doubt that, in the main, the Soviet régime has brought up a loyal younger generation, saturated with Communist ideas, feeling that it has a stake in the new order and ready to fight for it.   It is noteworthy that Hitler and Mussolini also have more enthusiastic ad-

---

[4] It is at least conceivable that some old features of home and family life will creep back if food and housing conditions ever become appreciably easier.

mirers who are under thirty than those over thirty. And this would suggest that there is something fallacious in the idea that individual liberty has a special appeal for youth. The full implications of liberty, and of the denial of it, are apt to come with maturity; and youth, at least in some countries, seems to enjoy the process of marching in step, of being bound together by compulsory common ideas — and of figuratively or literally knocking on the head critics of those ideas.

XIII

OLD RUSSIA IN NEW MASKS

"Thus developed the Moscow state. Now we can scarcely understand and still less feel what sacrifices its creation cost the people's welfare, how it pressed upon private existence," says V. Kluchevsky, in his *Course of Russian History*.

This is how one of the greatest and most eloquent of Russian historians interprets his country's development during the Middle Ages. And these words of Kluchevsky could well be the epitaph of Russia's Iron Age. The people who lived during that age certainly have some conception of what sacrifices of the people's welfare an absolutist state, intent on a grandiose project of natural reconstruction, can demand, of how heavily such a state presses on the private existence of the individual.

With nations, as well as with individuals, the past casts long shadows. There is so much that is strikingly, obviously, flamboyantly new in the Soviet system that the foreigner who spends a short time in Russia may quite naturally come to the conclusion that there has been a complete break with everything that antedates the Bolshevik Revolution.

But the longer I have lived in Russia the more I have been impressed by the tremendous grip which former administrative ideas and practices still maintain, by the numerous links and parallels, some curious, some humorous, some sinister, which unmistakably bind the autocracy of the

Romanovs, and of still earlier Tsars, with the Union of Soviet Socialist Republics. I am convinced that one can learn more about the spirit and the realities of the Soviet Union by reading a few good histories of Russia than by poring over innumerable speeches of Soviet leaders, with their stereotyped phrases and endless statistics.

The strongest link between old and new Russia is the absolutist character of the state, with its inevitable corollary: utter contempt and disregard for the rights and interests of the individual when these come into conflict with the supposed interests of the state. The Tsars ruled for their own glory and that of God; Stalin rules in the name of the dictatorship of the proletariat and the future world revolution. The masks are new, but the technique of government is strikingly similar; both the crowned autocrats of the past and the uncrowned autocrat of the present find it necessary to put to death and to hold in unpleasant places of exile what would seem in a Western country an abnormally large number of people. To make the parallel more complete, let us turn to Kluchevsky's description of the state of affairs under the Empress Anne, in the first half of the eighteenth century: —

Espionage became the most encouraged state service; everyone who seemed dangerous or inconvenient was eliminated from society. Masses were banished; altogether under Anne more than 20,000 were banished to Siberia, and it is impossible to find a trace of where 5000 of these were sent.

This was Russia in 1730. It would hold just as good for Russia in 1930, except that the number of persons banished would have increased more or less in proportion to the growth of the population. And how many more traits of likeness there are in the Soviet and Tsarist administrative psychology! The spirit of the pre-war organized pogrom lives again in the liquidation of the kulaks; the one was a race atrocity, the other a class atrocity.[1] The liquidation of the kulaks took far more victims. And the Tsarist prosecutors who worked up fantastic ritual murder charges against the Jews have found worthy successors in Gay-Pay-Oo examining magistrates who manufacture sabotage charges which are just about as credible as ritual murder — as when they accuse unfortunate bacteriologists of spreading poisoned serum or insist that elderly retired professors of history are promoting intervention from Germany.

In the autumn of 1929 many thousands of German colonists from Siberia flocked to Moscow and took up quarters in the suburbs of the city, asking permission to go abroad. As industrious and capable farmers with strong religious convictions they had suffered still more than the Russian peasants from the simultaneous Soviet drive against the well-to-do peasantry and against religion. Their behavior was perfectly peaceable; many of them belonged to the Mennonites and to other sects which are opposed on principle to the use of violence. They committed no overt act that might have justified the action of the Gay-Pay-Oo in carrying out a series of nocturnal raids on their settlement and forcibly deporting great numbers of them in freight cars either to

[1] I remember vividly a meeting at the large Kolomna metal factory at which I was present in the winter of 1929–1930, when a Communist woman agitator, with a peaked, fanatical face, urged the young workers at the meeting to go into the villages and help the authorities liquidate the kulaks. Perhaps this woman was a genuine self-sacrificing idealist; but the effect of her speech, for its victims, would be just as terrible as that of the address of a Black Hundred mob organizer of Tsarist times who would have been urging the masses to go and loot the homes of the Jews.

their abandoned homes — where food prospects were, to say the least, bleak, since they had been stripped of their grain by ruthless requisitions — or to concentration camps. (A minority of them were allowed to get abroad and finally settled in South America.) An official of the Commissariat for Foreign Affairs expressed great indignation to me because the plight of these refugees and their treatment by the Soviet Government had aroused comment in Germany.

"They are our citizens, are n't they?   We can do what we like with them," was his argument.

The irony of this attitude lay in the fact that this man had been obliged to live abroad, on account of his political convictions, under the Tsarist régime.   In those days he would doubtless have done everything in his power to enlighten foreign opinion about any case of oppression or maltreatment of the peasants by the Tsarist officials.   Now, himself a part of a new ruling system, he fell into the same formula with which a Tsarist official would have doubtless brushed away foreign protests against pogroms and other atrocities: "Our citizens.   We can do what we like with them."

When one begins to compare the Soviet Union during its Iron Age with Russia under Peter the Great, at the end of the seventeenth and the beginning of the eighteenth century, parallels are as thick as mushrooms.   Peter's basic idea of introducing in Russia the trades and industries which flourished in Western Europe had many obvious points of similarity to the Soviet five-year plan; and his success, measured by the number of factories and other enterprises which he started, was considerable, if one takes into account the almost universal illiteracy in Russia and the lower technical resources of that period.   The parallel with the five-year plan is further strengthened if one recalls that Peter's changes were accompanied by most severe deprivations for the population and by the ruthless smashing of many old beliefs and habits. It is a matter of historical record that Peter, who towers above almost all his predecessors and successors in energy and strength of personality and who had the sincerest belief that he was working for Russia's ultimate good, found himself obliged to squeeze more out of the population, especially out of the peasantry, than the sleepy early Romanovs who preceded him — a circumstance which, along with his innovations, convinced many of his subjects that he was Antichrist incarnate.

In reading Russia's classical economic history, M. Tugan-Baranovsky's *The Russian Factory in Past and Present*, I was surprised to find how many concrete problems of economic development in the time of Peter the Great and his successors were similar to those which confront Stalin and his associates at the present time. "Throughout the whole first half of the eighteenth century," writes Tugan-Baranovsky, "complaints of factory owners about the lack of workers do not cease."

Throughout the five-year-plan, Soviet factory managers, especially in new construction sites, were continually voicing the same complaint. The remedies which were found for the situation were not dissimilar. In Peter's time workers were "attached" to factories for a period of ten years; now excessive mobility among workers and slacking on the job are attacked by such methods as the widespread use of forced labor, the taking away of food cards from persistent "fliers," — or persons who "fly" from one job to another, — the exaction of pledges from workers to remain at their posts for fixed periods, and so forth.

Soyuzphoto

The Assembling Plant of the Stalin Motor-Car Works

We read in Tugan-Baranovsky that "the goods produced in Russian factories [of the eighteenth century] were distinguished by extreme expensiveness and low quality," and that this state of affairs persisted, despite the action of the state in fining the administrative department or guild which was responsible for the management of the factories. This seems to forecast the efforts, largely futile up to the present time, of the Soviet authorities to raise the notoriously low quality of factory output by prescribing sentences of imprisonment up to five years for managers, engineers, and others who may be found guilty of putting goods of defective quality on the market.

And there is a distinctly modern ring about Tugan-Baranovsky's statement, which refers to Russia in the eighteenth century, that "it was difficult to hold foreign experts, because they demanded much money and seldom adjusted themselves to Russian conditions." More than one American engineer or mechanic who quit the Soviet Union in a huff because of red tape, or hard living conditions, or a dispute with the authorities as to whether his contract called for payment in Soviet rubles or in some more solid currency medium, was unconsciously following in the footsteps of his British, Flemish, and German predecessors of two centuries ago.

The foreign technical assistant or advisor has been a constant figure on the Moscow scene for centuries, although his functions change, of course, with the passing of time and the new developments in industry. Foreigners are no longer physically segregated, as they were in the so-called *nemetzkaya sloboda,* or German Settlement, which existed in the seventeenth and eighteenth centuries. Yet the average foreign specialist or engineer who is employed by a Soviet trust is sharply differentiated from the Russians by the cut and quality of his clothing, by the food which he eats, and by his general style of living. And one suspects that, if a few natural allowances are made for conditions which change with time, the comments of a group of Americans, returned to Moscow for rest and recreation and assembled in the bar of the Metropole Hotel, after bleak and strenuous field work at Magnitogorsk, Dnieprostroi, or some other Soviet "industrial giant," would not be very different from those of the typical "foreign experts" of two or three hundred years ago who might have gathered in an inn of that time — a grizzled Scotch soldier of fortune, who was trying to make the Russian levies into passable regular troops; a Dutchman who was imparting instruction in the art of shipbuilding; a German who had charge of a new ironworks. One suspects that in both cases there would be much loud talk about dirt and discomfort, about the laziness and low productivity of the Russian workers and the generally strange living conditions of the country, coupled, perhaps, with silent reflection to the effect that, as jobs were reported to be scarce at home, it would perhaps be just as well to stick it out in Russia a little longer.

Foreigners in Russia have always been simultaneously spied on and pampered; they have never been subjected to the full rigors of the formidably indeterminate penal code which Tsars and Soviets have reserved for their own subjects. President Roosevelt's insistence, in the negotiations which preceded recognition, that Americans in the Soviet Union shall be free to establish their own churches has a parallel in the mediæval arrangement for the Germans; and a diligent research student even discovered the interesting fact that something in the nature of the present system under which foreign embassies are required to pay for food in some other currency than Soviet rubles existed in Moscow two or three centuries ago.   The virtues of Poor Richard have never been characteristic of Russian individuals, still less of the Russian state; and, if one excepts a period of a few decades immediately before the war, Russian currency has always been somewhat lacking in the qualities of stability and solidity.

Russia has always looked on the West with a peculiar mixture of superiority and inferiority.   "The rotten West" was a phrase beloved of the reactionary mystical Slavophiles who saw in autocracy, the peasant commune, and the Orthodox Church institutions which placed Russia far above the Western countries, with their cold liberal parliamentarism and capitalism.   The Young Communist of the present time is also trained to look with contempt on the "rotten West," which is always depicted to him as decaying and breaking up, while the Soviet Union, by contrast, is represented as moving from victory to victory.   Yet, along with this current of extreme national self-sufficiency, there has always been a contrary current in Russian life of excessive self-deprecation, of uncritical admiration of everything foreign. Peter the Great and Stalin have both, probably unconsciously, endeavored to solve this contradiction by borrowing from the West its technical achievements, while severely repressing any infiltration of the Western idea of individual liberty.

Perhaps as a result of its vast bulk and of its special geographical position, linking up Europe and Asia, Russia has always felt a vague conviction that it had a Messianic mission to perform for the whole world.   Nicholas I, who was in some respects the most perfect type of autocrat among

the Romanov Tsars, was not content to be an unlimited ruler
in his own country. He wished to make absolutism the
dominant principle of government throughout Europe.
When the Austrian Empire, after 1848, was rocked with
national and social unrest, Nicholas dispatched Russian troops
to help the Austrian Emperor maintain conservative "law
and order." Obsessed with this same conception of an
international mission, the Bolshevik leaders at the present
time, despite many disillusioning disappointments, are still
not ready to admit that the Bolshevik Revolution was a
national Russian upheaval and not a prelude to world
revolution on the same model.

Extreme secretiveness is another of the many administrative practices which the Bolsheviki have taken over, in
somewhat intensified form, from their Tsarist predecessors.
The Communist historian, M. N. Pokrovsky, tells how,
under Nicholas I, secrecy was carried to such an absurd
point that every document in the Ministry of Foreign Affairs,
however trivial, was marked "secret" or "very secret," so
that other means had to be found in order to mark out those
documents which really were of first-rate confidential importance. Pokrovsky derives from this fact the conclusion
that secrecy was the characteristic sign of a serf state.

One fears that he proved rather too much by this statement, because the annals of Soviet bureaucracy are full of
examples of exaggerated secretiveness which would seem
incredible in many other countries and which are no less
absurd than those of the "serf state" of Nicholas I. A
correspondent who recently inquired about the total number
of marriages and divorces in the Soviet Union was informed
that this was a state secret. The same answer was given by
an official of the Commissariat for Foreign Affairs when he

was asked for information as to the personnel of the Soviet War Commissariat. (This information, amusingly enough, was then found in an official publication of the Commissariat for Foreign Affairs.) Every journalist, every student of economic affairs, knows that statistical and other information which is given without a second thought in most countries is often withheld and cloaked with an atmosphere of profound secrecy in the Soviet Union, and that when it is given it is not infrequently far from reliable. A correspondent who had just returned from a trip through several districts of Ukraina and the North Caucasus, where local officials confirmed the universal peasant testimony of abnormal mortality as a result of hunger in the winter and spring of 1932–1933, went to the Commissariat for Health in Moscow and asked a responsible official in its foreign department what were the figures of mortality from famine. Perhaps taking the correspondent for a naïve and inexperienced foreign visitor, the official blandly replied: —

"Such a question could only excite a smile. There were no deaths from hunger at all."

Just at the time when the Soviet Government was prohibiting foreign journalists from traveling in the famine regions I happened to read a biography of Tsar Boris Godunov by Stephen Graham and was naturally struck by the following passage: —

He believed he could overcome rumor by silence. He believed he could hide self-evident truths by national pretense. The famine brought beggary and misery upon his reign and the injury to his good name as sovereign mortified him much more than the famine itself. He feared lest the catastrophe be noised abroad. So he organized prosperity parades before the foreign ambassadors in Moscow to make them think things were not nearly so bad as

they had been told.   At the beginning of 1603 it was forbidden
for anyone to appear in rags in the streets.   Conversation with
foreigners was forbidden, lest someone should tell them of the ruin
that had befallen Russia.

This passage described a Tsar's efforts to suppress news
of a famine that occurred in 1602–1603.   It could serve
almost equally well as a description of the Soviet Government's effort to hide from the outside world the famine of
1932–1933.

That the yoke of state service under Tsar and under
Soviets was a hard one is evident from the curiously similar
experiences of two men who broke away from it — Gregory
Kotoshikin in 1664, Gregory Besedovsky in 1929.   Kotoshikin was an employee in the Ministry of Foreign Affairs
who was beaten for making a mistake in writing the title of
the Tsar.   Becoming involved in a further scrape, he did
not wait for a second punishment, but fled across the frontier
to Poland and made his way thence to Sweden, where he
wrote a book which gave a most unfavorable picture of state
and private manners and morals in seventeenth-century
Russia.

Gregory Besedovsky, who had served for almost a decade
in the Soviet diplomatic service and had occupied the
responsible post of Counselor of Embassy in Tokyo, Warsaw,
and Paris, created a momentary sensation by leaping over
the wall of the Paris Embassy and appealing to the Paris
police for assistance in rescuing his wife and child, who,
he said, were being held as hostages for his return.   The
Soviet version of this curious diplomatic incident was that
Besedovsky had embezzled public funds; Besedovsky insisted that he was marked for execution on his return to
Moscow because he disagreed with Communist Party policy.

Whatever may have been the measure of truth in each version, Besedovsky promptly followed in the footsteps of his predecessor, Kotoshikin, publishing several books in which he gave a most unflattering picture of the methods of Soviet diplomatic missions abroad and of the foreign representatives of the Gay-Pay-Oo. Kotoshikin came to a bad end; he was beheaded because of a murder which he committed in the course of a private quarrel. It remains to be seen whether the twentieth-century fugitive from Russian diplomatic service will have better luck.

One could go on multiplying curious and ironical parallels between personalities and events in Old and in New Russia indefinitely. The similarities of administrative method between Tsarist and Soviet Russia are even more striking and more significant than the persistence of certain traits of Russian character: incurable unpunctuality, for instance, or keen popular enjoyment of music and drama.

Behind this tradition of the absolutist state in Russia lie, of course, definite and peculiar features of Russia's historical development. The mediæval Muscovite state grew up and expanded in a process of ferocious and protracted struggle with the Tartars and with other Asiatic barbarians. This struggle had two natural effects: a tremendous strengthening of the central governmental power, embodied in the Tsar (European visitors to Russia in the sixteenth and seventeenth centuries repeatedly expressed amazement at the absolute power of the Tsar, compared with that of their own sovereigns); and a certain brutalization of the national character as a result of the continuous sanguinary warfare.

Russia's history is notably lacking in those elements which placed a bar upon absolutism during the Middle Ages and paved the way for the ultimate emergence of democracy: powerful, semi-independent feudal lords, free cities, a Church which could face the State on equal or superior ground, a landed yeomanry, free from the shackles of serfdom. Russia has no such traditions as the English barons at Runnymede or John Hampden refusing to pay his ship-money levy on a question of principle or Luther nailing his theses to the door of the Wittenberg church. It knew only the unlimited power of the Tsars, the heavy bureaucratic rule of the Tsarist state machine, occasionally varied by fierce outbursts of anarchy such as the peasant rebellions of Razin and Pugachev.

Even non-Communist Russians are sometimes inclined to admire the tremendous scope of their country's revolution, to feel that, whatever its cruelties and blunders, it did create something new under the sun. In many respects, of course, this is true. But at the same time I seriously doubt whether the establishment in Russia of some form of liberal democracy, under which no citizen could have been herded into a freight car and shipped off to forced labor without open trial, would not have been a greater revolution, a greater breach with all the traditions of the Russian past, than the substitution of the Soviet dictatorship, with its Gay-Pay-Oo, for the Tsarist autocracy, with its Okhrana (secret political police).

Perhaps the strongest reason for disappointment with the final outcome of generations of Russia's revolutionary struggle, which had so many heroes and martyrs, is not that so much has been transformed and destroyed, but that so much of the Tsarist technique of government — stifling of free criticism, all-pervading espionage, arbitrary arrest and banishment of political suspects — has been taken over unchanged or preserved in aggravated form.[2] One feels that Rileev, the poet of the Dekabristi, or Sofia Perovskaya, who paid with her own life for the assassination of Alexander II, might not have fitted into the régime of Party dictatorship, might have felt uneasy and rebellious under the ever-watchful eyes of the Gay-Pay-Oo spies. But Nicholas I, the Tsar-provocator, who personally took charge of the cross-examination of some of the Dekabrist leaders in order to entrap them into full confessions, would certainly have been a useful recruit for the Gay-Pay-Oo; one is certain that he would never have let any *saboteur* go for mere lack of evidence, that he would have tolerated no deviation from the Party "general line."

It is the historical tragedy of the Bolshevik Revolution that, in the struggle to get and keep power, it unconsciously assumed so many features of the despotism which it set out to overthrow. This, incidentally, is a tragedy that has often repeated itself in various countries and in various forms.

Part of the tremendous fascination of the Soviet Union lies in the fact that it offers so much that is new and untried in economic and social fields; that it has changed the ideas and living habits of the people, especially of the younger

[2] That Soviet repression is more severe than that of the Tsars is scarcely open to denial. The Tsarist Government severely controlled and repressed opposition newspapers; the Soviet Government forbids them altogether. The Tsarist Government crippled the effective functioning of opposition political parties through administrative discrimination and through the agency of an indirect election system which gave very great advantages to the nobility and to the propertied classes in the cities; the Soviet Government outlaws all opposition parties and the Communist Party is quick to suppress any opposition groups which form within its own ranks. Far more people in Russia were executed or were banished to hard labor without public trial and for political offenses during the period 1928–1933 than during the last five years of Tsarism, 1909–1914.

generation, so greatly. But on the numerous occasions when one can see Old Russia peeping out behind the transparent new Soviet masks, when one can see the mentality of a mediæval autocracy curiously reproducing itself as part of the ideological armor of the dictatorship of the proletariat, one senses very strongly the profound skeptical wisdom involved in the French proverb: *Plus ça change, plus c'est la même chose.* ("The more it changes, the more it remains the same.")

XIV

THE HUMAN BEING UNDER COMMUNISM

One of the most debatable as well as one of the most important questions which the Bolshevik Revolution has raised is whether and how far a new social and economic system can change what is rather vaguely called human nature. How does the human being react to Communism, which takes away many of his old stimuli, destroys many of his familiar ideals, and offers him new ones in their stead?

My own opinion is that the Soviet régime has, in many ways, affected and changed human behavior without, however, necessarily altering the underlying motives of this behavior. A point that is often emphasized by Communists and by sympathetic foreign visitors to Russia is that wealth is not an ideal in the Soviet Union. The secretary of the Union of Communist Youth, Kosarev, once declared that no Soviet youth, if asked what he desired to become, would say that he wished to be a rich man; he would rather express a desire to be an engineer or technician, to be Stalin.

This is unquestionably true; but it does not prove that the younger generation in Russia is any more self-sacrificing or idealistic than the younger generation in any other country. Wealth is desired in most countries because it implies ease, comfort, security, social respect. It is not desired, at least by any rational person, in the Soviet Union, because there it implies precisely opposite things: degradation, persecution, endless worry, most probably ending in enforced transportation to Solovetzky Island or the Narim territory or some other highly undesirable place of exile and forced labor. As a matter of fact, a Soviet citizen at the present time could no more aspire to be a capitalist than an American or Englishman could aspire to be a slave owner. Every door that leads to the accumulation of a large personal fortune has been closed, barred, and triple-bolted. The limited concessions which were made to private business enterprise under the New Economic Policy have been swept away, and no one in the Soviet Union, to-day may own or operate the smallest kind of store, workshop, or restaurant, while private farming is also well on the way to elimination.

Under these conditions it is inevitable that the ambition which under a different system might find one means of expression in building up a fortune can find an outlet in the Soviet Union only through promotion in the state service. It is not the first time in history that wealth has been an object of contempt and reprobation. It is safe to say that the typical young man of the Middle Ages looked with more admiration and envy on the penniless knight who wandered through the world seeking adventures or on the barefoot monk whose words could sway huge audiences than on the Jewish money-lender, whose wealth was accompanied by marks of degradation and by constant insecurity of life and property.

The Soviet system does not offer wealth as a stimulus; but it does offer to men who rise high in the hierarchy of political and industrial administrators the equally strong incentive of power, accompanied by a standard of living which, while it is modest by comparison with what a wealthy man of luxurious tastes might choose to enjoy in America or Western Europe, is still far above the bleak Soviet average. True, a Soviet Commissar or "captain of industry" receives a moderate salary (although it may seem ridiculously small to a foreigner who is accustomed to think of the Soviet ruble as worth about two cents). But the position of a Soviet high official is something like that of an army officer in many other countries; the salary is small, but the perquisites of office are compensatingly numerous. A high post in the Soviet Union carries with it a comfortable apartment, the use of an automobile, the right to eat in a good restaurant at a nominal charge, admission to the best rest homes and sanatoria in vacation time, a private car for travel on the railroads, and so forth.

And the whole tendency in the Soviet Union at the present time is not to diminish material inequality, but to increase it by insisting that the more skilled and industrious worker in any field must receive more than his fellows. Equal wages may be the ideal of Mr. Bernard Shaw; it certainly is not the ideal of Stalin, who devoted some of his sharpest denunciation at the last Party Congress to those Communists who practise, favor, or condone *uravnilovka,* to cite a Russian term that is much in use but hard to translate, and that may best be rendered as "equalization" or "leveling."

"*Uravnilovka* in the sphere of consumption and personal life is reactionary petty-bourgeois nonsense, worthy of some primitive sect of ascetics, but not of a socialist society." Starting with this emphatic condemnation, Stalin added that there will be no *uravnilovka* even in the final phase of Communist society, when all are supposed to work according to their capacities and to receive according to their needs. Because, to quote Stalin again, "Marxism proceeds from the assumption that tastes and needs are not and cannot be the same as regards equality or quantity either in the period of Socialism or in the period of Communism."

All this is a far cry from the distinctly leveling tendencies of the first years of the five-year plan. In 1929 and 1930 the liquidation of the private traders in the towns and of the kulaks in the villages was interpreted by many rank-and-file Communists as the first step toward a society where material equality would prevail, where everyone would eat the same amount of food and be clothed in much the same way.

I met a vigorous exponent of this point of view in a former Red partisan who was fulfilling the tasks of a political organizer in a newly established collective farm in the lower Volga in 1930. "The liquidation of the kulaks is only a first step," he declared. "The next step will be that all state employees will enjoy the same standard of living."

"So you will earn as much as Stalin," I suggested, half jokingly.

"That certainly is our final ideal," he replied very seriously; "that there should be no classes and that no one should receive more than his fellow workers."

At that time village Communists often tried to force the peasants to organize complete communes, where all would eat at a common table and even such remnants of individual ownership as the family cow and chicken would be thrown into the common pot. In the towns Young Communists began to organize "living communes," where all put whatever wages they earned into a general fund, from which they received whatever was considered necessary for food and clothing.

Now such tendencies in village and city alike are severely

frowned on. A long process of trial and error has led to the recognition of the artel, where the peasant keeps his own house and garden, his cow and pig and chickens (if he is lucky enough to possess them), as the most workable form of collective farm. Anything that smacks of equal wages for work of uneven quantity and quality is considered thoroughly reprehensible; and the old ideal of the Soviet trade-unions, gradually to pull up the more poorly paid workers to the level of the more highly paid, is "right opportunism," a very abusive phrase in the Soviet Union.

Every kind of differential stimulus is being applied with a view to stimulating greater productivity in the factory, greater efficiency in the office, even greater proficiency on the part of students in the higher schools. Because of the low purchasing power of the ruble and the rationing restrictions, money wages alone are not as potent an incentive as they are in other countries. So all kinds of other inducements are pressed into service. The *udarnik*, or skilled and industrious worker, gets a better meal at the same price in the factory restaurant, receives first consideration when new apartments are ready for occupancy, is given preference when it is a question of admission to rest homes and sanatoria. A striking application of the principle of serving the *udarnik* first is to be seen at the State Opera House, where almost all the seats in the orchestra are marked with plates as reserved for *udarniki* of various institutions. The persons who occupy these seats are not necessarily manual workers; they may also be officers of the Red Army, engineers, specialists, employees, students, who are supposed to have performed meritorious service.

The stipends which are paid to students are also made dependent upon the quality of their work. The bright student receives a higher stipend; the hopeless dullard is struck off the state pension list altogether.

An oft-repeated slogan of the second five-year plan is "the creation of a classless society." [1] To a superficial observer this might seem to suggest greater material equality. But in its actual application the slogan seems likely to be conservative rather than revolutionary in its results. Once there are officially no more classes, there is no justification for class hatred and class envy. The unskilled laborer who in 1937 may grumble when he compares his Spartan fare and cramped living conditions with the higher standards of Soviet executives and engineers will be not a proletarian justly indignant at his lowly lot, as he would be in a "capitalist" country, but a misguided comrade, who must be instructed in the harmfulness of *uravnilovka* and the blessings of payment by piecework.

So Russian Communism, as it is working out to-day, shows no indication whatever of developing into a system of communal living and equal sharing. In this respect, indeed, the Soviet system is far less "communistic" than were the agricultural settlements established by the Doukhobors and by other sects which disapproved of private ownership of property before the Revolution. The whole emphasis of the very great change it has brought about is placed on the abolition of the possibility of employing one man by another for purposes of private profit, which, according to Communist economic dogma, is always a matter of exploita-

---

[1] It has never been quite clear to me why the abolition of classes is timed to coincide with the end of the second five-year plan. In one sense there are no classes in the Soviet Union now, since kulaks and private business men have certainly been effectively eliminated. If, on the other hand, abolition of classes connotes general material equality, this is not in the Communist programme for 1937, or for any other future date.

tion. Its concern is not that everyone should receive the same wage (indeed, this is definitely condemned as harmful and undesirable), but that the state should be, in one form or another, the universal employer and the general paymaster.

Communism has its non-material incentives. A large part of the huge national propaganda effort is devoted to praising efficient workers and denouncing slackers on "the labor front." In line with Stalin's declaration, on one occasion, that "the country must know its heroes," feats of scientific and labor achievement are described in the press; and such decorations as the Order of Lenin and the Order of the Red Banner of Labor are awarded to men and women who have especially distinguished themselves. In Moscow's Park of Culture and Rest one finds a proletarian counterpart to Berlin's Sieges-Allee in the Udarnik-Allee. Here, instead of the kaisers and princes of mediæval Germany, one can find the faces of *udarniki* — the shock workers — of Moscow factories, commemorated in sculpture by Soviet artists.

A system of "socialist competition" between factories, which endeavor to beat each other's records in increasing output and reducing costs, and between gangs of laborers in factories and on construction enterprises, has gone into effect. The groups or departments which are winning in such competitions are given such designs as airplanes or express trains; those who are behind are ridiculed in the factory newspapers by being shown with figures of camels or crabs.

All this doubtless has its effect on morale and psychology, especially in the case of the younger workers and engineers. A tragic case occurred in a Moscow factory in 1934 when a young engineer committed suicide because he had been held up to public reprobation and ridicule for an offense of which, as was later brought out, he was not guilty.

But up to the present time, at least, the rôle of these new "socialist incentives" is distinctly secondary. Experience has shown that the main motive of the Soviet worker or employee is not unlike that of the worker or employee in other countries — to improve his material condition in life. This is why the Soviet policy during the Iron Age of sacrificing the well-being of the population to the ideal of rapid and intensive new building seems, in retrospect, to have been of questionable economic advisability. It seems quite probable that the provision of more beefsteaks and shoes, more shirts and gramophones, would have stimulated higher productivity of labor and would have meant surer and more genuine, if less spectacular, industrial progress.

Quite typical of the relative importance of the materialistic and the propaganda inducements to work has been the experience with the system of singling out the more industrious and capable workers and calling them *udarniki*, or shock workers. When this system was introduced in 1929, the appeal was largely sentimental; the *udarnik* was supposed to get his reward in public approval, in the consciousness that he was "building socialism." But with the passing of time the system acquired much more prosaic stimulants, and now the *udarnik* is spurred on by the prospect of the material benefits which a more skilled worker would get under a capitalist system: more and better food and clothes, a better apartment in which to live.

No discussion of the human being under Communism would be complete without a description of the status of the industrial worker, in whose name the Revolution was made. Officially the Soviet state is a dictatorship of the proletariat. Hostile critics have described it as a dictatorship over the proletariat. And curiously enough both definitions possess some elements of truth. The proletariat — that is, the manual working class — has a far larger share of power and opportunity than it possessed in pre-war Russia. In some respects it obtains greater special consideration than the corresponding class in other countries. Yet at the same time the Soviet worker, the theoretical sovereign of the country, is more bamboozled than the worker in countries where the press is free, and less protected against exploitation than his fellow worker who may belong to a trade-union of his own choosing in a democratic country. For the experience of Russia's Iron Age would certainly indicate that the state, as well as the private employer, can be an exploiter.

The young Soviet worker has far greater educational opportunity, far more chance of entering a profession, than he would have enjoyed twenty years ago. If one can see the worst side of Bolshevism in a famine-ravaged village of Ukraina or the North Caucasus, one can find its most constructive achievements in an industrial town such as Ivanovo (formerly Ivanovo-Voznesensk), which was well known before the war as a centre of the textile industry. Here, among a number of post-revolutionary educational institutions, one can find a chemical institute with about a thousand students, mostly children of the workers of Ivanovo and neighboring towns. Over half the students in the Russian higher schools are of working-class origin. There is a rapid process of sifting out the brighter and more capable children of workers and promoting them to higher posts in the state service.

The industrial laborer in Russia also gets the benefit of a statutory seven-hour day,[2] with one day's rest in six; of a comprehensive system of health and accident insurance; of an annual two weeks' vacation with pay. A network of rest homes for workers and employees on vacation has grown up all over the country. While these places have suffered during recent years from overcrowding and from the general food stringency (the most comfortable conditions are to be found in the vacation homes reserved for high Party and Soviet functionaries and for Red Army officers and Gay-Pay-Oo officials), they represent a means of organized recreation for the workers that was almost nonexistent in pre-war days.

The worker to-day is reading more, is playing more organized games, and is therefore less likely to go on the debauch that was often the sole recreation of the laborer in Tsarist times. One sees a much higher percentage of workers at the opera, at theatres and concerts, than would have been the case before the Revolution. The manual worker is deliberately given preference in many details of daily life; while this works hardship and injustice to persons who lacked the good judgment to select parents of indubitably red-blooded proletarian origin, and while class favoritism in any form certainly does not promote efficiency,[3]

[2] The seven-hour day is pretty faithfully observed in factories, but is often exceeded in new construction enterprises. There is a legal six-hour day in mining, but the period is reckoned from the beginning until the end of work, not from the time of going into the pit.

[3] It has long been a pet theory of mine that the country which would make access to its higher educational institutions and promotion in its state service and in its industrial life dependent solely on merit, quite irrespective of wealth, birth, race, or nationality, would make amazing progress in every field of achievement. The Soviet Union, after making such a clean sweep of old distinctions of rank and property, might have

this fact strengthens the hold of the Soviet régime on the masses. It is almost taken for granted, for instance, that the director of a factory or the president of a provincial or city Soviet must be an ex-worker.

The active-minded worker also gets a good deal of satisfaction out of participating in the many commissions which exist in every factory. He has a good chance of being elected to his city or district Soviet, which means that he may investigate schools, hospitals, public institutions, to his heart's content, and offer suggestions for their improvement. Among workers who are Communists by conviction one sometimes finds a feeling that the factory where they are working is "their own," a feeling which is stimulated because Soviet social life is largely built up around the factory, with its club, sport teams, dramatic circles, and the like.

So much for the dictatorship of the proletariat. Now for the dictatorship over the proletariat. The worker in Russia is, after all, a cog in a state machine, the workings of which he has no direct means of controlling. Many of the biggest questions affecting his daily life are decided by a little group of men in the Kremlin in whose selection he

---

attempted to test out this theory by application. But any move in this direction was thwarted by the extreme class bigotry of the Soviet Union, which can only be compared with the racial bigotry of present-day Germany, with the inverted snobbishness which took the form of giving the workers, not the equal opportunity which they were denied under the autocracy, but heavily weighted favoritism — in the form, for instance, of very high quotas of admission to the higher schools, which excluded more gifted students if they belonged to other classes, and especially if they were of "bourgeois" origin. I was once talking with two Russian friends, one of whom remarked that in pre-war days offices were often given to incompetent noblemen, with the result that the actual work had to be done by someone else. "It is just the same to-day," observed my second friend. "Very often a high technical post is given to an inexperienced Communist worker, and some anonymous non-Party expert must do the work."

has no voice and whose decisions he has no means of criticizing or resisting. He has no more voice in deciding who is to manage the factory in which he is employed than an American steel worker has in the choice of the directors of the United States Steel Company.

In Western democratic countries, independent trade-unions protect the everyday interests of the workers. The Soviet trade-unions are thinly disguised organs of state, dominated by appointees of the ruling Communist Party, who are more interested in forcing up production than in voicing demands for the best possible real wages and working conditions. This tendency has always existed; it has been very greatly strengthened since the former head of the trade-unions, Mikhail Tomsky, was accused of "a trade-unionist deviation" and replaced by a more obedient executor of Stalin's policies in the person of Shvernik.

The sacrifices which the worker has been compelled to make for the sake of industrialization have not been as formidable as those which have been required of the peasant, but they have been heavy enough. While the average monthly wage of the Russian factory hand has increased between 1929 and 1933 from about seventy-five rubles to about one hundred and twenty-five rubles, his cost of living has doubled or trebled, even when one makes the most generous allowance for the fact that prices in his coöperative shop were controlled and therefore rose much less than prices on the free market. Nothing in all Soviet statistical practice is more mendacious than the recording of paper-ruble wage increases without reference to the all-important fact that many articles which could easily be bought at moderate prices without restriction as to quantity in 1926 and 1927 are now unobtainable or can only be had in minute

L. Kagan and I. Rappoport, Members of the O.G.P.U., in Charge of General Work on the Baltic–White Sea Canal

rationed quantities in coöperative shops, while prices on the free market and in commercial stores have risen five, ten, in some cases even twenty fold or more.[4]

If the worker wishes to have vegetables in the family larder he must often spend his free day working in his own or in the factory garden.[5] As against the legal shortening of the working day, by comparison with pre-war conditions, one must set the dreary hours which are wasted in queues, the fierce struggle to get on and off street cars, all the strain which the worker, like every other Soviet citizen, feels as a result of the lack of adequate housing, transportation, and supply.

The few soft things of life in the present-day Soviet Union go, in the main, not to the theoretically sovereign proletarian, to the man who is actually operating a machine or hacking out coal in a mine, but to the higher ranks of the Soviet bureaucracy. One of Russia's innumerable "anecdotes" tells how a worker, struggling for standing room in a packed street car, pointed to high-placed officials who were riding past in comfortable automobiles and sarcastically remarked: "I am the boss. Those people are just my clerks."

The fact that a Soviet trade-union is a department of state, rather than an independent class organization of the workers, is reflected in a number of Draconic laws and administrative practices which are designed to maintain labor discipline, but which would not be tolerated by the working classes in countries where they possess the right of free trade-union

[4] A cake of very poor milk chocolate which could have been bought for thirty kopecks in 1926 or 1927 is now priced at twelve rubles.

[5] The *subbotnik* is another means of encroachment on the free time of the worker or employee. While these labor expeditions on free days are supposed to be voluntary, a good deal of social pressure is brought to bear on people who are indisposed to join in them.

organization and of striking as a means of redressing grievances. Under a law which was promulgated in November 1932, any worker or employee who is absent without leave for a single day loses his job, his food card, and his room, if the latter is assigned to him by the factory or institution where he is working. A decree published on March 20, 1934, prescribes that workers may be docked of their wages when the quota for quantity and quality of work is not fulfilled, even if the worker is not personally at fault. There have been repeated instances when workers and employees on the railroad lines have been shot because they were held responsible for accidents — a measure, incidentally, which has not reduced the high number of wrecks on Soviet railroads. Strikes are outlawed in fact, if not in theory, in the Soviet Union. Anyone who began to agitate for a strike would be regarded as a "class enemy" and treated accordingly. Consequently the workers at those new construction enterprises where food and housing conditions are especially bad have developed a passive kind of protest by drifting in masses from one job to another — so far, of course, as they are free to do so. The exiled kulaks and other people at forced labor are compelled to remain where they are sent.

Both the real and important educational advantages and facilities for advancement which the Soviet régime has given to the working class and the hard conditions of daily life affect the psychology of the Soviet worker to-day. Which aspect bulks larger depends on individual temperament and psychology.

In every Soviet factory there is a group of "activists," mostly members of the Party and of the Union of Communist Youth, with a sprinkling of non-Party workers. This group stiffens the morale of the plant, pushes through every campaign which the Party initiates, and generally constitutes a nucleus on which the Soviet régime can rely in the factory. Along with these staunch supporters of the new order, who naturally occupy the leading posts in the Party organization and in the factory committee, there are middle-aged workers who are more interested in the bread-and-butter things of life. Their attitude is one of passive acceptance of the existing order, qualified by some bitterness and grumbling when material conditions become too difficult or when the factory manager presses on them too hard for higher productivity.

Finally, there are the young workers, who are unusually numerous because of the rapid growth in the number of workers and employees during the last few years. (At the end of 1933, there were 21,883,000 workers and employees, as against 14,530,000 in 1930. The number of manual workers in industry and transport during this period increased from 5,079,000 to 6,882,000.) This working-class youth, like Soviet youth in general, is more inclined than are the older workers to discount the hardships of the present and to take an optimistic view of the future.

Inasmuch as almost half the population of the Soviet Union consists of non-Russians, the feelings of the individual about the Soviet régime are often affected by its nationality policy. There has been no theoretical modification of this policy, which is based on the right of every people in the Soviet Union, however small and obscure, to use its own language in schools, courts, and public business. However, as a result not of racial chauvinism but of geographical accident, some of the bitterest hardships of the Iron Age occurred in non-Russian sections of the country — notably in Ukraina, in Kazakstan, and in Central Asia. These hardships, in turn, generated a mood of popular discontent which easily assumed an anti-Soviet nationalist hue.

On July 8, 1933, the Soviet newspapers published a statement from the Communist Party Central Committee announcing that N. A. Skripnik, formerly Commissar for Education in Ukraina, had committed suicide, and stigmatizing his suicide as "an act of cowardice, especially unworthy of a member of the Central Committee."

Behind that cold and dry *communiqué* was a poignant personal tragedy. Skripnik was a veteran Ukrainian Bolshevik, a man with a long pre-war record of underground activity, a participant in the Bolshevik Revolution and in the civil war in Ukraina. This old revolutionist was not so hard-hearted as some of the younger men whom Stalin sent to Ukraina with instructions to squeeze out the last bushel of grain and to drive through collectivization, even if the price of it was famine. He was attacked in the press and at Communist meetings as "too nationalistic" and found his way out in suicide.

Skripnik's suicide was only one dramatic symptom of the deep discontent which prevailed in Ukraina in 1932 and 1933, and which here and there led to the resumption of activity by the anti-Bolshevik Ukrainian nationalists that had once followed the leadership of Petlura, who was assassinated in Paris in 1926 and whose aim was an independent non-Soviet Ukraina. There were many arrests, especially among Ukrainian intellectuals, and as remedial measures the Party Central Committee proposed that there should be a careful purge of scientific and educational institutions where the presence of separatists was suspected; that the works of Marx, Engels, Lenin, and Stalin should be published in Ukrainian; and that "Bolshevik control" should be established over Ukrainian literature and art, evidently for the purpose of rooting out any traces of separatism.

This disaffection in Ukraina had its roots not in a systematic preference of Russians to Ukrainians in state offices, not in any suppression of the Ukrainian language, but in the ruthless agrarian policy dictated from Moscow, which led to hunger as early as 1931 and to widespread famine in 1932–1933. Some of the more fertile regions of Ukraina before the war had a fairly high percentage of peasants who were reasonably well-to-do, by Russian standards, and the lot of these peasants was changed very much for the worse by collectivization.

Against a different and Asiatic background this same drama of economic discontent finding nationalist means of expression has been played out in Central Asia and in Kazakstan in recent years. Toward the end of 1933, Maksum, the President, and Khadjibaev, the Premier, of the Republic of Tadjikistan — which borders on Afghanistan and includes the lofty Pamir area, "the Roof of the World" — were summarily deposed from office. The Secretary of the Communist Party organization in Central Asia, Bauman, accused them of committing or tolerating "too widespread an application of administrative measures, searches, and arrests," of permitting the torturing of peasants by the use of cold water and by placing iron hoops around their heads, and also of being national chauvinists. So, according to Bauman, Maksum and Khadjibaev had advocated the driving of all Russians from Tadjikistan and tried to discredit the local Gay-Pay-Oo as "a Russian body."

In view of the secrecy which surrounds the removal of

high Soviet officials from office, it is difficult to say with certainty whether Maksum and Khadjibaev were more objectionable because of their Oriental methods with recalcitrant peasants or because of their anti-Russian attitude; but their elimination was only an episode in a very fierce struggle which has been proceeding for years in Central Asia. Originally this struggle assumed the form of an effort on the part of the Communists to break down the traditional features of Mohammedan life — the veiling of women, the acquirement of brides by purchase, and so forth. More recently it has become sharper because of Soviet insistence that cotton, in many places, be planted instead of rice. In view of the general shortage of provisions, this enforced substitution of a market crop for a food crop sometimes caused hunger in the regions where it was carried out and excited strong resistance.

It is a significant and genuine achievement of the Soviet régime that no one is debarred by his race or by the color of his skin from rising to the highest offices of the land — provided, of course, that he adheres strictly to the Party line. But the autonomy of the various republics which make up the Soviet Union, never very real, has been still more curtailed during the Iron Age, with its intensive centralization. The head of one of the federated Soviet Republics has about as much power as the ruler of a "protected" native state in India; he is liable to swift political elimination if he ever fails to carry out the instructions which emanate from Moscow.

What kind of balance will finally be struck between the power of the state and the scope of the individual personality under the Soviet system is a fascinating question to which no final answer can yet be given. In the early years of the five-year plan the whole tendency was strongly in the direction of completely flattening out the individual under the huge collectivist steam roller.

Stalin's six conditions for the management of Soviet industry, proclaimed in the summer of 1931, heralded a turn in the tide, and since that time the Soviet leaders have shown a disposition to give the individual more leeway within the iron framework of an economic system which permits no private ownership of means of production. It is now a fixed rule of Soviet economic enterprise that the director of a factory shall have unlimited authority, along with full responsibility;[6] the whole trend of the reorganization of Soviet administration carried out in 1934 was in the direction of getting away from the *collegia*, or commissions, which were formerly in every Commissariat, and substituting the leadership and authority of the Commissar alone; the differential-wage stimulus is being more and more vigorously applied in industry and in agriculture.

Concessions to the individual are more slowly and grudgingly given by the Soviet leaders in the realm of thought than in the sphere of economic incentive, where an overwhelming weight of experience has shown that no satisfactory results in industrial development can be achieved except on the basis of rewarding good work and penalizing bad work and of giving the manager of a state enterprise generous authority along with strict responsibility. Yet it is a sign

[6] M. M. Kaganovitch, a brother of Stalin's chief lieutenant and himself a prominent official in the Commissariat for Heavy Industry, writes as follows in the course of an article about the proper management of Soviet factories: "It is necessary above everything to strengthen single-headed authority [*edinonachalie*]. It is necessary to proceed from the basic assumption that the director is the complete chief in the factory. All the employees in the factory are completely subordinated to him." Cf. *Za Industrializatziu* ("For Industrialization"), for April 16, 1934.

of the times that children in Soviet schools in the future are to be taught about the personalities of the outstanding Tsars and Tsarinas, as well as about the economic features of their reigns.

Confronted with the most formidable machine of state propaganda and compulsion of which history has any record, the human personality in Russia is still able to claim some rights; it is one of the paradoxes of Soviet development that the huge process of industrialization in which the Soviet leaders see the final triumph of collectivism is demanding, for its successful functioning, more and more regard for the interests and desires of the individuals who must operate it.   Indeed, one may say that a main general problem of the Soviet Union is to find out how much individualism must be conceded in order to make a collectivist system work, just as a main problem in other countries is to find out how much collective control must be established in order to make individualism work.

XV

CULTURAL LIFE IN THE IRON AGE

THE pontifical Dr. Samuel Johnson once announced that education in Scotland was rationed like food in a besieged city; no one starved, but no one had a full meal. However true this observation may have been as regards Scotland in the eighteenth century, it certainly has some application to cultural life in the Soviet Union.

By comparison with pre-war times, far more people in the Soviet Union can now read and write; there has been a sweeping spread in educatoin of all types during recent years; what with special trade courses, classes for training illiterates, new scientific research institutes, over and above the regular educational system, one sometimes has the feeling that the whole country, or at least the whole younger generation, is at study.

On the other hand, original creative thought, outside those purely natural sciences where there can be no plausible effort to organize a "class front," is certainly uncommon under the Soviet system. The decimation of the old intelligentsia through emigration, through sabotage trials, through the removal of non-Marxist professors from many departments of teaching in the higher schools; the bringing in to the high schools and universities of a vast raw mass of students from families where there were no inherited habits of thought, study, and criticism; the harsh insistence, backed

up not infrequently by administrative repression, that the
"Party line" must be the guiding rule in art and literature,
as well as in politics and economics — all this tends to place
on Soviet culture a stamp of dull uniformity, of unquestioning conformity to ideas and slogans which are handed down
from above.

It should be noted that the word "culture," as it is used
in the Soviet Union, has a different and much more practical
significance than one associates with it in America or
Western Europe. Soviet culture has nothing to do with
Matthew Arnold's "sweetness and light," or with ability
to decipher Greek and Latin texts, or with erudition and
æsthetic taste. It means rather an observance of the simple
rules of good manners and cleanliness and hygiene, in which
the Russian masses before the Revolution often had little or
no training.

A *kulturni chelovek* in Russian might be literally trans-
lated into English as "a man of culture." What it would
mean, under Soviet conditions, is a man who knows the uses
of a toothbrush, who bathes fairly regularly, who does not
get into drunken brawls or curse his neighbor with the traditional unprintable "mother oath" — in short, who shows
signs of developing into a model Soviet citizen. The un-
ceasing campaign for "culture" in this sense of the word
is an important phase of the general Soviet effort to remake
the country by means of propaganda.

The base of the educational system in every country is the
elementary school. Here, as in practically every field of
Russian life, there have been enormous changes during the
Iron Age. For the first time in its history, Russia now
has universal compulsory primary education, with a minimum
term of four years; and the number of pupils in the ele-

mentary schools has increased from 11,697,000 in 1929 to 19,163,000 in 1933. The number of students in middle schools has grown from 2,453,000 to 6,674,000, and the number in higher schools from 207,000 to 491,000.

The very speed of the development of the Soviet school system has led to some inevitable "growing pains." School buildings are apt to be overcrowded, and studies are often carried on in two or even three shifts. There is a shortage of trained teachers. Schoolbooks, pencils, and paper sometimes do not go around. On a walking trip which I took with some Russians in the high mountains of the West Caucasus, the children in one district asked every passer-by for a pencil, which was probably an ingenious local teacher's way of remedying the local deficiency in school supplies.

But, when one makes allowance for all these shortcomings, education has made unmistakable progress during recent years; and there has also been a substantial improvement in the quality of the instruction in the elementary schools. This improvement is the result of what might be described as a conservative revolution in Soviet teaching methods.

During the decade between 1921 and 1931, the typical Soviet school suggested something in the nature of a joyous bedlam. Discipline was so lax as to be almost nonexistent, and the authority of the teacher was at a minimum. New pedagogical methods, based on the more novel theories of Western educators, were tried out in quick succession, often with scant regard for the technical preparedness of the Russian teachers and schools. Such "bourgeois" means of testing pupils' fitness as marks and examinations were discarded. The teaching of separate subjects was supplanted by the so-called "complex" method, under which a class was supposed to work on a given theme, — a city street, for instance, or the season of the year, — learning in the process a bit of geography here, a bit of arithmetic or history there.

It is not surprising that such methods produced a scrap-heap, hodgepodge kind of knowledge on the part of children who were subjected to them. The Soviet school child got a very uneven kind of training and was apt to display precocious brightness in some things, along with a woeful lack of exact knowledge about others.

In 1931 the disadvantages of this state of affairs began to impress themselves on the Soviet authorities. An important factor in bringing about this realization was the failure of many young engineers and specialists, after graduating from Soviet schools, to measure up to the technical requirements of the posts to which they were appointed. Anatole Lunacharsky, who was more suited for oratory and for æsthetic criticism than for the practical administrative tasks which were connected with the direction of the Russian school system, was replaced as Commissar for Education[1] by the vigorous Andrei Bubnov, who had organized the propaganda and educational work in the Red Army. And Bubnov carried out such a sweeping reorganization of teaching methods that the Soviet schoolroom to-day is almost unrecognizable, compared with what it was a few years ago.

The teacher has become, if not an autocrat, at least an undisputed leader in the classroom, endowed with ample disciplinary powers for use against refractory pupils. Marks and examinations have been restored; and the importance of the traditional three R's and of other basic subjects — such as grammar, geography, natural sciences, and so forth — is

[1] Lunacharsky was subsequently appointed Ambassador to Spain, but died before he took up the duties of his new office.

again fully recognized. The "complex" method has been cast into the discard, and teaching is again by individual subjects. Efforts at group preparation of lessons, which were formerly encouraged as Communist in spirit, are now frowned on; the desirability of testing the individual capacity of each student is recognized.

The bad heritage of a chaotic and slovenly past has not been entirely overcome. *Izvestia* in 1933 published the following candid summary of an investigation of the knowledge of 65,000 Soviet pupils: "Bad grammar, abundance of mistakes in spelling, low level of knowledge of literature, insufficient acquaintance with mathematics, poor knowledge of the map in geography, superficial and often politically incorrect information in civics and social sciences."

But when one visited a Soviet school in 1933 or 1934 one carried away an impression that the pupils were working hard and acquiring definite knowledge — something which could not have been said of the Soviet schools of a few years ago. The restoration of conventional teaching in the schools, like the establishment of the full authority of the director in factories and other state enterprises and the insistence on unequal wages for unequal work, is an illustration of the flexibility which the Communist leaders sometimes show in scrapping experiments which have proved clearly inefficient or unworkable.

The organization of the higher schools has completely changed during the last few years. Universities, in the old sense of the term, have ceased to exist. In their place have come specialized "institutes," where students are trained as engineers in different branches of industry, agricultural specialists, teachers, doctors, and members of other professions. These institutes are under the direct control of the organizations which will later employ their students. So the Commissariat for Heavy Industry has charge of many engineering schools; the Commissariat for Transport supervises the training of future railroad engineers; medical students come under the Commissariat for Health, and pedagogical students under the Commissariat for Education.

In these specialized institutes, as in the elementary schools, discipline has tightened and there has been some improvement in the standards of study. At the same time, Soviet higher education still has its conspicuous defects. The selection of students, in part at least, according to considerations of class origin or Party allegiance, rather than in accordance with capability, does not make for the highest scholastic standards. The institute principle of organization, while it perhaps serves a utilitarian purpose by giving quick intensive training to some of the specialists who are badly needed everywhere, is open to the objection that it tends to produce a narrow and one-sided type of education. The genuine popular hunger for knowledge that is behind the many new educational institutions which have been springing up all over the country is one of the most hopeful features of contemporary Russian life. But in many cases the immediate effectiveness of the new schools is very much lowered by the hard and crowded conditions in which many students live, and by the absence, in some cases, of trained teachers.[2]

[2] I once heard an enthusiastic admirer of the Soviet régime describe for the benefit of a few newly arrived tourists a "collective farm university" which had been established in a remote town, hitherto bereft of educational institutions. The narrative went on swimmingly until one of the tourists quite innocently asked, "And who were the teachers?" The speaker paused, hesitated as if the question had hitherto not been considered,

Three very distinctive higher educational institutions are the Communist Academy, the Institute of Marx and Engels, which has now been fused with the Lenin Institute, and the Institute of Red Professors. The Communist Academy grew up as a sort of revolutionary supplement to the famous Academy of Sciences in Leningrad, which was founded by Peter the Great. Whereas the latter is mainly devoted to research in the natural sciences, the Communist Academy, which has departments in economics, history, law, and a number of other subjects, concentrates its attention upon the application of Marxian formulæ to the social sciences. According to its constitution, the Communist Academy is supposed to "work over the problems of Marxism and Leninism, struggle with bourgeois and petty-bourgeois distortions of Marxism, struggle for the strict observance of the point of view of dialectical materialism both in social and in natural sciences, and expose the remnants of idealism."

The Young Communist scholars of the Academy take these militant injunctions very seriously and are always quick to see the hidden hand of the bourgeoisie in the most remote crannies of art, literature, science, and architecture. A typical title of a lecture at the Academy is "Bourgeois Tendencies in Architecture and How to Combat Them."

While it was under the direction of the internationally famous Marxian scholar, D. B. Ryazanov, the Institute of Marx and Engels built up an impressive collection of material about the lives and times of these two founders of materialistic socialism. No such mass of material about Marx

---

and finally blurted out, "Heaven knows," following this up with a slightly lame anticlimax to the effect that "anyone who knew something about birds" undertook to give the collective farmers a course on ornithology.

and Engels has ever been housed under one roof before. Many unpublished letters and newspaper articles, written anonymously or under pseudonyms, have been brought together for the first time; and the Institute has published voluminous editions of the writings of Marx and Engels in Russian and in German. Its hundreds of thousands of volumes and tens of thousands of periodicals include, besides the mass of material on the lives and activity of Marx and Engels, rich collections relating to the French Revolution, to the Wat Tyler rebellion, to the Levelers of Cromwell's time, to the Chartist Movement in England, to the Revolution of 1848 in Germany and France, and to the writings of philosophers who especially influenced Marx and Engels, such as Hegel and Fichte. The Institute was recently fused with the Lenin Institute, which specializes in the collection and publication of all Lenin's writings, and lost its gifted head in 1931 when Ryazanov was accused of sympathy with an alleged Menshevik plot and sent into exile.

The Institute of Red Professors is training a future generation of professors of history, economics, law, political science, and philosophy who will teach these subjects from a strictly Communist standpoint. While candidates for admission to this Institute must be Communists, with a record of five years of membership in the Party, contact with advanced education seems occasionally to have corrupted the ideological soundness of some of them. The percentage of expulsions from the ranks of the Red Professors of Trotzkyists or other heretical sympathizers was considerably higher than the percentage in the Party as a whole.

Throughout the Iron Age, Soviet intellectual life has been

very much under the influence of two slogans: "Art on the Class Front," and the *"partiinost"* (Party character) of science. The strained, militant character of the period swept away what little æsthetic tolerance had formerly existed. The Glavlit, or Board of Censorship, always strict in its scrutiny of new books and new plays, became a veritable inquisition, eager to ferret out the faintest trace of·skepticism which might be tucked away in a novel or a drama; and its efforts were ably assisted by a group of militantly "proletarian" authors, such as the playwright and novelist Kirshon and the poet Bezimensky, who were always quick to denounce fellow authors in whom they detected any taint of heresy. Addressing the Communist Party Congress in the summer of 1930, Kirshon laid down what might have been described as the æsthetic code of recent years in the Soviet Union in the following terms: —

"In relation to bourgeois ideology, as on all fronts, we must pass over to decisive offensive, mercilessly liquidating the bourgeois ideology. . . . The class enemy on the literary sector becomes active. In a moment of sharpened class struggle any liberalism, any respect for æsthetic language, even though it may be directed against us, is direct aid to the class enemy."

Sometimes the efforts to link up everything under the sun with the application of the teachings of Marx and Lenin went to such absurd lengths that educated Communists themselves were moved to call a halt. For a time a group of physicians banded themselves together under the title "Leninism in Medicine." A certain Comrade Gubkin lamented the absence of Marxist-Leninist theory in Soviet forges and foundries and pronounced the judgment that "not one machine must be set up or ordered from abroad

without an adequate Marxist basis." A journal entitled
For Marxist-Leninist Natural Science blossomed forth with
such slogans as "For Party Spirit in Mathematics" and "For
Purity of Marxist-Leninist Theory in Surgery."

A well-known Communist professor, A. Stetzky, raised
a voice of protest against this tendency, observing that some
Soviet scientists, instead of mastering their subjects, preferred to indulge in pompous and empty generalities about
Marxism, and coldly inquiring, "What is the value of a
declaration about Party spirit in mathematics if the people
who proclaim this slogan do not know mathematics?"
Stetzky characterized as charlatans people who profess ability to teach "how to operate blast furnaces on the basis of
Marxism-Leninism, or how to build houses on the foundation of dialectic materialism." He recommended the dis-
solution of the special societies of "Marxist Physiologists,"
"Marxist Physicians," and "Marxist Mathematicians" which
had grown up around the Communist Academy.

But, while some of the more comical excesses of this
effort to place art and science on the "class front" occasionally
excited rebukes, the pressure on the author, the artist, and
the scientist to hew very closely to the "Party line" has
been tremendously strong and is clearly reflected in the
changed character of literature and drama after 1928. It is
not good for one's health to be an outspoken noncon-
formist. There was the case of an eccentric philosopher
named Losev, who played an amusing trick on the censorship by writing a book under the harmlessly dull-sounding
title *The Dialectics of the Myth* and loading it down heavily
with metaphysical matter which would conduce to boredom
and neglect on the part of the official who was charged with
deciding whether or not the book was fit to print. Then,

in the latter part of the work, Losev inserted the following "dangerous thoughts": —

"Proletarian ideologists are sometimes indistinguishable from capitalist snakes and jackals."

"It is impossible for Communists to love art. Once there is art, there is genius. Once there is genius, there is inequality. Once there is inequality, there is exploitation."

"To burn people at the stake is more beautiful than to shoot them, just as Gothic architecture is more beautiful than modern barracks, church bells than automobile horns, and Platonism than materialism."

The sequel to this joke was not so amusing; not only was the book confiscated, but Losev himself was sent to Solovetzky Island, and even distant acquaintances, who had no responsibility for the heresies of his book, were arrested and exiled. More recently an author named Erdman, who had written a play, *Mandate*, which was sufficiently Communist in spirit to be produced at the Meierhold Theatre, was banished, along with some associates, because they had been indiscreet in repeating satirical stories and making up humorous skits about Stalin and about Soviet conditions in general.

Apart from the possibility of falling into the bad graces of the Gay-Pay-Oo, the Soviet author is subjected to a kind of pressure which is milder, but probably no less effective. If his work deviates too much from the official point of view, it will sooner or later cease to be printed. Hence it is not surprising that during the last years, when the demands upon the authors not only for loyal but for enthusiastic support of Soviet policies and Communist ideas have been more and more insistent, many of the *poputchiki* — or "traveling companions," as Soviet authors who maintained some reservations about accepting the whole Communist programme and philosophy were called — should have gone much farther in professing allegiance and should have written novels glorifying all the characteristic features of Soviet policy, from new factories, electrical power stations, and collective farms, to sabotage trials.

Of course there were quite probably a number of genuine "conversions." The more impressionable younger writers and dramatists, especially if they have Communist friends, may well be carried away with enthusiasm by the new social order, by the ambitious new building which is going on everywhere. No one likes to think of himself as a hypocrite; and not infrequently the author who begins as a conformist from prudential reasons ends as a sincere believer in the things about which he is supposed to be enthusiastic.

But the element of potential repression is always there; and the drastic regimentation of the last few years has not been favorable to the artistic development of the more subtle and gifted Soviet writers. One suspects that some striking tragedies, both of personal life and of artistic creation, have taken place under a system which was once officially described to me by Mr. Felix Kon, head of the Fine Arts Department of the Commissariat for Education, in the following words: —

"Art is for the masses. It must aid in remoulding all economic life. Art organizes thought. And, as it formerly served the priesthood, the feudal classes, and the bourgeoisie, it must serve the proletariat in the Soviet Union."

There is undoubtedly a considerable class of authors and poets, playwrights and artists, who feel themselves so thoroughly in harmony with the existing régime that they are not conscious of any repression. There is Bezimensky, for

THE "AGITATION BRIGADE" OF THE KUKHMISTEROV WORKERS' CLUB, MOSCOW, WHO MAKE PROPAGANDA INFECTIOUS IN THEIR TOPICAL PLAYS AND SKITS

instance, who goes from Magnitogorsk to Dnieprostroi and from Dnieprostroi to some state or collective farm on the Don, inexhaustible in energy, in enthusiasm, and in a knack for turning out rather simple rhymes. There is Jack Althauzen, a very popular poet among the Young Communists, whom I recently heard declaim two of his better-known works, "The First Generation" and "The Beardless Enthusiast." The former was a glorification of the present Young Communist generation that has been mobilized to build factories and railroads, to work in mines and timber camps; that went willingly wherever it was sent, to the deserts of Central Asia, to the icy wastes of the North, conscious of its mission as the builder of a new society. "The Beardless Enthusiast" is the outburst of a Young Communist who regrets that he could not have given up his life on the battlefields of the civil war.

There are the Soviet artists who participated in an exhibition of paintings depicting scenes of the Russian civil war and of Red Army life and who sent to War Commissar Voroshilov a message with the following militant sentiments: "We artists with our works want to shoot at our class enemies as Red Army soldiers have shot and will shoot. You have taught us fighting art, class art."

There is Kirshon, an ambitious Young Communist who has made himself something of a dictator in Soviet letters and who achieved a kind of distinction by writing a play, *Bread,* in which every character looks, talks, and acts precisely like a wooden phrase in a *Pravda* editorial. Inasmuch as *Bread* is symbolic of the propaganda play which has dominated the Soviet stage in recent years, a brief description of its plot may not be out of place. Although the acting and staging of this play at the Art Theatre were excellent, as always, one felt that the characters should really have worn large distinctive labels: "General Party Line," "Left Opportunist," "Right Opportunist," "Class-Conscious Poor Peasant," "Kulak."

"General Party Line" in Kirshon's play is represented by Mikhailov, the model Secretary of a Communist Party District Committee, while the "Left Opportunist" who serves as a foil to Mikhailov's shining virtues is another Communist, Raevsky. In the first scene these two characters are so plainly stamped that their future development is easily predictable. While Mikhailov, wearing a collarless Russian blouse, is absorbed in his manifold administrative duties, Raevsky, dressed in suspiciously good clothes which he has acquired during a visit to Berlin, enters and begins to entertain Mikhailov's wayward wife, who is becoming tired of the dull life in a small town and, one suspects, of the everlasting righteousness of her spouse.

Grain has to be extracted from unwilling peasants. Raevsky first essays this task, lets himself be thwarted by the kulaks, and gives up in disgust. Then Mikhailov appears on the scene and obtains the grain by the simple device of telling the peasants that, if they point out the kulaks, the latter alone will have to deliver the grain, whereas otherwise all will have to contribute. Raevsky almost spoils the situation by arbitrarily imposing an extra grain levy on the village; but Mikhailov saves the situation by hurrying back, repealing the levy, catching some kulaks who try to murder him, and completing his record of good deeds by handing over for trial the crestfallen Raevsky, who has already been severely bumped on the head by the kulaks.

The other characters are just as dry and stereotyped as Mikhailov and Raevsky. The leading kulak is wily and sinister, as kulaks are in Communist storybooks; a one-armed poor peasant illustrates the working of economic determinism by stoutly upholding the Soviet régime; a former nun introduces the necessary note of antireligious agitation, first by living in free union with the kulak, second by expressing a fervent desire for the return to power of Nicholas II.

The Kirshons, Bezimenskys, Althauzens, are sincere and enthusiastic upholders of the Soviet régime; they may quite reasonably feel that in no other country would they have enjoyed such wide scope and appreciation. But they have made no serious permanent contribution to Russian literature; there is perhaps no more striking proof of the zigzag movement of literary achievement than the fact that in 1833 Russia's outstanding poets were Pushkin and Lermontov, while in 1933 they were the "proletarian" rhymesters, Demyan Byedny and Bezimensky. Vladimir Mayakovsky, a poet of greater stature and originality, who was especially beloved of the younger Soviet generation of readers because of his exaltation of the machine age and his glorification of raw, uncouth strength, violated one of the chief canons of the Communist faith by committing suicide in 1930.

While the prose and verse propagandists have possessed a broad and free field during the Iron Age, the more sophisticated and thoughtful authors have experienced increasing constraint, which is very often reflected in the quality of their work. Among the few novels which stand out by reason of merit of various kinds during the last few years one may mention Sholokhov's *Tranquil Don*, an epic picture of Cossack life before and during the World War and the civil war; Aleksei Tolstoy's *Peter the First*, which is especially successful in reproducing the atmosphere of

Peter's time; V. V. Veresaev's *Sisters,* a story of Young Communist and workers' life which was not sufficiently orthodox to win the approval of Soviet critics; and Kataev's *Time, Forward,* which was one of the best of the *genre* novels written on the overworked theme of new industrial building.

Maxim Gorky, who is a sort of author laureate in the Soviet Union, and whose efforts to relax the chains which Communist fanaticism is inclined to place upon literary creation may be weighed in the balance against his public endorsement of the action of the Gay-Pay-Oo in shooting without trial forty-eight specialists in the food industry, has returned to his old field of activity as a dramatist. His two new plays, *Egor Bulichev* and *Vassily Dostigaev,* which deal with different phases of the 1917 Revolution in a provincial town, are not comparable with his greatest work, *The Lower Depths,* but they are well above the Soviet dramatic average in color and spirit.

A very notable Soviet musical achievement is Dmitry Shostakovitch's opera, *The Lady Macbeth of Mtzensk County,* based on a story by the pre-Revolutionary author Lyeskov. Both the grim, sardonic character of the plot and the power and passion of Shostakovitch's music suggest the greatest of Russia's classical composers, Moussorgsky, and place Shostakovitch among the foremost modern composers. Painting has never been one of the arts in which Russia was predominantly represented, and its quality has deteriorated under the Soviet régime. Indeed, most of the paintings submitted by the artists who expressed to Voroshilov the desire "to shoot with our works at the class enemy" might easily inspire the thought that the authors might do well to forsake the brush for the gun. A high level of achievement is to be found only in cartoons and caricatures, which

are, of course, best adapted to the spirit of an intensely
propagandist age. The development of the Soviet moving
picture, an art in which the country a few years ago stood
very high, has been disappointing. Among the great producers, Eisenstein was absent for a long time in America
and Mexico, and Pudovkin has been groping during the
last years without repeating the distinguished work which
he achieved in *The Fall of St. Petersburg* and *Storm over
Asia*. The Ukrainian Dovzhenko, whose *Arsenal* was one
of the best civil-war films, produced an excellent work
entitled *Earth*, which depicted the struggle in the village
over the establishment of a collective farm. It was, however, sharply attacked, partly because the producer had not
directed enough attention to the required theme of class
struggle, partly because one of the scenes, in which a peasant girl tears off all her clothes in a fit of despair over the
death of her lover, offended the curious streak of puritanism
that sometimes makes itself felt in Communist leading
circles. *Earth* received very few showings in Russia.

When repressive censorship was at its height, from 1929
until 1932, scarcely any literary or dramatic work with a
spark of originality could escape the carping attacks of the
sticklers for one hundred per cent "class art." During the
last year or two there has been a little relaxation of the
pressure; and the new officially approved slogan for authors,
"socialist realism," permits somewhat greater latitude in
the selection of themes and the handling of characters.
However, until the censorship is abolished altogether or
at least restricted to purely political questions, it seems improbable that Russia will be able to produce literature and
drama worthy of the artistic taste and capacity of the people
and of the splendid interpretative powers of the theatres,

several of which easily rank among the best in the world.

It is true that a great Russian literature was created during the nineteenth century, in spite of Tsarist censorship; but there is a very great difference between Tsarist and Soviet censorship, as there is between Tsarist and Soviet methods of propaganda in general. The Tsarist censorship was purely negative and did not affect an author who was content to leave political themes alone. There was no effort in pre-war days to force novelists to sing hymns of praise to the Tsarist political and economic system; the few authors who did write what might be called monarchist propaganda found few readers and are now entirely forgotten. Very different is the situation to-day. Not only is open criticism of the existing régime, of course, forbidden, but the author is expected to strike a positive note, to show that all is working out for the best in the Soviet world. If he does not, the stigma of the class enemy may be affixed to him.

No one who reads the Russian classical authors, Tolstoy and Dostoevsky, Turgeniev and Gogol, would be likely to derive an idea that Tsarist Russia was a happy place for its inhabitants or that there was anything particularly admirable about the Tsarist system. No such attitude of neutrality is possible to Soviet authors who wish to be printed, and until a novelist in Russia is free to depict his characters more as genuine human beings and less as figures in a Communist morality play the literature of the Soviet Union will labor under the heavy handicap imposed by the stamp of official propaganda.

Other fields of intellectual life have suffered even more than literature and drama from the deadening effect of censorship, combined with the exclusion from activity of the older men of learning, and the failure, as yet, to develop new scholars of corresponding ability. Soviet history is a dreary waste, as I can testify from personal experience after having faithfully read through hundreds of books and historical magazines dealing with the Revolution and the civil war. Not much certainly can be expected in the way of integrity or originality when Communist dogma regularly takes precedence over facts and when a word from Stalin is sufficient to cause a wholesale rewriting of historical text-books and a suppression of relevant historical evidence.

Biography is in an even worse plight; it would certainly be difficult to name even one first-rate psychological study of a man of eminence in any field which has been written since the Soviet régime came into power. Intelligent studies of other countries are also conspicuously lacking; *Confrontation*, which purported to be a study of English life by Madame Sokolnikov, wife of the former Ambassador in London, is so full of absurd misstatements and exaggerations that it could only be compared with the most extravagantly hostile and superficial books which have been published abroad about the Soviet Union.[3] Here again the curious Soviet mediæval tendency to accept dogma as a substitute for reality has a paralyzing influence upon objective judgment. No one in the Soviet Union would be permitted to tell Soviet readers that the influence of the

[3] Among Madame Sokolnikov's "discoveries" in England were that most English girls over twenty have false teeth, that patients in charity hospitals are required to rise from sick beds in order to kiss the hands of visiting patronesses, and that education at Oxford costs more than a thousand pounds a year. She characterized the Lyons restaurants in England as "parodies on Soviet public dining rooms," but I think anyone who has eaten in both institutions would be inclined to feel that the parody was the other way round.

American and British Communist Parties on the working-class movements of those countries is negligible.

In the field of natural sciences the situation is distinctly less favorable. Chemistry, biology, geology, physics, and kindred branches of learning are most intimately bound up with any programme of industrial development along modern lines. The Soviet leaders have realized that science must advance if the Soviet Union is to have any chance of realizing their dream of "overtaking and outstripping the leading capitalist countries." As has already been pointed out, there has been a notable increase in the number of students in the Soviet higher and middle schools, and scientific, technical, and mechanical subjects are especially popular. The government has made appropriations for the maintenance of numerous experimental and research institutes in agriculture and in various branches of science, among which the Tsagi, the institute for aviation research, has attained the highest reputation.

The work of such scientists as Pavlov in conditional reflexes, Joffe in physics, Vavilov in applied botany, Gubkin and Fersman in geological research, has attracted international recognition. One is impressed by the number of scientific expeditions which scour the Soviet Union from end to end. There are continual experiments, with varying degrees of success, in acclimatizing plants in new regions.

There have been few inventions of major importance; the Kazantzev railroad brake and the discovery of a process for making synthetic rubber are exceptions to this rule; and it not infrequently happens that what is described in the Soviet Union as an invention is a clumsy copy of a foreign patent. The Soviet newspapers often print sharp criticisms of the neglect and bureaucratism with which new inventions are treated. On the other hand, the introduction of many new branches of industry in the country has brought with it an assimilation of foreign technical knowledge; Russian engineers and mechanics are making many machines and other articles which were not manufactured or were produced in negligibly small quantities before the mighty drive for industrialization went into effect.

There has been a good deal of exploration, accompanied by scientific research, in little-known and remote parts of the Soviet Union. Regions in Central Asia which were formerly almost unknown have been accurately mapped, and the Soviet Union has been especially active in investigating the resources of its huge Arctic territory. The names of such scientists and explorers as Samoilovitch, Vize, and Schmidt are known to Arctic students all over the world. The heroic epic of the *Chelyuskin*, a ship which was crushed by floating masses of ice while trying to sail around Siberia (the crew and the members of the expedition on board the *Chelyuskin* were saved by a series of brilliant flights in polar-weather conditions), showed that Soviet Arctic voyagers yield to none in the world in daring and hardiness, and also demonstrated the remarkable capacity of Soviet aviators for Arctic flying.

Against the genuine and in some cases distinguished achievements of Soviet science and exploration one must set a very dark feature of Soviet intellectual life during the Iron Age: the appallingly large number of scientists and men of learning who were imprisoned and exiled without any kind of fair or public trial, in most cases without any public statement of the offenses which they were supposed to have committed. A very brief and incomplete list of the more distinguished men who have been arrested during the Iron Age includes the following names: historians, Platonov, Lubavsky, Likhachev, Tarle; agricultural experts, Kondratiev, Chayanov, Makarov; the physicist Lazarev; the statistician Kaffenhaus; the expert in bubonic plague, Zlatogorov; the specialist in old ikons, Anisimov; the bee expert Butkevitch; the oceanographer Kluge. To anyone who is familiar with Russian science these names speak for themselves, and one could add to those I have mentioned hundreds, even thousands of scientists and technical experts. It was officially stated that two thousand persons, the great majority of whom were engineers and technicians, were arrested in connection with the trial of the "Industrial Party," and the numbers of agricultural experts arrested along with such distinguished men as Kondratiev, Chayanov, and Makarov, can scarcely have been less. A pithy anecdote which enjoyed surreptitious circulation during the worst period of inquisitorial persecution of the technical intelligentsia ran as follows: "I have three sons. One is an engineer; one is an agronome; the third is also in prison."

No reasonable person would be likely to deny that a primary condition for the advancement of science is the physical safety of its more distinguished representatives, the assurance to them of such elementary rights as open trial by jury in the event that they are accused of any offense. This condition has emphatically not been realized in the Soviet Union, which during its Iron Age has enjoyed the unenviable distinction of having a far larger proportion of its intellectuals in prison or in exile than any other country in the world. Science can scarcely be expected to reach its highest possibilities of development in Russia so long as Gay-Pay-Oo investigators, who are seldom distinguished by eminent scientific attainments, are given a free hand to frame up charges of "sabotage" whenever a scientific or industrial experiment turns out badly.

Looking back over the wide field of intellectual life in the Iron Age, one sees varied and contradictory tendencies. On the positive side there has been a sweeping extension of educational effort of all kinds. Opportunities have been created for large numbers of young scientists through the enlarged quotas of admission to the higher schools, through the opening up of many new research institutes. On the other hand, the same driving fanaticism that caused the Communist rulers of the country to redouble their efforts to wipe out illiteracy, to give the masses broader educational facilities, produced far less desirable results in the cramping limitations which were placed upon the creative artist in all fields with a view to making him toe the "Party line," in the morbid, ever-present suspicion of sabotage.

It is conceivable that in the long run the educational processes which have been initiated in the Soviet Union will prove more permanent and enduring than the excesses of state-inspired propaganda which have accompanied them. When large masses of the Russian people learn to read and appreciate Tolstoy, Turgeniev, and Dostoevsky they may well turn away with a bored yawn from Kirshon and Bezimensky. But one problem which is of the very essence of genuine cultural life, of scientific and artistic progress, has not been solved. This is the problem of intellectual liberty, which means for the writer and the artist the right to follow his creative bent free from state dictation; for the historian the right to describe events as they actually occurred; for the economist and the engineer the right to express without fear of reprisals their honest opinions of this or that governmental measure; for the scientist the right to pursue experiments without being afraid that, if they turn out badly, he may be hailed before some irresponsible Gay-Pay-Oo tribunal to answer to some fantastic charge of sabotage.

XVI

THE CRUSADE AGAINST RELIGION

ONE of the most novel and distinctive features of the Soviet régime is its determination to root out every form of religious faith in the vast territory under its sway. There have been many instances in history when one form of religion cruelly persecuted all others; but in Russia the world is witnessing the first effort to destroy completely any belief in supernatural interpretation of life. This uncompromising Communist hostility to religion, which has never wavered, although the methods of combating religious faith have varied considerably from time to time, is another strong proof that Communism itself may be regarded as a new fanatical faith, if not as a new religion.[1]

During the Iron Age every militant feature of Communism became greatly intensified; and antireligious activity was no exception to this rule. Propaganda effort was redoubled. The limited liberties which were granted to re-

---

[1] It is quite significant that two other fanatical faiths which now dominate large countries, Italian Fascism and German National Socialism, although they are not philosophically committed to dogmatic atheism, have become involved in a number of sharp disputes with religious organizations. The question of the education and training of the youth has been a bitterly contested point, both in Italy and in Germany. Fanatical nationalism, like fanatical Communism, is at bottom unwilling to concede that religion may make equal or stronger demands on human loyalty.

ligious organizations in the milder years of the New Economic Policy have been withdrawn or greatly curtailed — in fact, if not in name. It is now a real test of physical courage, of willingness to endure hardship and persecution, to be known as an active believer in any form of religion. To be a priest or a minister during the Iron Age was to be engaged in a still more dangerous profession than that of the engineer, the economist, or the agricultural expert.

All the familiar potent instruments of Communist propaganda have been brought into play for the purpose of making religious faith of any kind (the Communist antireligious agitation plays no favorites as between the devotee of the Russian Orthodox Church and the sectarian, the Jew and the Mohammedan) appear at once infamous and ridiculous. The basic tenets of religion, its ministers and practitioners, are ridiculed in cartoons, caricatures, posters, and moving-picture performances, denounced in books and magazines, satirized on the stage, held up to scorn and opprobrium in the antireligious museums which have now been installed in many of the most famous Russian churches and monasteries.

The general principles underlying the Soviet drive against religion of all kinds are very similar to those which guide the editors of the numerous virulent anti-Semitic newspapers and magazines in contemporary Germany. Truth and objectivity are of minor importance; the main purpose is to defame and denounce in every way. The late French statesman, Aristide Briand, once told an anecdote of an anticlerical newspaper, where the editor, from force of habit, placed the regular headline, "Infamous Act of a Priest," over a story of how a priest had saved a boy from drowning.

A Soviet editor would be very likely to do the same thing,

Citizens in Line to Visit Lenin's Tomb

if he were so careless as to allow any piece of news favorable
to a priest or a minister to appear at all. I was once an
unnoticed witness of a characteristic episode in the unremitting drive against religion. The scene was the Moscow
office of the Union of Militant Atheists. A discomfited
photographer was receiving a severe reprimand from one of
the officials of the organization. The photographer had
been taking pictures of some sectarian artisans, and the official was quite disgusted because the photographs revealed
nothing scandalous or incriminating. "You must show
them exploiting hired labor or doing something that will
discredit them," he told the photographer. "But I did n't
see them doing anything of the kind," was the plaintive reply
of the taker of pictures, who had evidently been imperfectly
grounded in the principles of "class photography."

One of the most widespread and successful weapons in
the campaign for universal atheism is the antireligious museum. When I entered Saint Isaac's Cathedral in Leningrad, a solid and massive piece of architecture, with huge
pillars of Olonetz granite, heavy bronze doors, gilded dome,
and richly ornamented interior, I found an incongruous combination of the traditional religious background of bas-reliefs
and paintings depicting sacred scenes and the numerous ex-
hibits of antireligious propaganda which have been scattered
through the edifice.

Just above a collection of religious books in Old Slavonic
which have been preserved in the Cathedral was a text from
the works of the Communist prophet, Lenin, to the effect that
the purpose of religion is "to justify exploitation and to give
a reduced-price ticket to heaven." Near by was the following citation from Karl Marx: "The destruction of religion,
the phantom happiness of the people, is a necessary condi-

tion for their real happiness." Another quotation from Lenin was to the effect that all oppressing classes require the executioner and the priest.

The attacks on religion in the depths and recesses of this vast cathedral were carried on with a variety of methods. The Orthodox Church was depicted as an upholder of serfdom and an oppressor of the people. Baptists and other evangelical Russian sects were displayed in photographs, with accompanying accounts endeavoring to show that such groups had always been counter-revolutionary and anti-Soviet.

Much was made of the so-called crusade against Russia which had been launched by foreign churches. There were several caricatures of the Pope, one representing him as standing beside cannon which imaginary foreign interventionists were supposed to turn against the Soviet Union.

The exhibition brought out the self-mutilation and the orgiastic sex practices of some of the wilder Russian sects, such as the Khlisti and the Skoptsi. It included a rather crude and imperfect study in comparative religion — figures of the dog-headed gods of Egypt, of Apollo and other Greek deities, being jumbled together with Buddhist statuettes and pictures of human sacrifices and other primitive religious rites, with little effort at order, arrangement, or explanation.

There were also a number of photographs of Soviet anti-religious activities. One of them showed the largest bell in Russia, which formerly belonged to the Troitzky-Sergiev Monastery, near Moscow, and weighed almost seventy tons, being carried off to be melted down for its metallic content. The demolition of the Saint Simon Monastery, on the outskirts of Moscow, and the giving up of wedding rings by women who have forsaken religion for Communism, were themes of other pictures.

In the former Strastnoy Monastery in Moscow and in other antireligious museums throughout the country the indictment of religion is hammered in, the attack proceeding along three main lines. First, there is the effort to prove that religion, in all its forms, has always been the enemy of the oppressed classes, especially of the workers. Second, there is an attack through the agency of natural science. Especially for the benefit of the peasants, who were formerly taught to regard natural phenomena as miracles, there is a systematic effort to give an antireligious turn to the most elementary facts of natural science.

Finally, there is a steady effort to represent religious belief of any sort as a kind of disloyalty on the part of the Soviet citizen. Red streamers with such slogans as, "Religion Is Incompatible with Socialism," and "Priests and Sectarians: an Obstacle to the Fulfillment of the Five-Year Plan," are frequently displayed on public buildings and on the streets.

It goes without saying that any representation of religion in fiction, on the stage, or in moving pictures must be derogatory; and some special atheistic plays and films have been produced. Two of the latter were entitled *Opium* and *Judas*. The former was a sort of pictorial antireligious museum; the latter showed priests and monks leading immoral lives and giving all sorts of treacherous aid to the Whites during the Russian civil war.

There is an especially vigorous atheistic propaganda among school children; and any teacher who, because of indifference or secret sympathy with religious faith, is lax in this field is liable to be dismissed. Important religious holidays, especially Christmas, are regular occasions for outbursts of antireligious agitation.

Indeed Christmas in Moscow is very different from Christmas in any other European capital. The sale of *yolkas*, as the Russians call Christmas trees, is strictly forbidden.[2] No festoons or ornaments are to be seen in the bleak shop windows; and one could scour Moscow in vain for a Christmas card. The bookstores display none of the Christmas stories which pour from the presses in other lands. By way of compensation Soviet children are offered a wide range of choice among books with such titles as *Against the Christmas Tree, Antireligious Work of the School with the Parents, The Attack on God*. A typical excerpt from one of these pamphlets, which bears the label *Library of the Young Atheist*, reads as follows: —

Millions of little children are brought up by very religious grandmothers. For such children the Christmas tree represents a very great danger. Not one Young Pioneer detachment, not one school and not one group of Young Atheists should leave children of pre-school age without attention during the Christmas holidays. The struggle against the Christmas tree is the struggle against religion and against our class enemies. Behind the back of Uncle Frost [the Russian name for Santa Claus] hide the priest and the kulak.

Scores of such pamphlets are printed annually and are distributed among Young Pioneers and among school children generally. This is only one aspect of the anti-Christmas campaign, which is waged every year with such vigor that one wonders whether the memory of the holiday in Russia

[2] In 1933, Christmas trees were offered for sale in the Torgsin shops, which accept only foreign currency — an amusing compromise of strict Communist principle for the sake of obtaining the much desired *valuta*.

will not some day be kept alive mainly by the strenuous efforts to suppress it. Among the other regular features of Moscow's anti-Christmas campaign are lectures by atheistic professors in workers' clubs, visits to antireligious museums, and tours of surrounding villages by fleet-footed evangels of unbelief on skis, who try to persuade the peasants to give up their private property holdings and their religious beliefs simultaneously.

The Soviet war against religion is characterized by extraordinary ingenuity and variety. The music hall, playing cards, and children's A B C's have all been pressed into service. Demyan Byedny, the unofficial poet laureate, wrote a coarse and violent antireligious skit entitled "How the Fourteenth Division Went into Heaven," for production in the chief Moscow music hall. It begins with a representation of the Russian and German Armies moving against each other, while priests on each side wave the cross and invoke divine aid. Then the scene shifts to a Russian village, where the priest is a thoroughgoing hypocrite and speculator, who robs an old woman immediately after he has administered the last communion to her.

Heaven, in the latter part of the sketch, is shown as a compound of a cabaret and a strictly policed state; the personages of the Trinity, Saint Peter, and the Archangel Michael are caricatured and represented as carousing with Rasputin. The Fourteenth Division of the Russian Army comes into Heaven *en masse*, because it has been annihilated by a German land mine.

Demyan Byedny fills his Paradise with old generals, aristocrats, landlords, capitalists, and such. The first shock comes when the general who led the Fourteenth Division sees with anxiety the Bolshevik Revolution of 1917. He eagerly looks forward fifteen years and at first is overjoyed to see that Russia in 1932 has a well-disciplined army and many new factories. But despair overcomes him when he learns that the hated Soviets are still in power.

At this moment news comes that the soldiers of the Fourteenth Division have mutinied. The denizens of Paradise promptly pass into oblivion, and the play ends amid the strains of a chorus to the effect that the Revolution has destroyed all gods and that Communism will create a Paradise in this world.

Even people who are so frivolous as to play cards may not escape the all-pervading influence of antireligious propaganda. A unique edition of playing cards has been issued with all the face cards decorated in such a way as to cast disrepute on some form of faith. The hearts show a Roman Catholic priest yearning for a woman; the diamonds caricature Jewish rites; the spades show the Orthodox Church in an unfavorable light; and the clubs depict the Oriental shaman, or medicine man, and Buddhist figures. The joker in the pack represents the Deity as a capitalist in evening clothes, holding the reins which control all the four forms of religion. On the backs of the cards is Mephistopheles carrying off the souls of the damned.

The effort to make Russian school children imbibe hatred and contempt with their A B C's, or rather with their A B V's, to use the Russian order of the letters, takes the form of an antireligious alphabet, in which every letter is illustrated with an atheistic slogan, accompanied by vivid pictorial representations. The letter B, for instance, is printed on a sheet showing a red broom sweeping out the Bible and the ikons, accompanied by the appeal: *"Bros'tye, bratsi, boyatsya bogov"* ("Give up, brothers, fearing gods").

V has a still more lurid device. A sinister-looking capitalist in top hat and monocle pours a stream of liquid out of a container marked "religion," while a homicidal-looking Easterner slashes his own face with a sword, a woman beats her head on the ground, and a man performs an orgiastic dance with a whip. Here the motto is, "Faith is harmful, more harmful than wine" — a philosophic principle which would not, of course, be applied to faith in Communism.

Another picture in the alphabet shows a cheerful young atheist carrying an umbrella to ward off the streams of religious teaching which are pouring from the lips of three highly unprepossessing ecclesiastics. Still another depicts a red tractor sweeping with the force of a Juggernaut over a village church, and over the bodies of two kulaks at the same time.

Churches and religious organizations are quite unable to reply to the enormous flood of violent, defamatory antireligious propaganda which rolls over the country year after year. The year 1929, which may be regarded as the first year of the Iron Age, witnessed a significant change of the Soviet Constitution and a still more significant change of Soviet administrative practice as regards religious organizations. Until 1929, freedom both of religious and of antireligious propaganda had been recognized as the right of every Soviet citizen under Article 4 of the Soviet Constitution. In 1929 this article was amended so that henceforward the Constitution recognized, instead of the right of religious propaganda, only the right of "profession of religious faiths." The right of antireligious propaganda, of course, remained. Along with this constitutional change went a sweeping prohibition of social, educational, and benevolent activities on the part of church organizations.

An authoritative interpretation of the significance of this alteration of the Soviet Constitution makes the points that the law now does not permit either "the winning of new groups of toilers, especially children as adherents of religion," or "any kind of propagandist and agitation activity on the part of church and religious people." [3] In other words, no church representative, no individual believer, may reply in speech or in writing to the attacks on religion in the numerous antireligious publications and in the antireligious museums. A priest or minister or rabbi is comparatively secure against administrative arrest only if he restricts himself in the very narrowest way to the carrying out of the prescribed ritual of his faith — sometimes not even under this condition.

Priests and ministers of all religions in the Soviet Union have always been classified with criminals and insane persons in so far as they were disfranchised and deprived of civic rights. The denial of the right to "vote" — that is, to hold up one's hand as a sign of approval of the list of candidates for the Soviet submitted by the local Communist Party organization — would be a trivial disability in itself. But it carries with it a number of social and economic deprivations which, in recent years, have become increasingly severe.

The children of a priest (Russian Orthodox priests are usually married) may not be admitted to middle or higher schools or to state employment (and very little employment in the Soviet Union is not state employment) unless they renounce and break off all connections with their father. Moreover, disfranchised persons have no right to food

[3] *Cf.* N. Orleansky, *Zakon o Religioznikh Obyedineniyakh RSFSR* (The Law about Religious Associations in the Russian Socialist Federative Soviet Republic), Moscow, 1930, p. 47.

cards, and under the stringent rationing restrictions of the last few years this is a great disadvantage.

Apart from these social and economic hardships any priest is in danger of being exiled by administrative order; and this statement is also true for persons who are conspicuously active in church affairs, such as members of the council which exists in every church and must represent the church in its dealings with the authorities. Very considerable numbers of priests have been exiled during the Iron Age; and not a few have been executed. Before the peasant resistance to collectivization had been crushed, first by the wholesale "liquidation" of the kulaks, then by the great famine of 1932–1933, there were many murders of especially hated Communist rural officials and organizers; and the regular Soviet judicial practice in such cases was to execute not only the actual perpetrators of the murder, but also anyone who could plausibly be represented as a moral instigator. The local priest often fell into this last category.

It is difficult to give a full documentary picture of the extent of persecution of individuals in the Soviet Union for religious convictions, because of the secrecy with which arrests are carried out and because of the ease with which the Gay-Pay-Oo (unhampered by any necessity for bringing the kind of concrete proof that would convince a jury) can accuse an actively religious man or woman of "counter-revolutionary activity." A few cases which have come to my personal attention, however, illustrate the general situation.

Several young men were studying privately for the priesthood. They were arrested and banished to an unhealthy part of Turkestan, not far from Chardzhui, where they are very likely to die of malignant malaria. Two girls whose offense was that they had been singing in a church choir were banished from Moscow to Tashkent. Several years ago the former Princess Sophie Lieven, who, like a number of Russian aristocrats, had found consolation in religion for the suffering which the Revolution had brought to her, was arrested because she had been reading the Bible to peasants. She was finally released as a result of private intercession undertaken by the British Embassy.

In one church on the Maroseika, in Moscow, which has now been pulled down, the entire personnel of the church council was arrested and sent into exile on three separate occasions. It is the generally accepted rule that only people who are not afraid to suffer for their convictions accept election into the church councils. When old workers belong to a church they are often selected for membership in the council, because the manual laborer, in practice, has a few more civil rights than the ordinary Soviet citizen and is therefore less likely to be arrested for religious activity. The other members of church councils are apt to be elderly people who are willing to spend their last years in exile, if necessary, for their faith.[4] It is a common practice for religious believers to go to various churches in order to avoid being identified too prominently with any one congregation by the spies who are active in the churches, as everywhere else in Russia.

The sole occasion on which foreign journalists were able to talk with the Metropolitan Sergei, Acting Patriarch of

---

[4] The contrast between the formal and the actual status of the church council in the Soviet Union is very similar to the situation which prevailed in regard to trade-unions during the decade before the 1917 Revolution. Formerly trade-unions were legal organizations. But members of their executive committees were very likely to be rounded up by the Tsarist police and sent into exile. Exactly the same rule holds good in regard to the church councils to-day.

the Orthodox Church,[5] afforded a vivid idea of the relations between Church and State in the Soviet Union. It was early in 1930, when antireligious administrative activity was at its height and arrests of priests and closings of churches were going on all over the country.[6] Sergei, very probably acting in obedience to a strong hint from the authorities, published in the official *Izvestia* a statement to the effect that there was no persecution of religion in the Soviet Union. The authenticity of this interview had been questioned abroad; and, with a view to establishing it, the Commissariat for Foreign Affairs made arrangements for Sergei to receive the foreign journalists in Moscow. There was a short period of waiting in the parlor of Sergei's simply furnished house in one of the outlying districts of Moscow, and one of the journalists said: "Perhaps Sergei is ready for martyrdom. Perhaps he will really tell us how many priests have been shot and exiled, how many churches have been closed against the will of the congregations."

But it was not for nothing that Sergei has retained for many years his post of Acting Patriarch, whereas his predecessor in office, Peter, was quickly shipped off to an unknown place of banishment. What he said during his brief talk with the journalists could not have given offense to

[5] No Patriarch has been elected since the death of Tikhon in 1925, partly because so many Bishops and Archbishops have always been in prison or in exile that it would be impossible to assemble a canonical quorum, partly because the Soviet Government would not permit the election, in any case.

[6] There was some relaxation of the intensity, although not of the fact of religious persecution, after Stalin had published his "Giddiness from Success" open letter to local officials in the spring of 1930. In this communication he sounded a warning against complicating the difficult task of winning the peasants over to the idea of collective farming by insulting their religious feelings or closing churches where the population did not desire it.

the most exacting official of the Gay-Pay-Oo. He was a plump, elderly man, with the full-flowing beard of an Eastern prelate and small shrewd eyes, in which cunning seemed to be mingled with apprehension during his short conversation with such unaccustomed and potentially embarrassing guests. He handed out three typewritten copies of replies to written questions which had been submitted to him in advance; and the replies contained nothing beyond what he had already stated in *Izvestia*. Unwelcome inquiries about the number of arrests and executions among his clergy were evaded or left unanswered. When the journalists attempted to learn more concrete facts by putting oral questions, Sergei seized the welcome opportunity to retreat, saying as he hurried out of the room: —

"Oh, I could n't answer any oral questions. I would have to consult — the Holy Synod."

One must confess that this remark excited irreverent smiles: for it was obviously a very different and decidedly unhallowed body that was giving Sergei instructions as to what he could and could not say for the benefit of the outside world.[7] His position under the Soviet régime is about as difficult as that of a Greek Patriarch under the rule of a fanatical Turkish Sultan.

The powerful combination of propaganda and terrorism has wrought considerable changes in religious faith, as in other fields of Soviet life. Under such strong pressure only

[7] Sergei's declaration that there was no persecution of religion excited a good deal of resentment among Orthodox believers, although some of them, of course, understood the helplessness of his situation. The protests against persecution of religion voiced by the Pope, the Archbishop of Canterbury, and other ecclesiastical leaders were warmly welcomed by religious Russians, in so far as they learned of them through the hostile outbursts of the Soviet press. Indignation in regard to these protests was confined to Communists.

persons with deep-rooted religious conviction tend to hold out, along with some of the older people who cannot give up the habit of going to church or of crossing themselves before the ikon. But the neutral, the passive, the indifferent, tend to drift away from religion under the Soviet state creed of atheism, just as they would profess religious faith under a strongly clerical régime. Very typical of this tendency was the simple remark of the wife of a Kolomna worker with whom I talked: —

"Before the Revolution everyone told me that I ought to go to church, so I went. Now everyone tells me that I should n't go, so I don't."

The youth has been brought up in an atmosphere of contempt and abhorrence for religion; and when one makes every allowance for the occasional counteracting influence of a religious family there seems little doubt that the majority of the Soviet younger generation, even those who do not belong to the Union of Communist Youth, are indifferent, if not actively hostile, to every form of religion.

So the future outlook for organized religion of any kind in the Soviet Union is dark. There are few young people to step into the places of the older believers who die off. According to official figures there are still about 38,000 Orthodox churches in the Soviet Union, as against about 54,000 before the war. The decline has been much greater in the towns than in the country districts; Moscow has less than 100 churches, as against over 600 before the war. The process of demolishing churches or of converting them to secular uses (the Stalingrad Cathedral was turned into a garage) has gone still farther in many provincial towns; and newly built Soviet industrial towns grow up with no churches of any kind.

What seems probable is that with the passing of time the number both of believers and of churches will continue to diminish. A few churches will be allowed to stand — as proof to foreign visitors that there is complete freedom of religion in the Soviet Union. It is quite conceivable that faith, among Orthodox and sectarians, Jews and Mohammedans alike, may gain in intensity among the few who cling to it. Underground groups of enthusiasts may emerge. But with the existing system of control of the spoken and printed word it is difficult to see how a new prophet could obtain a wide audience before he was detected and "liquidated" by the Gay-Pay-Oo.

Russia seems committed to the experiment of discovering whether a purely materialistic conception of life can permanently satisfy a large and varied population. If the experiment does not succeed, if the traditional craving of the individual for some extra-worldly interpretation of existence proves too strong to be permanently repressed, a revival of religion, perhaps in some form which cannot be foreseen at the present time, may occur. If, on the other hand, Communism proves able to function as a substitute for older creeds, it may well be that during the coming decades belief in religion will become uncommon, as much a sign of an independent and unconventional mind as skepticism or atheism would have been in the Middle Ages, when the whole weight of the existing political and social order was thrown in favor of religion, as it is now, in the Soviet Union, thrown against it.

XVII

SOVIET COMEDIES

THE Soviet régime, like all young dictatorships, has a tendency to be pompous, solemn, and dull in its official language. The man who is shot in the Soviet Union has the consolation of knowing that formally he is being subjected "to the highest measure of social defense." When the Union of Communist Youth on one occasion took up the problem of the dearth of humorous plays on the Soviet stage, the efforts of their spokesmen to suggest remedies for the situation took the form of publishing articles under such titles as "The Organization of Laughter" and "The Serious Business of the Smile."

Yet anyone who has lived in Moscow is apt to look back on it as one of the most amusing cities in the world. The sources of comedy are so numerous: the strangeness of many new features in Soviet life; the irrepressible Russian tendency, which even the Gay-Pay-Oo cannot suppress, to turn up a first-rate impostor now and then; the natural comic sense of Russians, whose psychology has not been completely made over in the propaganda mill; the funny figures which many foreign visitors to the country cut against the Soviet background.

The quality of the official humorous magazines in Russia deteriorated very markedly during the Iron Age. The contributors to these publications had to consider very care-

fully whether their stories or sketches would not expose
them to the formidable accusation of "pouring grist into the
mill of the class enemy" or "sowing opportunist lack of
faith in the creative power of the proletariat," to use two
phrases which were much in vogue. Quite typical of the
painfully strained propagandist humor which developed
under the increasingly severe censorship was a frontispiece
of the magazine *Krokodil,* showing conventional capitalist
figures bending over a broken-down automobile while a
Soviet car, painted in vivid red, drove triumphantly forward.
If one looked into another supposedly comic paper, *Lapot,*
one saw M. Poincaré, who for a time succeeded Sir Austen
Chamberlain as the main villain in the chronic intervention
scare (Poincaré has now given way to Hitler), giving the
following amiable counsel to an audience of vulture-faced
gentlemen in frock coats and military uniforms: "I recom-
mend the most profitable business — to turn blood into oil
and bones into coal."

Perhaps there were Communists so well disciplined that
they bent over and chortled with mirth when they looked
at such heavily propagandist efforts at wit, but I doubt
whether there were many of them. The main source of
humor in the Soviet Union is the ubiquitous, ever-changing
"anecdote," or satirical story, which is never written down,
for obvious prudential reasons, but which passes with amazing speed from person to person and from city to city by word
of mouth and then dies away, to be replaced by a more timely
successor. Thousands of these anecdotes have been put
into circulation since the Revolution; they are the best
substitute for the nonexistent freedom of speech and press;
and it is not surprising that in Germany also the "anecdote"
has become popular since the establishment of the present
dictatorship.

Anyone who could make a complete collection of Soviet anecdotes would have not only a good and varied assortment of jokes, but extremely valuable footnotes to the popular mood during various phases of the Soviet régime. Some of these jokes date back to the very early years of the Revolution, notably the saying that "everyone in Russia is, has been, or will be in prison" and the remark that "there is no news in the *Truth* and no truth in the *News*" (*Izvestia*, the title of the Soviet official newspaper, means "News," and the name of the Communist Party organ, *Pravda*, means "Truth").

Food plays a considerable part in the jokes of more modern vintage. So two Russians discuss who is the greater man, Hoover or Stalin. "Hoover taught the Americans not to drink," argues one of them. "That is nothing," is the reply; "Stalin taught the Russians not to eat." Another story represents Stalin as complaining to President Kalinin that there are mice in his cupboard. "There is a certain remedy for that," suggests Kalinin. "Put up a sign outside the cupboard: 'Collective farm named after Stalin.' Then half the mice will die of hunger and the other half will run away."

The Gay-Pay-Oo comes in for its share of satirical attention. There is the story of two private traders who pass the Gay-Pay-Oo headquarters. One turns away and replies to the other's question as to why he did so: "I don't like to look into the future." Then there is the tale of the host of rabbits from all parts of the Soviet Union who appear on the Polish frontier and ask permission to cross it. "The Gay-Pay-Oo has issued orders to arrest all the camels in the country," they explain. "But you are not camels," reply the Polish frontier guards. "Just try to prove that to the Gay-Pay-Oo," reply the terrified rabbits.

Stalin's six major conditions for the successful operation of the state industries have been parodied in an imaginary "six conditions for the intelligentsia." These six conditions are as follows: "Don't think. If you must think, don't talk to yourself. If you must talk to yourself, don't talk to others. If you must talk to others, don't write. If you must write, don't print. If you must print, deny it the next day."

The Soviet financial problem of forcing almost all citizens every year to subscribe to a new state loan finds its comment in the story of the man who was found drowned in the Moscow River, "with no signs of violence, except a few bonds of the five-year-plan loan." Then there is the story of how Stalin and Voroshilov, during a First of May demonstration, discussed whether the workers on parade were genuinely loyal to the régime. It was decided to test out the question by taking one worker out of the procession, leading him to one of the Kremlin towers, and telling him, as a proof of loyalty, to jump off. The worker complies with unexpected alacrity, is caught in a net which has been prepared in advance, and congratulated for his daring and loyalty, whereupon he disgustedly remarks: "Oh, to the devil with such a life as we are leading!"

A joke which has also been applied to other dictators has found application to Stalin. The Soviet dictator is saved from drowning and offers his rescuer any reward he may desire. "I have just one wish," says the rescuer — "that you don't let anyone know that I saved you."

Many of the anecdotes are untranslatable, because they are plays on Russian words. Typical of this type is the conundrum: "Who can live sweetly in Russia? Only Gorky." (*Gorky* in Russian means bitter; and the anecdote is a hit at the comfortable life which the Soviet author laureate leads in Moscow and in his villa at Sorrento, in Italy.)

Where these anecdotes originate is one of the unsolved mysteries of Russian life. No Moscow social evening is complete without the telling of a few of the latest ones (although it is not always safe for Russians to repeat those which affect Stalin personally in too large and mixed gatherings), and they will probably last as long as the Soviet régime itself.

The best comedy in the Russian language and one of the best in the world is Gogol's *Inspector General*. Its plot is based on the arrival in a sleepy small town of an unknown young man, who is generally taken for the government inspector who has come from St. Petersburg to look into the doings of the local officials. Inasmuch as they all have good reason for uneasy consciences, they begin to besiege the unknown visitor with offers of hospitality and more solid forms of attention in the shape of presents of money. The visitor plays up to the rôle which has been assigned to him and disappears with his spoils just on the eve of the arrival of the genuine inspector general.

This comedy has repeated itself in actual life more than once under the Soviet régime, sometimes with Russians, sometimes with foreigners. In the spring of 1934 Russians were horrified or amused, according to their turn of mind, on reading of the unmasking of Nikolai Petrovitch Sharov, a Party member who had given himself out as a revolutionary hero of the first order: a former worker, a Red Guard and Red partisan during the civil war, an active underground revolutionary who had suffered all sorts of persecution at the hands of the Tsar's police. Sharov's undoing came when he overreached himself and tried to obtain admission to what might be described as one of Russia's most exclusive clubs, the Society of Old Bolsheviki. His record was closely scrutinized and one after another of his self-assumed "revolutionary merits" disappeared in the process. It was found that he had never been a worker, much less an underground revolutionary, that he never fired a shot as a Red Guard or a Red partisan, that he had simply been an employee in the telegraph service and a perfectly loyal subject of the Tsar, who had even on one occasion offered his services to the police as a volunteer spy. In short, Sharov had been a very good specimen of a Soviet Khlestyakov (the latter was the hero of Gogol's *Inspector General*), and had developed with several other Party members what might have been called a "racket" in the shape of trading on glowing but false testimonials of heroic past deeds. Indeed the case of Sharov brought to light the existence in the Soviet Union of a large number of bogus war veterans, who had enrolled themselves as former Red Guards or Red partisans for the sake of material advantages which are granted to such civil-war fighters, without ever having done anything to qualify themselves for such privileges.

An equally amusing hoax of a different kind was perpetrated by the editorial board of the humorous magazine, *Krokodil*. With a view to testing the credulity of Soviet industrial managers the board decided to announce the existence of an entirely fictitious "Trust for the Exploitation of Meteoric Iron."[1] Knowing that nothing in the Soviet

---

[1] The meteoric iron was supposed to be obtained from fallen meteorites. The amount of such iron is, of course, far too small for profitable industrial and commercial use.

Union can be done without a stamp, and that with a stamp almost all things are possible, the organizers of the imaginary trust inserted a notice in a newspaper to the effect that the stamp of the trust had been lost.   Then they applied to the stamp bureau for a new stamp, received it, and set to work in earnest.

Armed with an imposing stamp which could be affixed to correspondence, and with a name that smacked of super-industrialization, the "trust" made remarkable progress. One state official after another expressed unbounded enthusiasm over the possibility of meteoric iron.   Food cards were issued for a number of nonexistent employees of the imaginary trust.   Orders for office equipment, for furniture, even for a new truck, were fulfilled without question.   Demands for meteoric iron began to pour in; and the "trust" was on the point of receiving an appropriation of 100,000 rubles from the Commissariat for Finance when an official in the Commissariat for Education became suspicious, called in the police, and revealed the hoax.   Although this was by far one of the best jokes the *Krokodil* ever cracked, its publication was forbidden, apparently because it would have been too injurious to the prestige of a number of Soviet "captains of industry" who had swallowed so easily the tale of the high virtues of meteoric iron.

A foreigner who, at least from the Soviet standpoint, was no better than a false inspector general was a Balkan author named Panait Istrati.   There was a time a few years ago when Istrati was regarded as the very foremost of "international proletarian writers."   He toured Russia from one end to the other, making enthusiastic speeches at the banquets which were tendered in his honor.   The directors of Soviet propaganda felt that here, at last, was a man who would contradict "the lies of the capitalist press." Soviet publishing houses vied with each other in publishing translations of Istrati's works and in thrusting honoraria on the author. But when Istrati left the Soviet Union the tone of his writing abruptly changed. One of the organizers of his reception, Boris Volin, lacking the discretion to keep silent about the lamentable end of this experiment in international propaganda, heaped reproaches on Istrati in the following terms: —

For a year and a half Istrati was a guest of the Soviet Union. He went hither and thither without obstruction, concluded agreements and contracts, took high payments from our publishing houses, complained that Gorky and Barbusse were paid at higher rates. He journeyed, issued greetings, collected money — and departed.

After his departure, according to Volin, Istrati expressed the following sentiments, which the Soviet publishing houses certainly did not anticipate when they were paying him: —

The working class is badly beaten down in the Soviet Union.
The devil himself created Russia for dictatorship.
Banditism and terror found their best expression under the so-called dictatorship of the proletariat.

A jovial Irish novelist named Liam O'Flaherty also proved a poor investment, from the standpoint of international Communist literary propaganda. Arriving in Moscow, as he tells us, with only eight depreciated Soviet rubles in his pocket, he was promptly conducted to the headquarters of the International Association of Proletarian Authors. Here he, along with other writers, was presented with the question: "What would you do in the event of war against the Soviet Union?" Thinking of the eight rubles in his pocket, O'Flaherty, although, as he assures us, he had no desire of firing another shot except against his creditors, solemnly enunciated: "If capitalist Europe makes war on the Soviet Union, I shall make war on capitalist Europe with all the means at my disposal." This gallant declaration was received with shouts of applause by the assembled "proletarian authors"; and O'Flaherty was overwhelmed with offers of payment for past, present, and future translations of his work into Russian. When he left Russia and wrote an amused and amusing sketch of his experiences, in which this episode figured prominently, he doubtless caused the credentials of every future "proletarian author" in Moscow to be examined somewhat more carefully.

Everyone who has lived in Moscow for a number of years can look back on a varied and entertaining parade of foreign pilgrims to the Soviet capital. There was the American woman tourist who, after being shown Lenin lying in state, inquired: "Who was the gentleman we just saw in there?" There was the married couple from the State of Missouri who, after hearing an edifying lecture on Soviet achievements in the protection of public health, asked in rasping nasal voices: "But what is the Health Commissariat going to do about the flies in the Grand Hotel?" There was the eccentric gentleman who was determined to set up a statue of Lincoln in every foreign capital; but found the Moscow Soviet coldly indifferent to his proposal. There was the enraptured lady who announced, after a brief sojourn in Moscow, that she could see "triumph written on the skies."

There was the woman enthusiast from London who was so overwhelmed with enthusiasm after her Moscow pilgrimage that she committed her emotions to verse, with the following amazing results: —

To My Beloved Comrades — Au Revoir

I longed to see your wondrous land,
I yearned to shake you by the hand,
And now at last my dream's come true
And I have seen and talked with you.
It's quite impossible to say
How happy you have made my stay.
You teach the lesson day by day:
Where there's a will there is a way.
You show that gold and greed can be dethroned
And all by all be justly owned.
Your children are a happy band —
Knowledge and freedom hand in hand.
I turn my face unto the West,
Feeling the East is doubly blest.
Comrades, the brightness of your light
Is needed to dispel our night.[2]

The unconscious humor of this effusion was enhanced by the fact that the *Moscow Daily News*, the English-language newspaper of the Soviet capital, unsatisfied with its adulatory tones, was unwilling to print it without a grave note of admonitory correction. China, India, and other Eastern colonial and semi-colonial countries, it informed the author, whom we may call Mrs. Modlin-Creighton, are certainly not "doubly blest." Exception was also taken to another line in the poem, in which Mrs. Modlin-Creighton had expressed the view that "perfect love can cast out fear."

Another figure, quite as comical in his way as the rhapsodic Mrs. Modlin-Creighton, was the genial Rotarian who

---

[2] I cite only part of this unusual poem.

turned up in Moscow brimming over with three great ideas: to persuade the Soviet Union to join the Rotary International, to donate the annual interest on one thousand dollars as a prize for the best schoolboy essay on "Rotary As a Force for World Peace," and to induce Soviet sport organizations to participate in the Olympic Games at Los Angeles. After encountering what seemed to him an inexplicable reluctance on the part of Foreign Commissar Litvinov to discuss these matters personally with him, the persistent Rotarian wrote a letter to the Commissar, in the style of, "As one free-born citizen of a great republic to another," giving Litvinov elaborate instructions as to where to communicate with him by mail or telegraph. What made the Rotarian's mission especially funny is that in orthodox Communist eyes the Rotary International would seem a most sinister "class organization of the bourgeoisie," while the Olympic Games have sometimes been described in the Soviet Union as a subtle means of preparing for hostile intervention. A worthy companion of the Rotarian was an exuberant journalist who wished to convince Soviet editors of the desirability of purchasing such products of American *Kultur* as "Krazy Kat" and "Boob McNutt." The idea of a provincial Communist Party Secretary in Krasnodar or Saratov trying to read class content into the adventures of Boob McNutt, or wondering what the antics of the Krazy Kat might have to do with world revolution, is irresistibly titillating.

Then there was a rather irascible newspaperman with a strongly developed sense of acid humor who insisted on expressing his grievances in long letters addressed to the highest Soviet authorities. He wore out the patience of the Commissar for Posts and Telegraphs by pointing out manifold deficiencies in its system of mail and telegraphic delivery, stressing the point that it took longer for a cable to come from the Moscow telegraph office to a near-by hotel than from New York to Moscow. When he received a letter with more than the usual evidence of having been opened, — in the shape of a telltale blot of green ink on the contents of the letter, corresponding with that which was used in rewriting the address, — he drew a circle around the offending blot, wrote out the brief message, "Fire that man," and sent the letter back to the censorship department of the post office. When the hot water failed to run in his hotel he addressed a letter to Menzhinsky, late head of the Gay-Pay-Oo, explaining in great detail just how the hotel furnace was being mishandled and ending with the suggestion that the Gay-Pay-Oo, as one of the few efficient Soviet institutions, might do something about the matter. The newspaperman asserts that the water was running piping hot the day after the letter had been dispatched.

Apart from these individuals who have consciously or unconsciously added to the gaiety of life in Moscow, there are standardized comic types and situations. There is the glowing tourist, or the member of a foreign "workers' delegation," who delivers himself as follows to the *Moscow Daily News:* "I have been in Moscow three days and I *know* that all the stories about hunger and forced labor are lies."

Then there is the not-infrequent case of the American or British engineer who leaves the Soviet Union in a soured and disgruntled mood and proceeds to sell an article to a conservative newspaper or magazine in which he paints both the technical achievements and the general living conditions of the Soviet Union in the darkest colors. The reaction of the *Moscow Daily News* in such cases has the regularity of an automatic reflex. The interpreter of the recreant engineer is interviewed; and, with visions of Solovetzky Island as a penalty for being suspected of giving his employer unfavorable information, the interpreter is most ready to describe the engineer as a drunkard, a moron, and, in general, an utterly untrustworthy and undesirable person. The Soviet state organization that engaged the engineer often contributes a few derogatory remarks; and on one occasion the *Moscow Daily News* even obtained an affidavit from a police official in Sverdlovsk to the effect that Engineer X, the latest author of an unappreciative article, had been on a perpetual debauch during his stay in one of the Sverdlovsk hotels, and had even gone so far as to shoot off the fire extinguisher in his room without any need. In explanation of this I might add that Sverdlovsk is about as bleak and dismal a place as one could well find; and that a foreign engineer, stranded there with no knowledge of Russian and nothing to do, might certainly yield to a weakness for drink.

The *Moscow Daily News* has no funny page, but is not devoid of amusing features. One of them, the rambling didactic reflections of a proletarian philosopher who employed the pseudonym of "Moscow Mike," and wrote in a queer ungrammatical jargon that was supposed to represent the language of a manual worker, has been discontinued; in fact, the author, detected in certain moral derelictions, was ingloriously expelled from the Communist Party, despite his views, which were more orthodox than those of *Pravda*, and has now left the Soviet Union. "Moscow Mike" on one occasion expressed special indignation over a satirical sketch of eccentric foreigners in Moscow which appeared in an American magazine. "You might think we was running a nut house here, and not a great big workshop for building socialism," was the expression which his offended *amour propre* assumed.

Because it is widely circulated abroad, especially in its weekly edition, and because it is printed in the English language, the *Moscow Daily News,* which is under the editorship of Michael Borodin, former advisor to the Chinese Nationalist Government, is even more strictly controlled and censored than are the regular Russian newspapers. Sometimes the censorship is amusingly evident. A headline will indicate that all is not well with some factory or state farm which is under description. But the article over which the headline is placed reveals no trace of the defects. The censor's shears have trimmed the article, but the headline has been allowed to stand. One of its best-known contributors once wrote an article about the Stalingrad tractor factory which began: "Those who say that the Stalingrad tractor factory is a failure are liars. Those who say it is a success are also liars." This was not regarded as a suitable introduction, and the sentences, after being subjected to the censor's revision, came out somewhat as follows: "Those who say the Stalingrad tractor factory is a failure are liars. Those who say it is a success at the present moment are perhaps a little premature in overlooking the existence of certain defects which will doubtless be ultimately overcome."

On one occasion the readers of Moscow's English-language newspaper rubbed their eyes when they saw a headline announcing the existence of appalling conditions of forced labor in Siberia. A day or two later there was a shamefaced explanation to the effect that, as a result of a regrettable printer's error, "Siberia" had been printed when "Liberia" had been meant.

Hotel life in the Soviet Union has its element of comedy. Although conditions in the leading Moscow hotels have been improving, there are occasional serious lapses from what the American tourist would regard as normal standards of service; and the *Moscow Daily News* once directed a battery of denunciation against the New Moscow Hotel, based on tourist complaints. The salient points in the indictment were as follows: —

The staff cannot tell a guest's name or room number, even though he has stayed two months. . . . Mail is handled very carelessly. To be sure whether one has mail, one must go through all the letters that come in. Telegrams are never delivered to the person or room when they arrive — in fact, a telegram is a bit of torn gray paper which falls from the packages of letters as tourists look over their mail. . . . The push bells do not work. . . . When shoes are put out to be cleaned, the owner must practically always go out and look for them in the morning, as they are never returned. . . . Laundry is returned poorly washed and pressed, sometimes, if you are lucky.

Still funnier, perhaps, was a feature of Soviet hotel life which I saw in the course of a visit to Ivanovo. Posted up in the lobby of the hotel, for all to read, was a chronicle of the sins and failings of Comrade Grishin, Second Manager of the Hotel Kitchen. Comrade Grishin, if one could believe this "wall newspaper" (every factory and public institution in Russia has its "wall newspaper," in which defects are pointed out and slackers are held up to public scorn), had been very naughty indeed. First of all, he was so intoxicated most of the time that "he couldn't move his tongue." Second, when one of the numerous Soviet commissions, headed by a doctor, had endeavored to inspect the kitchen, Comrade Grishin found power of speech enough to curse them with a familiar and unprintable Russian oath. Last and gravest offense of all, he endeavored to speed up some of his subordinates who were cleaning fish by seizing a large fish and beating them over the head with it. Where, except in the Soviet Union, would such skeletons of the business cupboard be brought out and paraded for public delectation?

It is perhaps appropriate that, in a country which has destroyed the private capitalist system, currency should be one of the chief sources of comedy. For a variety of reasons of expediency, the real status of the Soviet ruble is not discussed in correspondence from Moscow.

From 1924, when the Soviet currency was stabilized, until 1928, the Soviet ruble was a fairly respectable member of the international family of currencies. Faint signs of cracking began to appear in 1928. As a result of the frenzied finance which was a feature of the five-year plan (the Soviet Government printed about five times as much new money as had been contemplated in the financial section of the plan), combined with the acute shortage of food and manufactured goods and the spread all over the country of shops which accepted only foreign currency or precious metals in payment, the real value of the ruble shot downward with the speed of an arrow; and in the winter of 1933–1934 the unofficial market rate of exchange was about forty-five rubles to a dollar, although officially a dollar would purchase only one ruble and thirteen kopecks, as the nominal value of the Soviet currency had been adjusted to the depreciation of the dollar.

The situation has led to a constant, secret, but none the less intense struggle, with varying results, between the foreigners, who are eager to pay for everything in Soviet currency, and the Soviet commercial organizations, which prefer to be paid in anything else. The struggle is all the more amusing because neither side wishes to come out in the open. The Soviet Government is stubbornly unwilling to admit that the stability of its currency has been one of the sacrifices of the five-year plan; Soviet representatives in public statements insist, with entire gravity, that their ruble is one of the few currencies in the world that came through the crisis unscathed.[8]

The most amusing episode of the perpetual ruble comedy occurred in the autumn of 1932, when the Soviet authorities closed the food store which had hitherto supplied the needs of foreign diplomats and notified the latter that henceforward a Torgsin shop (where only foreign currency is legal tender) would attend to their needs. There were growls and mutterings of wrath among the diplomats; and on the last day when the ruble store was open for business it was stormed by representatives of all the embassies, eager to make the best use of their cheap rubles. The more enterprising embassies brought trucks to carry away their purchases.

At first the British had reason to feel that insult had been added to injury, for the pound sterling was pronounced an unstable currency, unworthy of acceptance in the Torgsin shop. (This was quickly rescinded.) A prominent British

---

[8] The Soviet Commissar for Finance, Grinko, once told of a case when a former Finance Minister of another country asked him how the Soviet Government contrived to keep the ruble stable. It is uncertain whether the ex-Minister was very naïve or whether he had a taste for joking.

representative announced that "it was a piece of confounded impudence for people who sell a third of their exports to Great Britain and are glad enough to take pounds in payment to place the pound on a par with the Afghan currency and their own wretched rubles and refuse to take it in payment."

Some ambassadors made formal representations on the matter to Litvinov. The latter, who has inherited the capacity for sarcasm, if not the intellectual culture, of his predecessor, Chicherin, retorted that the new arrangement was really a privilege for the embassy staffs, since they would henceforward be spared the bother of exchanging their foreign money for rubles at the State Bank — an institution where the exchange department has had amazingly few customers during the last few years.

At the time of writing the situation is that cheap rubles have their uses in hiring chauffeurs, purchasing benzine, buying railroad tickets (although the Soviet authorities do everything in their power to make it inconvenient and difficult to buy a ticket in rubles to a place outside of Russia), and, for some lucky persons, in paying rental. On the other hand rooms in the better hotels, new apartments, the better grades of food and liquor, and inclusive tourist tickets are obtainable only for foreign currency. The natural trend of Soviet policy is to contract the ruble area and to extend the "gold" area, so far as foreigners are concerned; and it will be interesting to see whether it will ultimately prove possible to put foreigners completely on a "gold" basis without confessing too openly the breakdown of the Soviet paper currency.

While there is much that is strained and drab in contemporary Soviet life, there is certainly no lack of diverting comedies. And no foreigner with a spark of inflammable humor can find life in Moscow dull so long as the supply of anecdotes holds out, tourist poets like Mrs. Modlin-Creighton and Rotarian idealists continue to make their appearance in the Soviet capital, and the *Moscow Daily News* remains on sale.

XVIII

EXCERPTS FROM MY RUSSIAN DAIRY, 1924–1934

Moscow, *October* 1924. — I have just returned with Sonya from a trip of six or seven weeks through a number of peasant districts in Southern and Southeastern Russia, including the lower Volga, the North Caucasus, and parts of Ukraina, ending up in Kursk Province, in Russia proper. The villages have certainly made visible recovery from the years of civil war and famine. There was plenty of food everywhere, except in a few drought-stricken provinces of the lower Volga, and there the authorities seem to be taking adequate relief measures.

The provincial towns give the impression of being rather badly down at the heel and there is a good deal of unemployment; the industries have not developed fast enough to take up the slack of people who have returned to the towns since the hungry years drove them into the country in search of food. There are still a good many ragged barefoot waifs, orphans of the civil war and famine, hanging about markets and railroad stations, looking for a chance to beg or steal.

The pre-war Russian gentry have certainly been driven off their lands forever; the former big estates have been parceled out among millions of peasant households. At the same time, the Soviet Government has its problems, present and future, in dealing with the peasants. The peasant has not the least natural inclination toward socialism; scarcely one peasant family in a hundred belongs to the communes and collective farms which the government wants to encourage; and the members of these farms, if you can believe their neighbors, are often the most shiftless peasants, who cannot make a success out of their own holdings and who hope to live at state expense if they join a commune.

Fitting the peasant into a socialist scheme of things is bound to be a hard task for the future; and in the present the local authorities have to reckon with a good deal of discontent and grumbling on the part of the peasants on account of the high direct taxes and the prices which are fixed for city goods, which are disproportionately high, compared with the prices which the peasants get for their grain, meat, oil seeds, and other products. There seems to be little conscious political disaffection in the regions where I traveled, except among the Kuban Cossacks, who mostly fought on the side of the Whites in the civil war and have something of the psychology of Southerners in America after 1865, and in some Ukrainian regions where there are still embers of anti-Soviet separatist spirit.

We stumbled on this quite unexpectedly in Karmava, a good-sized village in the central part of Ukraina. Some of the local Soviet officials went with us to the school, where the teacher had arranged a little entertainment. There were recitations of the poems of Ukraina's nationalist poet, Shevchenko, and the entertainment ended with the singing of the "Internationale." If we had left immediately after the entertainment, we should have gone away convinced that the teacher was an enthusiast for the Soviet régime. But we happened to visit him later in his home, and, after he learned that we were both foreigners and not Communists, he began to talk in a very different vein. He told with increasing enthusiasm of how, in the years when the Soviets were carrying out wholesale grain requisitions during the civil war, the peasants of Karmava and neighboring villages pulled out their old war rifles and went into the woods to lay ambushes for requisitioning parties and generally to carry on a guerrilla war. And finally, casting all discretion to the winds, he burst out: "The Communists said we were bandits. But I think we were like Garibaldi."

Of course it is hard to decide how much of this secret hostility, which is half economic and half nationalistic (this teacher was an ardent Ukrainian nationalist and looked on the Soviet régime, even though it had given the Ukrainians freedom to use their own language in courts and schools, as something that came from Moscow), survives. The sharp edge has been taken off the peasants' discontent by the substitution of a regular tax system for requisitioning. And, although there are comparatively few Communists in the rural districts, and these are mostly local officials, they are certainly not asleep. They already have in the making a crude but extensive propaganda machine, which may accomplish a good deal with the peasants, especially as some of them are illiterate and more are semi-literate.

In the same Ukrainian village, Sonya and I attended a propaganda meeting where a local Young Communist harangued the assembled peasants on the international situation, painting the machinations of the capitalists everywhere in the darkest colors. After the speech the meeting was thrown open for questions, and one tall peasant, in bast shoes and trousers made out of sacking, spit out the sunflower seeds which are rural Russia's substitute for chewing gum and ventured the question: "Who is Dawes?" "Dawes? He is the main bandit who is robbing the German railroads," flashed back the Young Communist oracle. From an orthodox Communist point of view this was a perfectly accurate description of the Dawes Plan.

But actual and not metaphorical railroad bandits had been all too numerous in Ukraina during the civil war, and one felt that Mr. Charles G. Dawes had been permanently impressed on the minds of the peasants as the leader of a gang engaged in derailing and robbing German trains. "How much money did the imperialists press out of China?" inquired a younger peasant, feeling himself in deep water as he stumbled over the long word "imperialists." Here the Young Communist was stumped for a moment, but quickly recovered himself and replied, "They pressed out so much that it would be impossible to count it."

At this point Sonya lost her patience and scribbled down as a side comment on the notes she was taking: "Ignorance talking to ignorance."

But, while the peasants of Karmava were getting some rather weird conceptions of international politics, it was the first time, no doubt, that many of them had ever been aroused to think on the subject at all; and this is only one aspect of the constant campaign for propaganda and education which the Soviet régime is carrying on. In the struggle which is going on in the country districts between the new apostles of Communism and the men of the older generation who still possess influence, — the priest, the well-to-do peasant, the teacher who is secretly not in sympathy with the new régime, — time and governmental power are two powerful weapons in the hands of the Communists.

June 15, 1925. — One thing in Moscow and in Russia generally that has not changed with time and revolution is the large number of beggars, professional and occasional. Contrary to the romantic belief which is sometimes encountered abroad, most Russian beggars are not former generals, princesses, or people of education and former wealth. Of course there are exceptions to this rule, among beggars and itinerant salesmen. There is a one-time judge of the Moscow Municipal Court who found himself excluded from work because of his pre-war position, and, in a quite Russian mood of philosophic resignation, took to selling matches on the street near the University. The professors often stop to talk with the cultivated match seller, whose guest they had been in pre-war days; and there is a story that the French Ambassador, Jean Herbette, having stopped to buy a box of matches, found himself greeted in perfect French, and entered into a long and animated conversation.

But such instances are rare. Most beggars are either professionals or very poor people who have taken to begging as a result of want and unemployment. Among the professional beggars there are several recognizable individuals. There is a gaunt young man who looks as if he might have been shell-shocked in the war, who boards street cars, dressed in a pre-war student's uniform, and asks for alms in two or three European languages, besides Russian. There is a little boy, noticeable among many of his kind, who gets on the car at one of the principal stations and holds out his cap for copper coins, meanwhile singing plaintively about his hard life. A picturesque figure that one hesitates to classify as a beggar is a white-haired old man who goes about the streets at night and can always be found outside the opera houses after the performance, playing the most familiar melodies from *Aïda, Carmen, Sadko,* or whatever the night's performance may have been. The old man is a genuine artist; he holds tightly to his flute while he plays, and refuses to break off a melody in order to receive benefactions.

Russians, despite their poverty, seem to be more generous to street beggars than Western peoples would be. They perhaps share the Oriental feeling that the beggar, if not a holy man, is a more or less inevitable and respectable figure, who should be pitied and helped to the best of one's ability, and not roughly asked to go to work. And so long as this attitude persists it seems likely that the droning whine of the beggar will be one of the most familiar of the Moscow street sounds.

October 15, 1925. — The recent resumption of the sale of vodka at the pre-war alcoholic strength of 40 per cent was the signal for a wild orgy of a considerable part of the Muscovite population. Long waiting lines have been forming outside the shops where the fiery liquor is sold, and it is no uncommon sight to see a customer pull the cork out of his bottle and gulp down the entire contents amid a circle of envious and enthusiastic onlookers. There has been an enormous increase in public drunkenness during the two weeks since the *sorokgradusni* (40 per cent) went on sale. Excessive use of the new stimulant has caused a number of deaths, and the police have had their hands full attending to cases of drunkenness and disorderly conduct. In some cases parties of boisterous merrymakers have boarded street cars and created so much disturbance that they had to be removed by force.

Thirty per cent vodka was legally sold before October 1; and at first sight it seems surprising that an addition of 10 per cent to the alcoholic content of Russia's strongest beverage should have such a conspicuous and disastrous effect upon the sobriety of the city. However, it seems that Moscow took the restoration of vodka of pre-war strength as a huge holiday, which had to be properly celebrated.

The official justification for the legal return of vodka is that all efforts to prohibit it broke down as a result of the widespread drinking of *samogon*, or home-brewed vodka, which sometimes attained an alcoholic strength of 70 per cent and was considered more harmful than vodka, both in its physical effects and in its waste of grain. The euphemistic explanation for the return of vodka is that it is a "means of fighting *samogon*." While this consideration doubtless carried weight, the action of the government was also influenced by the fact that the Russian peasant is reluctant to part with his grain until he sees something which he may buy with the money which is paid him. It is expected that vodka will help to fill up the void which is created by the shortage of manufactured goods.

February 12, 1926. — The hand of the dictatorship has made itself felt more than is usually the case in the present theatrical season. The Repertory Committee, which decides what may and may not be produced, has condemned Wagner's *Lohengrin* as "mystical," Schiller's *Maria Stuart* as "religious and monarchical," and Massenet's opera *Werther* on the ground that "it is irrational in our age to cultivate Werther moods." The Committee has also forbidden the stage production of Dostoevsky's *The Brothers Karamazov* and insisted on the deletion of a scene from Tchaikovsky's *Eugen Onegin*, on the ground that it depicted "idyllic relations between the landlords and the peasants."

An ordinary Soviet citizen would have little chance to criticize publicly a decision of the Repertory Committee, but a well-known Communist named Larin leaped into the breach and published a spirited denunciation of the censorship, suggesting that the Repertory Committee had earned the humorous prize which was recently offered for "the biggest Soviet fool" and declaring, "It is an insult to the intelligence of the workers to impose such a stupid censorship on works of genius." Larin has a reputation as champion of lost causes, and I am afraid that he may be maintaining this tradition when he runs counter to the system of thought control which, to the Soviet régime, is just as important as the control of industry or foreign trade.

December 15, 1926. — Whatever other forms of repression there may be in Russia, there is certainly no tyranny of dress. You can never be sure from a man's clothes whether he is a government official, a ruble millionaire, a university professor, or a worker in a textile factory. Sonya and I just had a good practical illustration of this at the opera. During a performance of *Sadko* we were sitting next to a man in high boots and the familiar Russian collarless blouse, and opened up a conversation with him in the hope of finding out how a worker enjoys his new opportunity to hear operas in the orchestra seats. As Russians often are, in quite casual talks with strangers, our neighbor was quite frank and talkative, and we were soon surprised to learn that, although he had been a worker before the Revolution and had fought in the Red Army during the civil war, he was now a man of property, the owner of a number of clothing workshops. Whereas most Nepmen (as private traders and small employers are called in Russia, since they were only allowed to resume activity after the introduction of the Nep, or New Economic Policy) complain bitterly about taxes and labor requirements, our acquaintance was inclined to strike an optimistic note. He made a fair living, as he said, and had accumulated about a hundred thousand rubles. He evaded some of the trade-union payments by sending out much of his work to the homes of his employees.

November 7, 1927. — For one man, at least, this tenth anniversary of the Bolshevik Revolution, celebrated with the usual huge parade centring in the Red Square, with troops drawn up and new recruits reciting the oath of service, while cannons boomed and airplanes circled overhead, has been a day of bitter tragedy. This is Leon Trotzky, who, together with Preobrazhensky, Muralov, and a few other faithful lieutenants, made a last desperate effort to break through the iron bars of the Party dictatorship by organizing a counter-demonstration and addressing the crowds.

The Trotzkyist efforts were a failure; they were broken up by groups well trained in whistling, jeering, and throwing missiles, men which the Secretary of the Moscow Communist Party organization, Uglanov, had prepared for just such an emergency. And, even if Trotzky had been left free to speak, I doubt whether his eloquence would have had the magic effect of ten years ago. It was one thing to stir up the undisciplined masses of 1917, promising them rivers of milk and mountains of honey if they would overthrow the feeble government of Kerensky. It is quite another thing to reach the Soviet masses of 1927, regimented and taught to look for their orders from above by the very dictatorship which Trotzky himself helped so much to establish, and also taught by experience to be skeptical about the fulfillment of promises of a quick improvement of their lot by revolutionary means. The soft, jellyfish intellectuals to whom Kerensky looked for support are very different from the hard-boiled men of the present Party machine whom Stalin has taught to obey him exclusively and who have a very direct stake in the maintenance of the existing order.

Taine's likening of the French Revolution to the crocodile, devouring its own young, seems to have a modern Russian application to Trotzky; only he is denied the swift martyrdom of the guillotine. What he can expect is exile to a remote place and perhaps a chance to write his memoirs. What memories he must have had to-day of the turbulent upsurge of 1905, which failed for lack of decisive, clear-cut leadership; of the victory in 1917; of the crowded years when he was war lord of revolutionary Russia; then of the slow process of elimination from leadership which reached its climax to-day, when any of Uglanov's henchmen could hoot and whistle at the man who could order his enemies to execution in 1918 and 1919.

One does not like to be too specific about names and events in Russia, even in a private diary; but it has been striking and a bit amusing to see how some of the Trotzkyists in the Communist ranks have brightened up at the reversion to the old illegal methods of work: secret printing presses, clandestine distribution of leaflets, code words, underground meetings, and all the rest of it.   But these men are the exceptions; the average Soviet citizen, including the average Communist, has lost the taste for revolutionary romantics. So the Soviet Juggernaut will roll over the Trotzkyists, as it has rolled over countless heretics before and after them.

DNIEPROPETROVSK, *August* 1928. — How the Revolution loves to change names. This windy town on the Dnieper was formerly Ekaterinoslav. Its neighbor, Alexandrousk, further down the river, is now Zaporozhe, which literally means "Beyond the Rapids." In general the Soviet régime has been insistent on rechristening places which bear such familiar names of Tsars and Tsarinas as Nicholas, Alexander,

Catherine, and Elizabeth. So we have Gandzha, instead of Elizavetpol, in the Caucasus; Zinovievsk, instead of Elizavetgrad, in Ukraina; Sverdlovsk, instead of Ekaterinburg, in the Urals; Novo-Sibirsk, instead of Novo-Nikolaev, in Siberia; Leninakan, instead of Alexandropol, in Armenia. This desire for change applies to other things besides names of towns. A policeman is a "militiaman." The term "officer" apparently excites no pleasant memories of pre-war times, and the Red Army officer is a "commander." "Soldier," like "officer," is out of fashion; the Soviet soldier is a *krasnoarmeyetz,* or "Red Army man."

All this is rather a digression from the episode which impressed me most strongly during the trip which Sonya and I have been taking in the country districts of Southeastern and Southern Russia. When we stopped in a village not far from here, the local Soviet directed us to the house of a peasant for accommodation, and we were most surprised to find, along with the simple whitewashed walls, the benches and a few plain chairs of a typical Ukrainian peasant's house, a tiled floor — the only one we have ever seen in a peasant's possession.

It seems that our host, whose grandfather had been a serf, had so far enriched himself during the years of the New Economic Policy that he had more rubles than he could spend in the sparsely supplied coöperative store. So he invested in his tiled floor, which had been torn out from some landlord's mansion and had been lying about in the hands of the local Soviet. The peasant is afraid, however, that his burst of luxury may cost him dearly, since he is being talked of as a kulak, and this is likely to bring on him very heavy taxes and many other inconveniences. In general this peasant, like many others with whom we talked, feels a vague foreboding of big and unfavorable changes. Last spring, for the first time since the introduction of the New Economic Policy, the local authorities used threats of force, and in some cases actual force, to compel the peasants to sell their surplus grain; and there is a feeling that this may be only the prelude to still worse things in the future, and especially to a drive to make them join communes or collective farms, which the majority of the peasants certainly regard with little enthusiasm.

Among the more capable and ambitious peasants one often hears the idea, expressed with more or less clearness, that the government is checking their development, preventing them from becoming as prosperous as they might be under another system. The limitation of the amount of land which one family may till and the insecurity of tenure are familiar causes of complaint. One Ukrainian peasant spoke with envy of relatives and friends in Poland who could buy land and have it as their own possession. "But don't the Poles oppress your Ukrainian language?" I asked him. "You can't eat language," he gloomily replied.

CHIATOURI-GEORGIA, *August* 1929. — If there is one part of the Soviet Union for which I will certainly have a feeling of nostalgia if I ever leave the country, it is this Caucasus Region, in which Sonya and I have been traveling for the last two or three weeks. There are few places in the world where one can find such a picturesque medley of races and tongues, so many old customs, which are only beginning to yield to the impact of the Revolution — all against a magnificent natural background of towering snowy mountain peaks, magnificent gorges and ravines, splendid waterfalls and wild, rushing glacial rivers.

I think the place of all others that won our hearts on

this trip was Daghestan, a rocky mountainous little country on the shore of the Caspian Sea, with perhaps a million inhabitants and more than a score of languages and dialects. With the aid of an automobile which was most kindly placed at our disposal by the Daghestan Government (the Communist officials in Makhatch Kala, the capital of the country, certainly maintained the traditional Eastern hospitality of the country in dealing with us), we reached Gunib, far in the interior, a little village perched on an enormous mass of rock which is historically famous because it was the scene of the surrender of Shamil, the great Mohammedan leader of the peoples of the Eastern Caucasus, after a protracted and heroic struggle against the overwhelming military forces of Tsarist Russia.

The tribesmen of Daghestan showed that they had not lost their fighting spirit during the civil war. They first wiped out the Cossack garrisons which the White General Denikin placed in the country. Then, when they suffered misgovernment, requisitions, and offense to their religious feelings at the hands of the newly installed Soviet Government, they rose in fierce revolt in all the mountain fastnesses of the country. It took eight months of hard campaigning in the mountains (the Daghestan mountains are not so high as those of the Western Caucasus, but they are craggy, bare, and in some cases represent wonderful natural fortresses) and cost the lives of five thousand Red soldiers to put this rebellion down.

Now the country is quite peaceful; and one sees the best side of Soviet nationality policy in the entire feeling of equality which prevails between the Russians who are here as officials and technical experts and the dark-skinned men of the mountains. Walking through the few streets of

Gunib, we heard the curious cadence of an Eastern song, to the accompaniment of a musical instrument; and going into the house with our guide, who was the village teacher, we had the rare experience of hearing the village blacksmith deliver an eloquent declamation of an old ballad which described the defense of the *aul* (mountain village) Choch against the Russians in the days of Shamil.   The blacksmith was a little diffident at first in the presence of strangers, but he soon became quite engrossed in his song; his eyes brightened, his body swayed to the rhythm, his voice rose and fell like that of a mullah calling the faithful to prayer.

The daughter of the blacksmith, incidentally, was a living example of the progress of feminism in these remote wilds.   While her mother and some other girls and women left the room as soon as the singing began, she remained, discussing the songs and taking part in the conversation on a basis of equality that would have been inconceivable for the Daghestan maiden of pre-war days.   Her background, of course, was unusual.   She was one of a few mountaineer girls who had been sent to study in Makhatch Kala.   But the contrast between her attitude and that of the old-fashioned Daghestan woman, who springs up, submissively casts down her eyes, and remains silent as soon as a man enters the room, was so striking that one can easily imagine the big leavening change which the spread of education among women is likely to bring to this patriarchal Eastern land.

The Caucasian trip brought us many other vivid impressions and memories.   Immediately after primitive Daghestan we saw the vast oil fields around Baku, to which an energetic state director, Serebrovsky, had brought back from a trip of study in America all sorts of modern ideas, from the cracking method which increases the benzine yield of raw oil, to cottages for the workers and sanitary drinking cups for office use. (The office of the Baku Oil Trust was the only place in the Soviet Union where I have seen such cups.) There was the magnificent spectacle, on a distant road near the frontier of two Caucasian republics, Azerbaidjan and Armenia, of a host of nomad herdsmen on the march. The families moved in wooden carts, drawn by patient water buffaloes, with household belongings and domestic animals all piled into the carts and dogs trotting alongside. There was an element of gypsy romance in this cavalcade, with its camping by the river bank, the women often with babies strapped on their back like Indian papooses, the little girls with crescent-shaped earrings.

In Erivan, the rapidly growing capital of Soviet Armenia, we unexpectedly encountered an English-speaking Armenian from New York, who was assisting in the settlement of Armenian refugees in new towns on Soviet territory which bear the names of Arabkir, Kharput, and other places in Turkey where Armenians may no longer dwell. There was ever-charming Tiflis, the capital of Georgia, where, in some mysterious way unforeseen by five-year plans, the people always seem to be a little gayer and to have a little more to eat than in Russian provincial towns. Finally, there was Chiatouri, with its manganese mines in all the surrounding hills and a genial Georgian engineer as a guide, who, after vainly trying to initiate us into the art of riding spirited Caucasian horses properly, entertained us at an improvised banquet, where he insisted on drinking toasts, in fiery Georgian wine, first to all the eligible living beings, then to such inanimate objects as the stocks of manganese in the surrounding hills.

SAMARKAND, *May* 1930. — A trip, hot but most interesting, to the opening of the Turksib Railroad, which runs close to the frontier of Chinese Turkestan and will link up Siberia with Soviet Central Asia, has included as a climax visits to those wonderful old cities of Inner Asia, Samarkand and Bokhara. Tamerlane, ruthless son of the Central Asian steppes, made out of his capital, Samarkand, one of the great centres of Mohammedan architecture; and even to-day, when many of its huge mosques have partly crumbled away, it is easy to imagine what the city must have been in the days of its mediæval splendor.

In the beautiful ornamentation of the Shach-i-Zinda one can see a meeting of streams of art from many parts of Asia: blue tiles from Persia and Irak; the representation of a heron among tree branches, — contrary to the Mohammedan prohibition of the representation of living beings, — suggesting the Chinese art of the Ming epoch; inlaid ivory from India. Even more impressive is the tremendous ruin of Bibi-Khanum, the largest mosque within a radius of thousands of miles, built by Tamerlane in honor of his favorite wife. A mediæval chronicler describes it in these flowing phrases: "Its cupola would have been unique, if the sky had not been its repetition; its arch would have stood alone, if the Milky Way had not been its fellow."

It may seem a far cry from the forgotten drums and tramplings of Tamerlane's conquests, from Shach-i-Zinda and Bibi-Khanum, to present-day Soviet Turkestan, with its problems of forcing the extension of cotton plantations, its class war against the kulaks. Yet an archæological expert who showed us some of the rare monuments of Samarkand and explained their significance suggested, perhaps quite unconsciously, the existence of certain common traits between the dictatorship of Tamerlane and the dictatorship of the proletariat.

"Tamerlane forced all the skilled artificers and decorators whom he captured to work for him," said the expert. "If they refused he cut their throats" — with an appropriate gesture. "Despite these methods of compulsion, not all his enterprises turned out successfully," he continued. "Tamerlane attempted building feats which were beyond the mechanical power of his age. Some of his largest arches and buildings tumbled down soon after they were set up. But he was never willing to admit the real cause of these misfortunes. He always found people whom he held personally responsible and whom he hanged."

Was the archæologist merely recording historical facts? Or was there just a little shadow of suggestion that Tamerlane had found modern imitators? This was obviously no question to put to him before a mixed audience.

STALINGRAD, *August* 1930. — As Sonya and I were toiling up a hill, after a hot day in the newly built Stalingrad tractor factory, in order to attend the trial of two American mechanics who were accused of "racial chauvinism" for having become involved in a brawl with the sole Negro employed at the works, we were startled to hear, all of a sudden, a voice from nowhere, in English, bellowing: "You —— —— ——!" The startled feeling gave way to amusement when we realized that the threatening voice proceeded from a loud-speaker and that we were hearing the Homeric threats which preceded the scuffle between Mr. Lewis, a mechanic from Alabama, and Mr. Robinson, a West Indian Negro, in which Mr. Brown, another white worker, had become involved, apparently mainly as a mediator.

The scuffle ended very quickly without bodily harm to

anyone, but the Russians saw an excellent opportunity to hold a demonstrative trial on the subject of race prejudice. Mr. Lewis was lodged in the Stalingrad prison; and no less than ten amateur prosecutors, of different races and in different languages, held forth on the evil of racial chauvinism as a weapon in the armory of the capitalists against the workers. The effect of this on the three hundred American mechanics who had been imported from Detroit and other centres of the automobile industry did not, however, seem to correspond with the wishes of the organizers of the trial. Indeed, it seemed to strengthen them in their racial chauvinism. I talked with a middle-aged mechanic, of the type who probably earned fifty or sixty dollars a week before the depression, regularly voted the Republican ticket, and belonged to the Methodist Church. Lost on him were the finest efforts of Communist oratory. He was an active figure in the hastily improvised American committee to aid Lewis which had been organized when the trial set in.

"You know, brother," he began almost tearfully, "it 's been most humiliating for us, as Americans, to hear a lot of furriners get up and jabber about how our government was no good and how we could n't make laws to suit ourselves. And what they 're trying to do with this trial is to force on us something no white American will stand for: social equality with the colored race."

With a worried expression, my companion produced a grimy sheet of paper, saying that he wanted me to see just what Lewis had signed. On it was written a rather amusing and obviously dictated apology, on the part of Mr. Lewis, beginning with the statement that racial animosity was a favorite instrument of the capitalists and going on with expressions of regret "to the ladies of the American colony, to the workers of Russia, and to the workers of the whole world" for the disturbance in which he had become involved. It did not require much exercise of psychological imagination to realize that "the ladies of the American colony" had been mentioned at Mr. Lewis's inspiration, while the apologies to the workers of the Soviet Union and of the whole world were part of the price required to commute a prison sentence to simple expulsion from the country.   One line in the apology, however, was heavily crossed out; and I asked the reason.

"That was a direct apology to the nigger," was the mechanic's reply.   *"We crossed that out."*

KEM, KARELIA, *March* 1931. — This is the first time that our wanderings have taken us to the Soviet Far North, almost to the Arctic Circle.   The occasion for our trip to Karelia — a country of forests and lakes, with a Finnish-speaking native population, in Northwestern Russia — was a statement by Premier Molotov, addressing a recent Congress of Soviets in Moscow, to the effect that there was no forced labor in the Soviet timber industry, coupled with an invitation to foreign journalists to travel and investigate the situation for themselves.

Our experience would indicate that this invitation was not meant to be taken very seriously.   Practically all the accounts appearing in the foreign press about the use of forced labor in the Soviet timber industry referred specifically to camps under the charge of the Gay-Pay-Oo in Karelia and in the neighborhood of Archangel.   The Karelian Government officials at Petrozavodsk, the capital of the sparsely populated country, were unable to grant us admission to these camps; the Gay-Pay-Oo was quite outside their sphere of authority. And an application to the head of the camps here at Kem for permission to visit them was curtly refused, so that one is confronted with the alternative of thinking either that the Gay-Pay-Oo is above Molotov's authority or that the Premier was not altogether sincere in expressing an invitation to foreign journalists to investigate the forced-labor situation.

At the same time the trip to Karelia has by no means been wasted. Although one's freedom of travel and investigation has a very definite and concrete limitation in the shape of the barbed wire which surrounds the Gay-Pay-Oo concentration camps, it is easy by merely traveling through the country, seeing long lines of freight cars packed with prisoners and considerable numbers of men being marched off to work in Kem itself under armed guard, by talking with railroad workers and fellow passengers on trains, to find abundant confirmation of the general impression in Moscow: that Karelia has been used as a place of exile and forced labor on a gigantic scale. As for the system in vogue in the little forest-ringed peasant hamlets where there were no prisoners or armed guards and which we were permitted to visit, it was a kind of compulsory labor such as one might expect to find in an indifferently administered African colony or mandated territory. Every Soviet received an order from the higher authorities as to how much timber must be cut; the Soviet in turn distributed this work among the peasant families; those who failed to carry out the allotted task were liable to fine or imprisonment. The labor was paid for, but in rubles which have shrunk in purchasing power quite as much in Karelia as in other parts of the Soviet Union; and this diminution in the buying power of the ruble is really the root of the peasant dissatisfaction with the system. Nature itself predestined the people in this northern territory, where farming possibilities are limited, to be woodsmen, and they would work in the forests gladly enough if they could get a fair return for their labor.

In short, I am carrying away from Karelia an impression

quite similar to that which I obtained in the collective farms
of the lower Volga last summer: that the government is
trying to extract from the peasants more in products and in
labor than it can give them fair compensation for. Hence
the discontent, and the actual or potential compulsion which
is becoming more and more a feature of Soviet economic life.
The Communist attitude, of course, is that the country is
being built up and that the people must make sacrifices.
The peasant attitude was pretty well summed up by the old
izvoschik who drove us from the Petrozavodsk station to the
town's unpretentious hotel and who growled out: "This
country is n't Karelia any more; it is *katorga*" (the Russian
word for exile at hard labor).

Moscow, *July* 1931. — Sonya became involved in a
verbal duel with a no less redoubtable adversary than Bernard
Shaw to-day. We were at lunch with Shaw and the
members of his party at the Metropole Hotel. Shaw had
celebrated his seventy-fifth birthday the night before by
delivering a speech full of enthusiastic encomiums for the
Soviet régime; and, among other things, announced that as
he approached the Russian frontier he had become convinced
that there was no food shortage in the Soviet Union, and
had therefore thrown out of the window all the hampers of
foodstuffs which apprehensive friends had given him.

"I think, Mr. Shaw, many Russians would have appreciated it if you had thrown away that food in Russia and
not in Poland," Sonya began.

"Where is there any food shortage here?" retorted
Shaw, pointing to the well-appointed dining room of the
Metropole Hotel, largely patronized by foreigners with
comfortable bank accounts, with a gesture that suggested
Marie Antoinette's "Let them eat cake." Sonya is literal-

minded and persistent, and she returned to the charge.

"I have a four-year-old daughter. As a foreigner I can buy all the milk she needs. But if she had depended on the Soviet milk ration she would have had milk only once or twice during this last winter."

"Why don't you nurse her yourself?" inquired Shaw, with a trace of irritation.

"I think she is a little too old for that," replied Sonya with a smile. "Oh, nonsense," said Shaw, with Dr. Johnson's determination to win the argument at any cost. "The Eskimos nurse their children until they are twenty years old."

"Well, Mr. Shaw, I 'm not an Eskimo," was Sonya's final shot.

It is a little amusing and surprising that Shaw, who has such a genius for stagecraft, seems to be quite oblivious of the really superb histrionic efforts which are being made for his benefit during his ten-day sojourn here.

October 1933. — We have just returned from one of the most interesting and certainly from the saddest of our many trips in the Russian villages. For as soon as the long-withheld and reluctantly granted permission to travel outside of Moscow was received we went to the North Caucasus and to Ukraina, to find out how much truth there was in the rumors of wholesale starvation among the peasants there during the past winter and spring. What we found was little short of the worst we had heard, and certainly explains the extraordinary action of the Soviet authorities in forbidding, over a period of several months, all travel in the famine regions by foreign correspondents. Everywhere a death rate that ranged remarkably close around the average figure of 10 per cent, according to the testimony of responsible local officials. Stories of whole families that had died off, leaving one or two survivors. Stories of cannibalism. A dreary, poverty-stricken, miserable population, shaking with malaria, in the once-fertile Kuban Valley, now overgrown with a thick crop of weeds.

Quite by chance the last village we visited was at once the most terrible and the most dramatic. It is called Cherkass, and it lies about seven or eight miles to the south of Byelaya Tserkov, a Ukrainian town southwest of Kiev. Here the "normal" mortality of 10 per cent had been far exceeded. On the road to the village, former ikons with the face of Christ had been removed; but the crown of thorns had been allowed to remain — an appropriate symbol for what the village had experienced. Coming into the village, we found one deserted house after another, with window-panes fallen in, crops growing mixed with weeds in gardens with no one to harvest them. A boy in the dusty village street called the death roll among the families he knew with the stolid impassivity that one sometimes found among the peasants in the face of the catastrophe of the preceding winter and spring.

"There was Anton Samchenko, who died with his wife and sister; three children were left. With Nikita Samchenko's family, the father and Mikola and two other children died; five children were left. Then Grigory Samchenko died with his son Petro; a wife and daughter are left. And Gerasim Samchenko died with four of his children; only the wife is still living. And Sidor Odnorog died with his wife and two daughters; one girl is left. Gura Odnorog died with his wife and three children; one girl is still alive."

The secretary of the local Soviet, a young man named

Fischenko, put the tragedy of the village in concrete figures. During the previous winter and spring, 634 out of the 2072 inhabitants of the village had died. During the past year there had been one marriage in the village. Six children had been born; of these, one had survived.

"It 's better not to bear children than to have them die of hunger," said a woman in the office of the Soviet.

"No," argued a boy; "if no children are born, who can till the land?"

I think the individual tragedy which stood out most strongly in Cherkass was that of a woman with whom we talked who had lost her three children. "They were such good children, such *uchenie* [learned] children," she said, weeping bitterly. To me the right of these unknown children, and the uncounted others of whom they were only the symbol, to live is higher than the right of the dictators in the Kremlin to launch a programme of overstrained and overhastened militarist and industrial expansion, to force on the peasants a system so hateful that it could only be finally clamped down with the use of the last and most terrible weapon — organized famine.

December 1933. — Kalinin made a curious reference to the famine in addressing the All-Union Soviet Executive Committee. He said: "Political impostors ask contributions for the 'starving' of Ukraina. Only degraded disintegrating classes can produce such cynical elements."

So, according to the Soviet President, the famine in Ukraina is nothing but the malicious invention of "degraded disintegrating classes." And not one Ukrainian delegate in the Soviet Executive Committee had a word of contradiction. I wonder whether Kalinin's speech will reach Cherkass, and what effect it will produce there.

XIX

FAREWELL TO RUSSIA

Moscow, *March* 1934. — Now that a new journalistic appointment is taking me away from Russia for many years, if not forever, I feel I should try to set down how I feel about the country and the régime which I have seen at a very important stage of historical development. I have always had a cordial contempt for the "Me and Russia" type of book. For an outsider to pay a fleeting visit to a country which has experienced such a tremendous upheaval and to see in it nothing but an annex for his own personality, to write a book under some such title as "I Saw Russia" or "What I Think of the Soviets," has always seemed to me to reveal a lack of sense of proportion that borders on impertinence. It is something like endeavoring to photograph oneself with Mont Blanc as a background.

At the same time no one with sensitiveness and imagination could live in the Soviet Union for more than a decade without feeling strong reactions of some kind to the dramatic events which have played themselves out on this huge stage. If the "Me and Russia" type of reporter seems out of place, I am also unable to sympathize with the observer who looks on human beings, if they happen to be Russians, as anæsthetized guinea pigs or pawns on a chessboard, and sees in the "liquidation" or wiping out of great numbers of them nothing but a necessary, if perhaps unpleasant, phase of an "interesting experiment."

There are certain aspects of Russia, which have nothing to do either with Tsarism or with Bolshevism, that have for me the greatest charm and appeal. Certainly few peoples are more naturally gifted than the Russians in many fields of art and culture. A century ago Russian literature was only beginning to exist; but who among authors in other lands can exceed Turgeniev in rich, mellow, all-embracing human sympathy, or Tolstoy in epic breadth of scope, or Dostoevsky in fierce dramatic intensity and psychological depth, or Gogol in sharp and salty humor? Equally impressive have been Russia's achievements in music, and in many branches of science. In the face of some particularly barbarous episode, past or present, I have sometimes been tempted to feel that the methods of Russia's rulers place it among the backward Asiatic countries, but I always come back to the thought that its thinkers, artists, and scientists have won it a high place in European culture.

I have come to regard the pre-war Russian educated class as the most charming of its kind in the world, perhaps because it was younger, fresher, warmer, and stronger in its appreciation of the cultural values which other countries are too much inclined to take for granted. Among the masses of the Soviet Union, among the workers and peasants and people of all occupations and of various races whom I have met in many trips through the country, there are qualities of hospitality, frankness, natural wit, friendliness to a foreign visitor, that leave the most pleasant impression. I personally enjoy some sides of Soviet life which are distasteful to many foreigners; I like the absence of a showy and gaudy night life in Moscow, and the sartorial freedom which is perhaps the only kind of liberty that does unquestionably exist in the Soviet Union.

When I first came to Moscow in 1922, my attitude toward the Soviet régime was more than friendly; it was enthusiastic. I sometimes look back with a shade of amusement to the rhetorical articles in praise of the Bolshevik Revolution which I published in radical newspapers and magazines at that time, animated, as I can see in retrospect, by little knowledge and much faith. And, if I am sometimes tempted to laugh at the outbursts of Mrs. Modlin-Creighton and other enthusiastic tourists, I must remember that in 1919 and 1920 my own attitude was very similar. How ready I was in those years to believe the most fantastic yarns of the well-disposed returned visitor to the Red Mecca of Moscow! And how I was inclined to denounce the mildest and most reasoned critic as a base traitor and defamer! Proceeding from the belief, which I still hold, that the World War was the supreme crime and folly of the century, I jumped to the conclusion, which I have long abandoned, that revolution on the Bolshevik model is the panacea for war and for all social injustice.

Not that I have completed the absolute psychological somersault which I have witnessed in some acquaintances who came to Russia avowed Communists and left the country expressing hopes for the complete overthrow of the Soviet régime. For some achievements of the Revolution I have the sincerest respect, especially for its spread of education among the masses, for its policy of absolute nondiscrimination among the races and nationalities of the country, for its exaltation of labor, for its promotion of health and recreation. I always come away from a workers' rest home or from a workers' club, situated perhaps in a former slum district,

Gut, Champion Diver of the Soviet Union, Prac-
tising at the Dynamo Water Stadium, Moscow

with a conviction that a vast amount of useful social and educational work has been and is being done under the auspices of the ruling Communist Party.

Industrialization was a reasonable goal for a country with the population and natural resources of the Soviet Union; and the Soviet leaders have certainly displayed tireless drive and energy in creating a network of steel and chemical plants, tractor and machine-building factories, and electrical power stations. The industrial progress of the country during the last few years is striking, even though one should bear in mind the fact, overlooked by some admirers of the Soviets, that pre-war Russia was developing its railroads and its industries very rapidly. I see no reason to doubt that the Soviet leaders and the majority of the Communist Party members believe sincerely in their cause and think they are working for the well-being of their country. I have repeatedly been impressed by the obvious devotion of the more idealistic of the Young Communists and of the veteran *podpolshchiki,* or former underground revolutionaries.

And yet, when one sums up all that can fairly be said about the constructive sides of the Soviet régime, there remains a formidable burden of facts on the other side. There is the permanent and odious system of terrorism and espionage. There is the decimation of the intelligentsia through secret arrests and banishments and most unconvincing "sabotage" trials. There is the subjection of the peasantry to wholesale deportations and to a "military feudal exploitation" that reached its terrible and inevitable climax in the great famine of 1932–1933 — all for the sake of imposing on the peasants an alien and unfamiliar system which certainly has yet to prove its productive advantages.

How can one reconcile such apparent contradictions:

establishment of children's nurseries and sending of some children, with their kulak parents, to Arctic wastes; setting up of technical research institutes and application of inquisitorial methods to scientists of world eminence — to mention two of the more obvious? It is my personal belief that the Bolshevik Revolution and the Soviet régime which grew out of it can only be understood as an example of historical tragedy of the deepest and truest type, a tragedy of cruelty, of the crushing out of innumerable individual lives, not from sheer wanton selfishness, but from perverted, fanatical idealism — always the surest source of absolute ruthlessness. And behind this tragedy lie several conceptions which are implicit in Communist philosophy; and the longer I have seen these in practice, the more I have come to regard them as sentimental fallacies.

The first, the oldest and the most demonstrable, is the conviction that the end justifies the means. I think the overwhelming weight of historical evidence is to the effect that the means determine the end, and that an idealistic goal, pursued by brutal methods, has a tendency to disappear from view. Such major atrocities as the liquidation of the kulaks as a class, the state-organized famine, and the persecution of the intelligentsia have harmful results that go far beyond their immediate victims. They brutalize the society that is taught or forced to look on them with indifference or even with applause. I have often felt that even more terrible than the commission of these atrocities was the fact that no voice could be publicly raised against them in the Soviet Union. A distinguished historical novelist of the last century, Aleksei Tolstoy, in his introduction to his novel of the times of Ivan the Terrible, *Prince Serébrany*, writes: —

"I throw down my pen in indignation, not so much at the

thought that Ivan the Terrible could exist, as at the thought that a society could exist which would look on him without indignation."

I think there could be some very pointed modern applications of this statement.

A second sentimental fallacy of Communism is its virtual ignoring of the grave problems involved when the few men who must inevitably guide the whole political and economic life of the country, under the system of the so-called dictatorship of the proletariat, are granted enormous power with no kind of effective check or control. Lenin was so obsessed with the idea that "capitalism," the private ownership of the means of production, was the root of all human ills that he never seems to have foreseen the abuses, equally serious, if of a different kind, which might emerge when all power, political and economic, would be in the hands of a dictatorial state.

I have talked with few if any peasants in the Soviet Union who do not consider the Soviet state a harder taskmaster than the Tsarist landlord. Russia's whole experience, especially during the Iron Age, certainly indicates most vividly that the possibility of exploitation is not eliminated when factories and mines, banks and railroads, are transferred from private to public ownership. A dictatorial state may exploit — more than that, *has* exploited — workers and peasants alike, not for the sake of private enrichment, but as a result of blundering mismanagement, of grandiose ambitions for quick industrial and military expansion. Incidentally, I think it is decidedly improbable that the Soviet state, after arrogating to itself the most absolute power over the lives of its citizens, will some day obediently fulfill Lenin's formula and "wither away." Lenin could doubtless imagine an abstract conception, "the state," withering away. It is very difficult, after seeing the atmosphere of special privilege with which high Party, Soviet, and Gay-Pay-Oo officials are surrounded, to imagine this new ruling class, or caste, voluntarily merging itself with the mass of Soviet citizens and "withering away" in any future, however distant.

The materialistic conception of history is a Communist dogma with which I am in vigorous disagreement. This effort to explain all human activity in terms of the play of economic forces seems narrow, inadequate, and unconvincing. It becomes positively ridiculous when there is an effort to explain a jolly overture by Glinka as "Russian trade capitalism expanding" or a melancholy song by Tchaikovsky as "Russian landed aristocracy in decay." More serious than these amateurish experiments in artistic misinterpretation is the tendency to regard the individual merely as a member of this or that class. This impersonal approach is an easy road to pitiless hardness.

Then the practice of "the dictatorship of the proletariat" in the Soviet Union has in it a large element of inverted snobbishness. Reasonable people would generally agree that labor with hand or brain is a title to respect. But I am quite unable to comprehend why work in a factory is intrinsically more ennobling than work in an office, or on a farm, or in a research laboratory. By its avowed and systematic discrimination against "non-proletarians" — that is, against non-factory laborers — in educational opportunity and in promotion in the state service, the Soviet Union is handicapping itself just as much as any state which resorted to some of the more familiar forms of class or race discrimination.

One among many points of faith common to apologists of

Communism and of Fascism is an overweening contempt for civil liberties, which are represented as unnecessary and inconvenient barnacles on the ship of progress. The longer I have lived in the Soviet Union, where civil liberties — freedom of speech, press, assembly, and election — are most conspicuously lacking, the more I have become convinced that they are of vital and tremendous importance, and that their existence or absence is as good a test as any of the quality of a nation's civilization. The Communist (or the Fascist; their trend of thought in this question is strikingly similar) talks of civil liberties as of the outworn fetish of a handful of disgruntled intellectuals who are unable to rise to the necessary vision of the high and noble character and purpose of the Communist (or Fascist) state. But my own observation in Russia has led me to believe that a great deal more is at stake than the freedom of thought of the educated classes, although it seems rather obvious that culture becomes impoverished when the historian must alter his record of the past, the author must give a prescribed coloring to his characters, and free research in any field can be cut off by the will of an all-powerful state.

It was during my trip through the famine regions of Ukraina and the North Caucasus that I became utterly and definitely convinced that democracy, with all its faults, weaknesses, and imperfections, is enormously superior to dictatorship as a method of government, simply from the standpoint of the common man. Is there any recorded case in history where famine — not poverty or hardship or destitution, but stark famine, with a toll of millions of lives — has occurred in a democratically governed country? Is it conceivable that the famine of 1932–1933 could have taken place if civil liberties had prevailed in the Soviet Union, if newspapers had been free to report the facts, if speakers could have appealed for relief, if the government in power had been obliged to submit its policy of letting vast numbers of the peasants starve to death to the verdict of a free election? The countless graves of the humble and obscure famine victims, the peasants of Ukraina and the North Caucasus, of the Volga and Central Asia, are to me the final grim, unanswerable refutation of the specious Communist contention that freedom of speech and press and political agitation is only humbug by which the bourgeoisie tries to delude the masses.

If I have one wish for the future of a country where I spent many of the best years of my life and for whose people I feel only the warmest friendship, even though I disagree so strongly with many of its present-day political, economic, and philosophical beliefs, it is that somehow a little leaven of doubt and skepticism might filter into the pure yeast of Communist dogma. It is not a matter of discarding methods that prove ineffective; any ruling group with elementary capacity for governing will do this. It is a question of coming to believe that there might be one per cent of a chance that the fundamental dogmas of Marxism and Leninism are wrong, or at least that they represent not infallible truth, but a working hypothesis, to be verified by trial and error.

I believe that the progress of civilization in Russia will go hand in hand with the progress of skepticism. When the Communists are no longer so self-righteously certain that they are leading the country to a future millennium, they will perhaps not be so ready to impose on it some of the characteristics of a present-day purgatory.

XX

THE SOVIET UNION TO–DAY
AND TO–MORROW

PROPHECY always has its risks, especially prophecy about a country which has passed through a great and unprecedented revolution. But no description of the Soviet Union in its Iron Age would be adequate without some effort to summarize the main characteristics of the present era and to forecast the probable future lines of development.

Barring war, the stability and the continuity of the Soviet régime seem quite assured. The very magnitude of the hardships and sufferings which it imposed on the population in the name of industrialization and collectivization is, in a sense, a testimonial of its strength, of the invincibility of its highly developed technique of government by means of a combination of propaganda and repression against any forces of internal discontent. War is the unknown possible factor which may confound all predictions about the future of the Soviet Union, or, indeed, of almost any other country. The Bolshevik Revolution was a child of the World War. Although there were many elements of weakness and decay in the Tsarist system, the Russian Revolution would probably have taken a very different course if the war had been averted or indefinitely postponed. In such a case the propertied peasantry which was emerging as a result of Stolypin's agrarian legislation would have had a far stronger voice in

shaping the course of events. Successful war is the sole means by which Communist revolutions are likely to be promoted in other countries. Unsuccessful war is the only conceivable means by which the Soviet edifice might be suddenly and violently overthrown.

Assuming that the Soviet Government does not become involved in war, what should I expect to find if I should revisit Moscow in 1940? There would probably be some improvement in material well-being, although the majority of the people would still be overcrowded and underfed. Perhaps by that time meat and milk and butter and fruit would be as easy to get as they were in 1925 or 1926. Moscow's subway would presumably be in operation, with a consequent relief for the hopelessly overburdened street cars. Its first period would perhaps be marked by a few collisions and other accidents, which would not be mentioned in the newspapers, while their casualties would be exaggerated in popular rumor. The Gay-Pay-Oo would have ceased to exist — under that particular name. Its functions of spying, arresting, and deporting undesirable Soviet citizens would be carried on by an organization with a more innocent title, which would include all the veteran officials of the Cheka and the Gay-Pay-Oo, but which might, in deference to outside opinion, have given up the practice of shooting people without any kind of public trial.

Going into the country districts, I should hope and expect to find no more evidences of recent famine and no acute food shortage, except perhaps in years of severe drought. On the other hand, I should be very agreeably and very much surprised if I should find the majority of the collective-farm members enjoying a standard of living which a West European or even a Baltic or Balkan peasant would

regard as well-to-do. The individual collective farms would probably have gained more autonomy; the dictatorial control over the farms now exercised by the machine-tractor stations would have proved in practice unwieldy and un-economic.

By 1940, rationing would probably have disappeared or have considerably diminished in scope; one result of this would be that the Soviet ruble would have assumed more of the normal functions of a genuine unit of currency. Real wages in the Workers' Republic would still be extremely low, and discreet inquiry in the proper quarters would probably reveal that possessors of foreign currency could obtain a very different rate of exchange from that quoted in the State Bank.

The shops would have assumed a more Western ap-pearance; more automobiles and buses would be coursing about the streets; the traffic policeman would perhaps be the most overworked man in the Soviet capital. There would be a brand-new crop of anecdotes, mostly centring around the subway, the real or alleged architectural defects of the Palace of Soviets, and the accidents of the infant Soviet automobile industry. There would still be some dutiful talk about the Soviet proletariat as the vanguard of the World Revolution, but that happy event would have visibly receded in popular expectation to a vaguer and vaguer future.

A certain type of American or English business man would be holding forth in the bar of the Metropole Hotel on what a wonderful market Russia would be if the governments at home could only see the light and advance considerable sums of the taxpayers' money in order to enable the Russians to purchase more of the goods which the business man was interested in selling. A hard-bitten engineer, just returned

from a copper smelter in the Altai Mountains, would inject the 1940 equivalent for "Oh yeah?" — accompanied by a profane and vivid description of what was wrong with the copper smelter. The enthusiastic tourist would be packing up to return to New York or London, all ready to lecture on how Russia, in all Europe, was the sole country with Hope and a Plan.

The three long-term trends in Soviet life which seem to me most significant at the present time (1934) are greater stabilization, growing nationalism, and increasing material inequality. A dominant feature of Soviet life since 1928 has been the crisis of agrarian production, which at its height reduced the town population to a very meagre food supply and caused famine in many country districts. There was a turn for the better in 1933, and, while unfavorable climatic conditions may further delay a process of agricultural reconstruction which is bound to be slow and difficult in any case, the probabilities are that the extreme low point of the agrarian crisis has been passed. The peasants have more or less reluctantly resigned themselves to the collective-farming system which has been forced on them so ruthlessly. The Soviet Government, on its side, seems to have given up the idea of pressing the peasants into full-blooded communes and is lavish with its promises of more manufactured goods. The struggle between the government and the peasantry, which reached its most ferocious form of expression in the famine of 1932–1933, is not over. It cannot be over until the peasant obtains more freedom in determining the conditions of his labor, more voice in disposing of his products, a fairer share in the national income. But it will probably go on now in milder forms, which will not be so destructive to agricultural productivity.

own resources and by its own efforts, with slight benefit of foreign capital. This will make Russia's industrialization more painful for the population than would otherwise be necessary. But at a time when defaults, moratoria, and frozen credits are the order of the day in countries with similar economic systems it does not seem probable that there will be any rush of adventurous capital into the Soviet Union.

The Soviet régime has been contradictorily interpreted to the outside world as a menace, a challenge, an inspiration, and a laughingstock. I should not personally subscribe unconditionally to any one of these sweeping interpretations, although, like all big historical movements, the Bolshevik Revolution has its separate aspects of horror, of heroism, and of absurdity. The Soviet system may be considered the most dramatic and most spectacular effort to solve, along new lines, what seems likely to be the major social problem of the twentieth century: to ensure economic security for the masses while preserving a reasonable measure of liberty for the individual.

That the Bolshevik method of solving this problem by completely destroying individual ownership of property and placing the whole responsibility for the economic as well as for the political administration of the country in the hands of an absolutist state will be imitated in other countries seems highly unlikely. I remember quite vividly the moment when I definitely came to feel that Bolshevism would never conquer Western Europe or America. It was in the autumn of 1930, when I was spending a vacation in the Austrian Tyrol.

A procession with bands and music was passing through the streets of the little mountain village. The marchers were mostly local peasants in holiday costume, with green coats and feathers stuck in their hats, and every man had a rifle slung over his back. As it happens, I had made a trip through some collective farms in the lower Volga just before leaving Russia; and as I watched the Tyrolean peasants, who looked like worthy descendants of the ancestors who put up such a magnificent fight against Napoleon, march swinging past I thought of a very different scene which I had recently witnessed in a lower Volga village. A local Communist official there had been telling the peasants how much grain they had to give up, what quotas of milk and meat would be taken away from them, what they had to plant and how they had to work in the collective farm. The peasants grumbled, sometimes cried out in protest at the amount of the requisitions; but one felt that with their serf tradition, and with the stern lesson of the liquidation of the kulaks before their eyes, they would submit. But a Communist grain collector, even if he had brought a regiment of Gay-Pay-Oo troops with him, would have had a hard time in that Tyrolean village. One felt that Austrian peasants would have turned their mountain valley into a cemetery before they would have submitted. And I certainly doubt whether forcible collectivization would have better chances of success with the farmers of Kansas and Nebraska, or with the French peasants whose Revolution, in contradistinction to the Russian, really did give them the land.

And the landowning peasantry and farmers represent only one of many stumblingblocks which Russian Bolshevism would encounter in other countries. So what seems most probable is that the Soviet régime is destined neither to serve as an ultimate model for the rest of the world, as its admirers believe, nor to go down in violent ruin and destruction, as its enemies hope. Barring the ever-unpredictable contingencies of large-scale war, the system will stand in its main features, subject of course, like other systems, to evolutionary modification and change. It will be the Russian solution of a problem which has already been solved in different fashion in Germany and in Italy, and which will doubtless in time find further solutions, varying with national temperament and economic circumstances, in America, England, France, and other countries. The failure of the pre-war economic system to regain its old balance, to function in the traditional automatic fashion, seems to mark out for every country a greater measure of state control and state regulation of its economic life. But how this control and regulation will work out in practice will probably vary from country to country as greatly as Russian historical development, for instance, varies from British, or German from American. That the Russian solution should at once have proclaimed the most glowing and ambitious ideals and should have taken the greatest toll of human lives and human suffering is certainly in full harmony with certain traits of Russian temperament (extremism, lack of the instinct for relativity and moderation, contempt for the individual personality) and with that Russian past which so often casts its long shadow over the Soviet present.

INDEX